THE RELUCTANT SATELLITES

THE MACMILLAN COMPANY
NEW YORK · CHICAGO
DALLAS · ATLANTA · SAN FRANCISCO
LONDON · MANILA

IN CANADA
BRETT-MACMILLAN LTD.
GALT, ONTARIO

LESLIE B. BAIN

The Reluctant Satellites

An Eyewitness Report on

East Europe and the

Hungarian Revolution

The Macmillan Company   New York   1960

First Printing

The Macmillan Company, New York
Brett-Macmillan Ltd., Galt, Ontario

Printed in the United States of America

Library of Congress catalog card number: 60-5406

Parts of this book have appeared in different form in *Look* and *The Reporter* magazines, as well as in newspapers affiliated with the North American Newspaper Alliance. Permission for including in this book previously published material is gratefully acknowledged.

For *M. L. S. and L. J. S.*

CONCERNING THE USE OF NAMES IN THIS BOOK

Many who speak in this book are now in prison, awaiting trial, or are refugees in foreign lands. The author has no reliable information as to the whereabouts of others, nor is it quite clear what charges were brought against those who are under arrest. Hence it is incumbent upon him to protect, as far as he is able to do so, those whose thoughts and actions are presented in this book. Moreover, even where people enjoy a comparative safety at present—as in Yugoslavia and Poland—tomorrow may bring a renewal of persecution and terror. Names and sometimes localities have, therefore, been changed or deliberately distorted.

On the other hand, people who are beyond retribution, and those whose actions and views were published in their native land or abroad, are quoted directly.

THE AUTHOR EXPLAINS

Man lives by revolutions in two ways. He rotates around a central axis which is the life of the species, and periodically he makes fundamental changes in the organization of his social existence. Whether he knows it or not, his life, as well as the lives of his ancestors and of his progeny, responds to a stimulus which originates in the evolutionary process of which he is an increasingly dominant part. We do not know much about this process; we merely know about its workings. Much like electricity, which we can measure, use, develop, and marvel at but which we do not really understand, this process working in the human species has many measurable qualities; nevertheless, it is still a mystery, a part of the great unknowable.

Whether history is interpreted according to Marxian materialism, or in terms of national fairy tales with which history books abound, or in terms of Carl Jung's atavistic archetypes, the evolutionary pressure which periodically erupts in revolution is clearly visible throughout. That evolution should express itself in revolutions may be a farfetched notion. Yet, as a line is but a succession of points, evolution also seems to be made up of myriads of revolutions, some spontaneous and some reflex responses to outside events. It may be difficult to see and to understand what an unarmed man walking up against a Soviet tank, in Budapest, has to do with the educational process in Malaya or with income taxes in America; nevertheless, the connection is there.

This book deals mostly with unarmed man in revolt or in process of revolt, and merely intends to present a brief view of an important part of mankind in ferment. The random pieces of mosaic shown here do make a pattern. The true victims of the war between the giants, still called the "cold war," are the peoples between and around them. They are condemned to stand still under a stopped clock, and are severely punished for fidgeting, even though their nerves are strained to the limit of endurance, and their hearts and minds ablaze.

Contents

PART THREE

Repercussions

PART ONE

Summer of Ferment

I

Cleaning Communism's House

It was hard to believe that the gaunt woman who strode toward the lectern in an ill-fitting housedress had been but a few years ago one of the belles of Budapest. Of the famous charm of Mrs. Laszlo Rajk, wife of the former minister of the interior, minister of foreign affairs, high mogul of Communism in Hungary, nothing remained but a certain erectness of body which, added to her cultured and emotional voice, heightened the drama of her appearance.

"Comrades," she began, "you will never know what it means for me to appear before you. After five years of unspeakable horrors in jail, robbed of my husband and child, condemned to silence, this is the first time I am permitted to speak."

The tightly packed audience in the huge auditorium of the Red Army Club in Budapest watched her, fascinated. This was no ordinary Communist party meeting; it was a carefully timed land mine designed to explode under Matyas Rakosi's regime in Hungary. The invitation for the meeting had stated that former underground fighters and partisans wished to meet with Hungarian intellectuals to talk over the state of affairs in Hungary, and the policemen downstairs had carefully checked each invitation to make sure no outsider would listen to the words which Communists were about to hurl at other Communists.

Mrs. Rajk leaned across the lectern, its light throwing deep shadows on her bony face. "They want to rehabilitate my murdered husband and me. Comrades, can murderers rehabilitate their victims? Shall they be permitted to rehabilitate? No, never!"

Suddenly the audience awoke. Shouts and applause broke from all parts of the hall. A few of the more timid looked around in amazement. This was unreal, unbelievable.

The woman on the platform was supposedly a traitor, a conspirator against the proletariat in the pay of Western imperialists, whose husband, the foreign minister, together with his fellow conspirators, had been executed for their unforgivable crimes amidst general rejoicing.

Heavily gold-braided officers among the audience looked uncomfortable. Up on the rostrum, conducting the meeting, were seated nine top Communists of Hungary; among them were Colonel General Szabo, member of the Politburo, the highest party organ, and Karoly Kiss, president of the Control Commission of the party, the lord high executioner of the Communists. But no one dared to dissent as the encouraging shouts and applause mounted.

"Where were you, comrades," shouted Mrs. Rajk at her enthusiastic audience, "when all these things were happening? How is it that you stood by in silence and permitted this horror to descend upon us? Did you not know that they were framing us—lying in their frenzied effort to grab all power to themselves? How did it happen that the West knew? How did Western journalists know the truth all along, while you did not? Or were you afraid? Are you cowards? Now is the time to prove yourselves!"

At this point Mrs. Rajk's pointed references to Western journalists nearly became my undoing. The blue admission card with which I had entered the hall was given to me by a well-known Hungarian writer whom I was honor-bound to protect. Throughout the evening several of the men seated on the rostrum had been watching me

4

making notes. When Mrs. Rajk, in her speech, reached the passage about Western journalists, those watching held a brief consultation and one came down and asked me what I was doing. People nearby heard our exchange, and one of them hissed at the official, "Haven't you covered up enough of your crimes?" The man returned to the stage.

Now came the dramatic climax of Mrs. Rajk's appearance. She asked the audience to pledge to the memory of her martyred husband an unrelenting crusade to punish those who were guilty of ruining Hungary.

Again facing the speaker's table with blazing eyes, she shouted: "You not only killed my husband; you killed all decency in our country! You destroyed Hungary's political, economic, and moral life. There is only one answer to you: You must be punished for your crimes!"

As she stopped speaking and turned toward the steps leading from the stage, the entire audience, including the now chalk-faced officials on the rostrum, rose and gave her a standing ovation.

For minutes the cheering, applauding, shouting Communists demanded that Mrs. Rajk continue. But she broke down and, fighting against upwelling tears, made for the door.

After Mrs. Rajk's speech the tone of the meeting hardened. Speaker after speaker denounced the leadership of the country and that of the Communist party of Hungary. Although no one dared to utter the sacrosanct name of Rakosi, the party boss, the meaning was unmistakable.

Dr. Hajdu, a veteran of fifty years in various Marxist movements, brought his audience to its feet with a vivid comparison in his closing words: "In ancient Ethiopia," he said, "when a man outlived his usefulness, he lay quietly down outside the stables of cattle, mules, and other dumb animals, and had himself trampled to death. I ask you, old comrades, are we to lie down before our assorted dumb animals and let ourselves be trampled to death?"

Earlier, Dr. Hajdu, a witty and brilliant speaker, had turned on the autocrats of the Communist party of Hungary, and cried: "The comrades always speak in the name of the workers and peasants— how do the comrades know what the workers and peasants say or think? They are surrounded by yes men and bootlickers who parlayed

5

the art of kissing the behinds of our almighty comrades into a plush living. These lackeys report to them only what they want to hear. Where else would they get their information? They never ride streetcars or buses. They ride in their chauffeur-driven limousines. They never go to the markets because they have their special stores. Not even when ill are they exposed to ordinary people, because they have an all-high, all-private, all-exclusive hospital of their own."

The meeting broke up in the early morning hours; and as the limousines of the high officials pulled away from the ornate building, hundreds of lower-echelon Communists who had organized the meeting remained on street corners and gathered in bars and clubs to continue the debate and plot their future course. For obviously this was part of a country-wide movement to undermine the still-entrenched Stalinists and blast them out of power. It was June, 1956, nearly three months after Khrushchev's speech to the Twentieth Party Congress in Moscow, in which he denounced the bloody tyranny of Stalin and his henchmen. Nothing that Khrushchev said was new to the long-suffering peoples within the Soviet orbit: but that things of this sort could be talked about was delightfully new.

Whereas a year before in Hungary I had to go to great lengths to make people talk to me in confidence, and had wound up my visit to the country with a heated row in the Foreign Office when I showed them the material I had collected and asked for denial or confirmation, this time I was eagerly sought out by all sorts of Communist functionaries and intellectuals. The atmosphere was still heavily laden with the oppressive humidity of crowded prison cells, torture chambers, and internment camps, but the slight cool breeze which had begun to stir throughout the country was intoxicating.

I had known before the meeting that a plan was afoot for a thorough housecleaning in Hungary. "Plan" is perhaps the wrong word. Nearly everyone I talked to—managers, party functionaries, writers, journalists, artists, intellectuals—spoke of the need for immediate changes. They were asking, agitating for them, and the sum of their plaints amounted to a vague plan. There was no conscious direction of the movement; but writers and intellectuals were printing stories, exposing the cruelty, wastefulness, and inhumanity of the regime, and tirelessly organizing meetings to

6

castigate the leadership. They planned their steps one by one, but as an overall plan for Hungary they had nothing but a set of high-sounding principles. Slowly the tantalizing wine of freedom began to go to their heads. After one successful anti-Rakosi meeting they quickly set about gathering material for the next. They heard the call and became crusaders. My question "Crusaders *for* what?" was always met with "Crusaders *against* this vile system which we blindly helped to build."

While the rebellious Communists appeared to be in the throes of a moral revulsion against themselves and, driven by guilty consciences, were trying to atone for their past, to an outsider the Hungarian scene in the summer of 1956 showed signs of a much deeper disintegration. As one by one the planks of the ideology of the Marxist state were freely examined, they were found to be in an advanced state of decay. The more the pieces were tested, the flimsier the structure was found to be. The process was all the more interesting because Hungary for years had tried to be a mirror of the Soviet Union, faithfully copying Soviet practices in an effort to become the living proof of the superiority of Stalin's ideology to the heresies of Marshal Tito.

As one who held for many years the view that the inner contradictions of Communism would cause its disintegration, I did not now trust my own judgment regarding the situation in Hungary. For one thing, it appeared too good to be true. Moreover, my informants up to this point were intellectuals who, even though sincere, were not in touch with daily events and were apt to exaggerate or project their own feelings. That they were also high-ranking Communist functionaries did not greatly alter my view of them, because during my previous visits they were just as eager to justify the regime as they now were to deprecate it. I did want to hear their stories, but I needed facts at firsthand before I felt I could evaluate their opinions.

That they were in the midst of a great emotional upheaval was obvious; the fact that they were risking their liberty and conceivably their lives almost daily spoke eloquently for their sincerity. But intellectuals, while always in the vanguard of history, often are too far ahead to have a clear and accurate view of what is behind them.

7

I had been greatly impressed by a story written by a Hungarian journalist, Tibor Meray, recounting a gigantic mixup at the new electric plant at Tiszapalkonya, and I decided to retrace his steps. It seemed to me that the ramifications of the story cut across the economy of the entire country, and that a detailed examination would not only reflect the workings of Communist planning but would also afford a close look at the mechanism on which the country's economy rested. This, I decided, should be a painstaking, minute examination of the system from the ground up.

2

Failure of the Five-Year Plan

On my way to Miskolc, I studied the official facts and data issued in connection with the Second Five-Year Plan, which included the proposed plant at Tiszapalkonya. It was, even without the official adjectives, a truly massive undertaking: four turbines to generate 225,000 kilowatts, enough to supply electric power to the entire agricultural section alongside the river Tisza, as well as to the huge new chemical combine a few miles from the power plant, where nylon, Orlon, fertilizer, and other chemicals were to be manufactured. The generators were to be built in Czechoslovakia, and natural gas from Romania was to be piped to the boilers. It was described as a triumph of socialist planning, a mighty cornerstone of Communist power.

At the Kossuth Hotel in Miskolc I met Istvan, secretary of the Communist party district, who came to "correct" the wrong impressions I might have gathered reading Meray's report.

The scandal at Tiszapalkonya began with a Party Day, a monthly boosting session arranged by the Communist party to siphon off widespread dissatisfaction in the country. At this particular meeting the main speaker was Deputy Minister Kilian, who waxed lyrical in describing the joys of socialist labor and the grandeur of Communist planning. Speakers following the minister were more pragmatic; they spoke of the large labor turnover and other assorted ills, due, no doubt, they said, to indifferent comrades who were not quite conscious of their great mission. One section leader proposed the establishment of forced-labor camps to remedy the labor situation. The nearly one thousand workers listening to the official speakers were unimpressed. Then a fifty-four-year-old worker, Jozeph Soltesz, rose and demanded the right to be heard.

He told the functionaries on the stage that it was not forced labor that was needed, but a decent chance to earn a living. Amid growing applause from the audience, he explained that he had come to Tiszapalkonya as a veteran member of the Communist party to help this all-important undertaking, but that he could not sit still when he heard comrades talking about forced labor.

"At the time when old mistakes are being remedied by amnesties and rehabilitations, it is a shame to talk about forced labor, when our marching song reminds us: 'Once labor was a burden, today an heroic deed. . . .' The comrades are just not telling the truth."

And he proceeded to tell it.

For twenty-five days of labor he received 132 forints base pay (the equivalent of $5 in purchasing power) instead of 1,060 forints, the official minimum. With extras his pay came to 210 forints for the month, less than one-sixth of the regular pay. As a family man with four children, he asked, "How do the comrades expect me to stay and work there?" Moreover, when he had asked for the reason for his low pay he was put off with double-talk, but was given no acceptable, valid explanation.

"When I came here six weeks ago, twelve of us reported to work on the same morning. More than half are gone because, as one put it, 'The waters are too muddy here.' Not one of us could earn a living wage no matter how hard and devotedly he worked. My output has always been over 130 per cent, and my pay is less than 20 per cent.

The grim-faced plant chairman, Andras Nagy, vainly tried to bring the meeting to order after Soltesz stopped speaking. The hall was in an uproar; the hitherto apathetic audience came to its feet. The words had been what they wanted to hear, but they could hardly believe that Soltesz, the little stoop-shouldered, white-haired mousy man, had read the riot act to the tin gods seated on the stage.

The ensuing investigation brought to light for the first time what nearly everyone in Hungary knew: "socialist planning," the key to Communist heaven, was a wasteful, cruel, unjust system that was robbing the country of its resources and its people of their wealth and health.

Now, Secretary Istvan was sitting across from me to explain.

"The truth is the truth," said Istvan. "Soltesz did get a big hand from the audience, and it was wrong for the chairman to try to silence him. The party does want criticism and will see to it that justified complaints are rectified. But," he added, "there is always trouble with the press. They come here for a few hours and write rhapsodies about the brilliant achievement at Tiszapalkonya, and about how many new cities it will supply with power, and as a result of this constant propaganda no one is taking the trouble to look into the mess we have here."

"What mess?"

Istvan became evasive. "Well, this is a big thing, and can't be built overnight . . ."

"Why were Soltesz and his co-workers paid such a paltry sum for a month's work?"

Istvan tried the tack the chairman had taken at the meeting so unsuccessfully. "There were many loafers," he said, "in the brigade Soltesz directed, and that brought down the pay for everybody in it." He went on to explain that workers did not get paid for their individual production. Ten or more men in a brigade worked as a team and got paid as a team. What the brigade earned was then divided among its members.

"But why should Soltesz be penalized for the bad work of others? Isn't Soltesz a first-class, above-norm worker?"

"Yes," Istvan replied, "Soltesz did work very hard; everybody knew that. But because the ministry set the production rate at 6,600 forints per man for the base pay of 1,060 forints, when the brigade's production was added up it did not come to more than 20 per cent of the base pay. Nevertheless we lent Soltesz 300 forints, deductible in six monthly installments to tide him over."

Istvan went on to tell me about some saboteurs and loafers who did not yet understand the meaning of "socialist conscience," but his heart was obviously not in it.

"Isn't it true that the reason for the low production of the brigade had nothing to do with loafers and saboteurs but was due to mismanagement?" I asked. "Wasn't there an investigation which showed that not only Soltesz but thousands of workers were victimized by a haphazard supply system that broke down constantly?"

The question had to be repeated three times before Istvan got around to admitting that "that too" played a role.

The following day at Tiszapalkonya, Istvan's defense had shifted: the saboteurs were people somewhere higher up who delayed raw materials so that the workers at Tiszapalkonya had to sit idly around, day in and day out, waiting for supplies. Of course, he said, "No work, no pay; the socialist state can't waste its money on nonproducing people."

The chairman, too, began by saying that a "nonproducing worker can't live on the fat of the producers," and was visibly perturbed that Party Day had not ended with the singing of the International as it usually did. The workers, encouraged by Soltesz, had begun to air their grievances, and a minor revolution was at hand.

Walking through the plant, I met countless people who were eager to tell me their troubles. While a bricklayer was telling me that he hadn't seen a brick in six weeks and consequently could not earn enough to keep his family in cold water, let alone food, a building carpenter was detailing how many days he had had to stop working because the lumber gave out. An electrician reported that when he went to the party secretary to complain about the lack of materials for his work, he was told: "Better shut your mouth or you will find yourself working in Szederkeny." (Szederkeny, a new city in construction for future workers at Tiszapalkonya and at the Chemical Works, was being built by prison labor.)

I sought out the Soltesz brigade. What was the truth of the matter? Who was responsible for the starvation wages the men were getting? Several explained simply: When there was cement to mix, sand was missing. When the sand came, the trucks with the gravel did not arrive. After days of loafing, they at last had all the ingredients but had to stop mixing cement because the foreman told them the structural steel had not come and therefore the cement could not be poured.

And so it went. They were assigned now and then to work to fill in their time, but at work which had a low pay-rate and at which there was no way for them to approach the minimum norm required for the minimum base pay.

The vast construction job at Tiszapalkonya soon began to look like an insane patchwork to me. Thousands of workers, hundreds of supervisors, miles of blueprints, tons of reports, requests, estimates, orders, regulations, slogans, all over the place, thousands of legs and arms scratched bloody because mosquito netting had not arrived for the bunkhouses, swearing, cursing workers, bullying foremen, harassed engineers—all within a few square miles, and all milling around the stark walls of the imposing new edifice of this Triumph of Socialist Planning.

Late in the afternoon I sat with a young engineer on the bank of the river and we tried—as an experiment—to estimate the daily loss at Tiszapalkonya. As the wasted working hours, days, and months mounted, we added the time of the engineers, managers, planners, bureaucrats, party delegates, and police supervisors swarming around the project. Then we tackled the "channels" through which every nail, grain of sand, or mouthful of bread had to travel before it reached Tiszapalkonya, and made a rough estimate of the people involved, their salaries and working hours, to add to our total at Tiszapalkonya.

"You know," chortled the engineer, "I'm not much of an engineer. This is merely my third year out of school, but I could build at least two more Tiszapalkonyas with what we are wasting here while building—if that is the word—this one."

"But can't you people do something about this? You are the experts."

My friend was vastly amused. "Go and see my boss. He's a big shot, the big boss of the project. Go talk to him!"

I did.

Director Jenei was a harassed, distraught little man who could

13

not help being constantly aware of his exposed position. His position corresponded to that of an American on-the-spot general manager of a large project. He was, like all Hungarians, mercilessly hemmed in by the three organs of the state: his superiors, whom he must serve with absolute obedience; the political police, which was ever present and which was the keeper of his constantly updated dossier; and the Communist party, to whom he had to account for every word and every act—official or private—and had to justify himself in line with the currently issued party directive.

He had endured the atmosphere around him as long as he could, but at the time of my visit he was obviously at the end of his tether. It was unkind to press him, because I had an uneasy feeling throughout our conversation that he might blow up and really put his finger on the sore spots, thereafter living in constant terror of the three ogres above and around him. I restricted my questions, therefore, to his immediate problems. I had, by then, a definite line which I wanted to follow: I would obtain a series of step-by-step interviews with people in charge of the project in order to confront the ultimate source of socialist wisdom—whoever he or they might be—with data which could not be explained with a slogan or a quotation from Lenin or Marx.

Jenei's story was very simple. He did his best and more. He used his friends and family connections to get things "in the black" for his project, but it was an uphill, infuriating job.

As he unfolded his story, it appeared that he had been fighting day and night for raw materials and supplies.

"But wasn't your project planned? My understanding was that it was carefully planned from the top down through dozens of offices and in the minutest detail."

A gleam came to his eyes and he snorted. "Planned, did you say?" He continued vehemently: "What is planned about the fact that right this minute I need 1,200,000 bricks to keep working and I have here a certificate for 80,000? Then, when I scream my head off, go from one office to another, making enemies as I go along, I am graciously given 500,000 more. Do you know what happens to a plan which operates that way?

"Look around you; that's what happens. But there is more: here in the neighborhood is a brick kiln. I could get brick from there within a few hours. But, no, I have no trucks! I get my bricks from a city hundreds of kilometers from here and wait weeks to get them.

"Enough? Oh, no! If I get the bricks from my neighbor it would cost me twice as much as I am paying for them from the distant place. Why? Because I can't get the railroad to transport the bricks from my neighbor, and truck transportation costs three times as much. I have the certificates. For less than half what I need. Now, all I have to do is go from one bureaucrat to another up and down the land to get railroad-car allocation for my bricks. Planned, did you say?"

"Why did you bother with the cost of transportation? You aren't working for capitalists; it's all state money."

The director looked at me pityingly and explained that he had a budget. Somebody, somewhere—sitting maybe on a cloud—decided that Tiszapalkonya should be built for so much and no more.

"What do you think?" he asked savagely. "Why have so many engineers been jailed for sabotage? Because they could not build for what the man on the cloud said they should build it for. They 'wasted' state money. Why do you suppose we have to let our Solteszes earn less than starvation wages? Because we are heartless machines? No, because we can't afford to be saboteurs."

Then he gave me a long list of materials that were missing, including several hundred tons of construction steel, insulating material, electric wires, cement, and lumber. For each of the missing items, he said, he had to wage a major battle.

"Of course we can't keep workers here!" he said. "Not only is our labor turnover intolerable, nearly 60 per cent, but our best workers are the first to leave us!"

As I listened to the director, the plant chairman, the party secretary, and several engineers and foremen, it appeared that they were just as much caught in an inexorable net of circumstances as the thousands of Solteszes in Tiszapalkonya. When they were endeavoring to justify their actions before their superiors, they were merely trying to defend their own jobs and often their skins. They appeared to be humane, kind, and just men who were charged with impossible tasks and who were trying to the point of exhaustion to fulfill them. They were clearly aware of the lot of the workers, and that the cost of this senseless circus had to be taken out of the hides of the little men and their families. Even the bully among them, the plant chairman, Andras Nagy, who had tried to silence Soltesz, admitted that the men were mistreated and that he had been fighting with the higher-ups for months to get some chairs, tables, beds, mosquito netting, spoons and forks for the barracks. But many of them still ate with their hands, slept on the floors, had nowhere to hang their clothes, and had to endure all night the onslaught of billions of mosquitoes from the river because he could not get what the plan for Tiszapalkonya called for.

The director's steel shortage was not one man's doing. His requisition left the local committee to go to the district office of the Power Development Corporation; from there, properly endorsed, it arrived at the office of the National Power Development Office; there the requisition was again examined, and sent to the Ministry of Construction, and from there to the Ministry of Heavy Industry. Then the arc began to incline downward; from the Ministry of Heavy Industry to the Steel Trust, from the Trust to the district steel-production office, and at last to the steel plant itself.

The requisition for transportation of the steel had to follow the same arc to its final destination—the railroad office allocation officer and his numerous minions.

While tracing the route a requisition for anything had to follow, I had the sensation of seeing a weird super-Rube-Goldberg machine with its thousands of arms interlocking and Director Jenei trying to pull a lever to make the thing move. And when it finally did move, the machine made the most ungodly motions and noise man's fancy could invent.

To climb over this entire monstrosity of a bureaucratic spiderweb seemed a hopeless task, and I decided to take short cuts.

My next stop was the chief engineer of the Power Development Office, who sent me to the general national director of the outfit called National Power Development Corporation.

But first the chief engineer gave me a brief outline of his major troubles: chronic shortages. "If it's not steel, then it's lumber or cement or tools or any of the hundreds of materials we need here. Why? How should I know? We just don't get things here on time, and every once in awhile the whole gigantic project comes to a halt. But even if the whole project were not stopped at once, parts are always lagging. Then one part has to wait for the other to catch up."

The director of the National Power Development Corporation was Ferencz Pikler, a knowledgeable, efficient, and devoted engineer. I gave him all the information that I had accumulated about the project at Tiszapalkonya, and asked him: Why?

"Because the plan [The Five-Year Plan] was not in line with our capacity. We engineers knew this when the plan was debated in the Parliament, and we warned the Council of Ministers—but they wouldn't listen to us. We just haven't got the wherewithal to build all these large projects. They looked beautiful on paper; all the facts and figures—well padded with wishful thinking—balanced well, and the comrades made impassioned speeches, and the first thing we knew the plan was adopted and we were elected."

He would not name the responsible persons, but merely made it clear that he had no bed of roses and that he wished some of the comrades would wake up and establish a more workable priority over the projects. With a wry grin he added, "Let's save at least one or two before they all collapse."

I was getting closer, now, to the top level, the last stop on the line of alibis.

One more stop on the road up was Deputy Minister of Construction Kilian. The burden of his song was the same: the plan was not planned right. Even *if* they had the materials, there was no reserve to make up for miscalculations. But even if they had had all the materials needed on all the projects, there would be not enough transportation facilities to take care of them.

"The only reason we haven't a critical breakdown of our transportation system right now is the shortage of materials. That's our silver lining," he said.

He mentioned other large-scale mixups besides the one at Tiszapalkonya. Coal development had not been able to take care of new factories and plants, and the gigantic projects were either half idle or were supplied with coal from faraway mines at excessive cost.

17

The chemical combine near Tiszapalkonya was being built while no one had the slightest idea of its purpose; its technology had not been worked out.

"What will happen if the combine isn't able to produce the required materials once its technology is established?"

"We'll rebuild it," he said with a shrug.

The trail now ended. I had spoken to nearly all of the technicians and managers connected with Soltesz's income. It was time to tackle the political figures who decreed Hungary's economy. I had enough facts and figures to ask anyone: Can you defend on any ground this mess which goes under the title of Scientific Socialist Planning?

I first fired this question at the Communist party's (then called Hungarian Workers' party) Secretariat for Economic Matters.

Here a brief explanation is in order. On record, the government was the executive organ of the state. But no executive or legislative prerogatives were exercised in Hungary (or in any other Communist-controlled land) without direct control of the respective section of the Communist party. For instance: The minister of culture was, on record, the highest officer in educational and artistic matters. But nothing he said or did was formulated by him, but by the Section for Cultural Matters of the party. It may have happened, as it often did, that the minister was at the same time also a high functionary of the section of the party which governed his activities.

Therefore it seemed to me that there was little sense in my pursuing my quest among government bureaus. The more direct route was by way of the party secretariat where the theoreticians, economists, and scientific Marxists, interpreters of Lenin, Stalin, and Rakosi, were dwelling.

My first encounter was with Academician Fogarthy, a respected pillar of the Communist party. "Professor," I asked, "why do you build huge industrial projects for which you have no fuel and for which every ounce of raw material has to be imported? And, to make it worse, you haven't even got the money for the imports."

"In the first place," he replied, "we will not need money for imports because we will develop our own resources—in time. In the second place, without basic industries such as we are building the total economy of our country could not be developed."

"I take it that you refer to a new economy for the country, since Hungary has been in existence for a thousand years and often has been very prosperous?" I asked.

"Yes, the economy of the country must be planned scientifically," he said, "to reach the highest peak of its capacity."

"Assuming for the moment that you have a valid point, before I can accept what you say with any degree of confidence I must ask you to tell me why you find it necessary for Hungary to compete with highly industrialized countries whose efficiency and productive capacity you are unlikely to equal and whose production costs, under any circumstances, would be much lower than Hungary's."

"This is a revolutionary stage of a world-wide struggle," said the professor, "and we must be industrially ready for the struggle."

"How can you think of entering into an economic struggle against the West when your industrial plants can't function without Western resources and Western markets? Moreover, isn't this so-called struggle outlandish, when you can't feed your own people?"

"That is the core of our striving, our revolutionary planning: to make us independent of you," answered the professor.

We were getting nowhere, so I said: "I won't embarrass you by asking you how good your plans are or how valid this whole theory of revolutionary necessity may be. I won't even ask you whether you consulted your people when you decided on this plan, for if you say, yes, you did, you would not be telling the truth, and if you say, no, you did not, you would be a traitor to Marxism. But I will say this: If I have understood the Marxian point of view, then the justification of socialist planning rests on the theory that the new world would be more efficient than the old, that the Marxian system would therefore build better, more economically, and to the greater benefit of the people than the old system, our system, democratic capitalism. How then do you explain the horrible waste, suffering, inefficiency, and real hunger which prevails in this normally rich country?"

I had shown economic data, ranging from the ridiculous to the tragic to Professor Fogarthy at the beginning of our discussion. Now I wanted to hear his justification.

"Some of the waste you spoke of was the result of the economic blockade which you Americans have decreed against us. Some was the result of mistakes. We are still at the beginning of our career as a socialist state and we make our share of mistakes."

Professor Fogarthy had no justification—no real explanation for me. When I asked him why the workers were condemned to pay for the mistakes of the higher-ups, the professor blandly told me that no one was permitted to go hungry in the country. I could not make up my mind whether he was lying or really didn't know. A third possibility occurred to me later: he may have been afraid.

Some other members of the secretariat pointed to the fact that the party's political bureau was really the final word on all matters, and its first secretary, Matyas Rakosi, was the fountainhead. There were mistakes, they said, but they were in the process of rectification. The Second Five-Year Plan was to be revised, and more attention would be paid to consumer goods. In addition, the wage and production structure of the country would be overhauled to eliminate "errors."

Nothing they said answered the key question: Why was it necessary to build what they were calling "socialism" at such a horrible price?

3

The Intellectuals

Ten days of intensive research throughout the country brought me back to Budapest by late June, and to a new series of encounters. While visiting schools in the country I met many bewildered teachers who were at a loss to know how to interpret the changes taking place in the Communist world. What were they to teach? Continue with Stalin the Great General, Stalin the Great Scientist, Stalin the Great Benefactor? What about the "new line," the new "interpretation" of Holy Marx, Lenin, and their Beloved Hungarian Apostle Rakosi?

Mrs. Ferencz Vadasz, deputy minister of education, agreed to discuss with me the problems of the educators and their obsolete textbooks.

A warm, motherly person, intelligent, and far above the run-of-the-mill Communist officials, Mrs. Vadasz was obviously devoted to her calling. A friend who gave me a short biography of Mrs. Vadasz before I met her described her as a "consecrated person whose sole concern is the education of youth" and who is not overly sanguine about Marxism. To Mrs. Vadasz, my informant said, Marxism was but an adjunct to, and not the goal of, education.

Mrs. Vadasz began the interview by showing me some impressive figures. In 1917, she said, at the annual mathematics competition, only three university men were able to solve the same problems which at the 1955 competition were solved by 1,500 middle-school (equivalent to U.S. junior-high) students. She went on to describe the curriculums of various schools, and when she came to political education I asked her whether she would care to tell me about the changes in that field. She readily acknowledged that it was a troublesome job. For one thing, the printing presses of the country were not able to replace all the textbooks which had to be canceled. She estimated it would take three years to bring the textbooks into harmony with the party line.

"Meanwhile?"

"Meanwhile we send our detailed instruction sheets to the teachers."

"Would you care to give me a set of those?"

After a slight hesitation she agreed, and I was handed a set of mimeographed sheets entitled "Suggestions to Middle School Teachers for the Use of the Directives of the Twentieth Congress."

Mrs. Vadasz did not attempt to minimize the troubles educators were encountering in trying to make students unlearn what they were taught earlier. She said that the most frequent complaint was that the students objected to being asked questions at the examinations which called for different answers from those they were taught during the school term.

Mrs. Vadasz, during our talk, often returned to her pet theory that education should be directed toward the development of thinking.

"But, Mrs. Vadasz, does not the present unrest in schools, particularly in higher educational institutions, arise from students throwing off their yoke of formalized, dogmatic thinking and trying to cut new paths for themselves?" I inquired.

"Yes, but it is a healthy trend," she said.

22

"Would not the encouragement of individualism lead to questioning a whole set of presently applied Marxian assumptions?"

Mrs. Vadasz hesitated for a long time, and finally explained that Marxism was not a dogmatic creed but a constantly evolving system.

"Isn't what you say contrary to the government's present practice of enforcing compliance with certain dogmas by all the police power of the state?" I asked.

"You are talking about Stalinism," she replied; "but that is a thing of the past. It was a perversion of Marxism."

The young Foreign Office attaché who accompanied me on my visit to Mrs. Vadasz was gloomy when we left the building. I asked him how he could explain the difference between what Mrs. Vadasz had said and the rigid police controls and careful scrutiny we encountered upon entering and leaving the building.

Victor, the attaché, was a bewildered young man. As an orthodox Communist, he was watching the entire structure of his values slowly crumble before his eyes. Earlier, while we drove to a factory, we had passed the huge Stalin memorial and I asked him how long it would be tolerated there. He was momentarily outraged. But suddenly recalling Khrushchev's exposure of Stalin, he lamely said that though Stalin in his later years made "mistakes," his statue would remain forever because Stalin's errors were far outweighed by his great services to Communism. I laughingly offered him a bet that the huge monstrosity would be gone within a year.

Mrs. Vadasz, as well as a number of intellectuals and writers, had given me the name of a Professor Gyorgy Lukacs as the foremost theoretician of the avant-garde, anti-Stalinist, prodemocratic Marxists. Dr. Lukacs had been rehabilitated just a few weeks before my arrival in Budapest and had been permitted to resume his teaching of Marxian ethics at the university. Imre Nagy, another recently rehabilitated anti-Stalinist leader and former prime minister, also was teaching at the university. I wanted to meet them. A well known writer, a friend of both of them, agreed to arrange the meeting.

In the meantime, I had issued invitations to a number of writers and intellectuals, who were then openly attacking the regime, to be my guests for a weekend at Lake Balaton. The resort town of

Balatonfoldvar was chosen for the meeting because it was somewhat off the beaten path and because only skeleton crews were running the hotels; we hoped they would not keep strict records of my guests. The season on the Balaton began on July 1st, after which all hotel accommodations were centrally controlled by state bureaus; but until then there was a fair chance for our little get-together to go unnoticed.

During the weekend I received, at various times, twenty-two guests. For reasons which were explained earlier, I cannot, even at this late date, identify them. To avoid confusion in describing parts of our discussions, I have assigned to them first names which bear no relation to their real names. Of these guests, seven were writers whose names were well known in Hungary, five were university professors, five were engineers, three were Communist party functionaries, and two were athletes. Of the twenty-two, eight were women, one of whom was the secretary of the Communist party in an important industrial district.

"If I have understood you correctly," I said, during one of our discussions, "you accuse the late Stalin of having caused grievous damage to you in three fields: First, there is, as you say, serious damage to your ideology and moral standing; second, his economic policies were wasteful and inhuman, thereby retarding Communist advance; and, finally, Stalin almost irreparably damaged the relations between Russian Communists and all other Communists. These things Stalin did in the name of Marxism. However, in the words of Mrs. Rajk, you members of the party not only followed him blindly, but nearly deified him."

Ivan, whose by-line in various Communist newspapers and magazines made him a familiar figure, replied: "We knew from the start that our ideology was at variance with our practice. However, until the late twenties we hoped that the bitterness and terror which prevailed in Russia following the various attempts by White armies to unseat the Bolsheviks would be mitigated and gradually eliminated. But the shock caused by the abrupt regimentation of Russian economy delayed from day to day the dismantling of the dictatorship. At least, that was what we were told and that is what we believed.

"Every pressure from the party for legality and decency was answered by Stalin's conjuring up another emergency. Thus, using real and pseudo emergencies, Stalin first violated and later overthrew altogether Marxian morality and ideology. Then he proceeded to substitute his personal interpretation of Marx and Lenin, and anyone who objected to Stalin's perversions was dealt with summarily by his personal palace guard."

"Would it be correct to say that you accepted Stalin because of fear?" I asked.

Before Ivan could answer, Mariska, the party secretary, interrupted to say: "No. That was a small part of it, at the beginning at least, because we did believe that Stalin's harsh methods were justified and necessary. The sinister aspect dawned on us only when we began a closer examination of the entire Stalin period after Khrushchev's speech to the Twentieth Congress this spring. Although since the war there had been tensions both inside and outside Russia, Khrushchev's speech directed our attention to the real source of our troubles. But the truth is that we all believed in Stalin. We worshiped him; he was our hero. There is no denying that."

Pointing to Ivan, she continued: "Ivan wrote many of the most fulsome hymns to Stalin ever printed anywhere. We were spellbound by our own propaganda, and accepted the idea that Stalin knew best what to do and why."

Another writer added: "All through the war, during the Nazi and Nyilas regimes, and even before them, we were looking for salvation, trying to escape the horrors of the years between the two wars. Frankly, the West failed us; the Germans and their Hungarian henchmen were murdering us, and we turned to Stalin as our savior. We needed a belief, a creed which at best promised a new life for us. That's why we believed so thoroughly in Stalin and that is why everything is collapsing around us now that he has been exposed as a monster."

"I don't want to bait you," I said, "but again echoing Mrs. Rajk, how could you ever have believed in the righteousness of such horrible terror as prevailed here and in other Communist countries?"

Klara, the matronly professor of botany at the university, said: "I know, I know. I can't believe that I could have been that stupid, that gullible. I just can't explain it. But perhaps if I tell you what happened to me, you will at least understand the process of believing, even though you may not agree."

She proceeded to tell the following story. She had a colleague, a respected professor, whom she knew well and admired greatly, who disappeared one day. Sometime later it became known that he had been arrested as a Western spy. Klara was outraged. It was impossible for her to believe that her friend could have been a traitor to anything. He was much too honest, much too outspoken to conspire.

"The more I investigated," she said, "the more party higher-ups I talked to, the more it appeared to me possible that unscrupulous Western agents had taken advantage of my friend. It never occurred to me that it could have been a frame-up or that my friend was really a spy. We, I thought, were too honest to be parties to such a miscarriage of justice. On the other hand my fallen friend was too gullible to have been able to defend himself against the wiles of enemy agents.

"Today," she continued, "it seems incredible even to me that I could have believed this, but what else was I to do? It sounded weird and unreal to accuse my comrades of senseless injustice. The result was that for some time, I and some of my friends became even more careful in our contacts with Westerners."

Klara's theme was enlarged upon by several others. They had begun to see things around them which *appeared* cruel and unjust, but they could not bring themselves to believe that such a monstrous betrayal of their ideals was possible. Many of them had fallen back on the easy way out. The authorities were in a position to know best what was going on. But many had become alert and questioning. And toward the end of 1955, after nearly seven years of credulous bewilderment, their slowly dawning suspicions had become a conviction: they were trapped and betrayed.

"Did you believe," I asked, "after Stalin had been exposed, that your system would become viable and humane and would, in fact, create an earthly paradise?"

The question was protested as being unfair. In the babel of voices which were trying to outbid one another, Laszlo, the novelist, managed to be heard.

"Don't let anyone fool you," he said. "We are Communists and we shall remain Communists. What is happening to us is not a rebellion against our ideals, but against the misuse of those ideals. We can't stand by and watch the further perversion of socialism, and we won't lend ourselves any longer to immoral practices."

Gyula, a party functionary, added: "We erred, we confessed, and we are ready and eager to make amends; we are making them and shall continue to make them until we are on the right track."

One of the most interesting statements was made by Ivan, who claimed that Stalin was anti-Communist. I asked for a bill of particulars.

"Stalin was anti-Communist, first, because he was responsible for the loss of moral excellence without which Communism cannot exist. Second, Stalin suffered from Caesaromania, and infected the entire Communist movement with it. And, finally, had Stalin been a true Marxist he would have known that the great new inventions and new technology outdated the Soviet system of 1924, and he would have realized the urgent necessity of major revisions in the Soviet structure."

Stalin, Stalin, Stalin. All our conversations revolved around Stalin and his Hungarian henchman Matyas Rakosi, who was widely advertised as the "best beloved disciple of the great Stalin." I had the uneasy feeling of listening again to Germans after the war blaming everything on Hitler. It was too pat, too glib. After all, no matter how Stalin had perverted Marxism, these people at one time accepted his rule as truly Marxian.

"Tell me," I asked, "aren't you using Stalin as a whipping boy? You seem to be gnawed by guilty conscience and to be blaming everything—your own misdeeds—on Stalin and Rakosi. But it seems to me that that is not all of it. The changes which you are now making—including the exposure of Stalin—may also be explained by the fact that the people here, as well as in Russia and in other Communist countries, exerted such pressure against your leadership that in order to avoid an explosion you had to make these changes. Stalin's death, however it came about, seems to have been a bonanza to you."

Tihamer, a respected professor of the Pazmany University, and formerly an alternate member of the Central Committee of the Communist Workers' party, expressed the consensus:

"True, had Stalin lived, the changes would have had to come, anyway. Stalin's death merely made it easier for us to revolt against what we were doing. Communism, as practiced by us and the

27

Russians, led to an economic and moral vacuum. There was no way out. We met a dead end. The forced industrialization cut the living standard of our people below an endurable level. Only terror kept the workers at their jobs and kept them from revolting. But terror was immoral as well as anti-Marxian. So a choice had to be made between continuing in one form or another the statism of the past or stopping and returning to Marxism. We made the choice. But it is running away with us. It is carrying us toward reexamination of the whole theory of 'salvation from above,' of a handful of Communists telling the people what ought to be good for them. This, too, is anti-Marxian because it is antidemocratic, and there can be no genuine socialism without democracy. Now we have to evolve— slowly, so that we won't bring down the whole edifice. Nevertheless, by the time we get through it will be substantially a new building."

"What kind of building?"

"I don't know. I know that it started with Marx and was continued by Lenin and that now we shall reshape it to suit ourselves and the requirements of the second half of the twentieth century."

Everyone became uneasy after the professor's statement. What he said came uncomfortably close to treason, and despite the brave words of my guests freedom was still too elusive in Hungary to be taken for granted. Except for a few fire-eaters, most of those I had spoken to during the weekend were acutely aware of the ominous fact that whatever freedom existed in Hungary was granted from above and could be withdrawn from above just as easily. Rakosi still was the boss of Hungary, and while I was assured by high party officials that the Central Committee had an anti-Rakosi majority, the executive organ of the party, the Politburo, renamed Presidium, was firmly in Rakosi's pudgy hands. And no one was willing to hazard a guess as to how strongly Rakosi was "in" with the Russians, to whom the last word belonged in all matters affecting life in Hungary.

There were straws in the wind, however, indicating that the Russians were willing to grant the country some political autonomy. Suslov, the man in charge of satellite affairs in the Russian Politburo, was in Budapest, and I had been informed that he was trying to talk Rakosi into resigning but that he forbade the complete rehabilitation of Imre Nagy, the former prime minister, whose return to power would have been accepted by Hungarians as a guarantee of better days. The Russians, however, regarded Nagy as a super-Tito, a man who was Hungarian first and Communist afterward and who, in a pinch, could not be relied upon to remain faithful to Moscow.

Hungarian Communist leaders also feared Imre Nagy. He was the prime minister who in 1953 had ordered a searching investigation into the activities of the political police, granted the right to peasants to leave the collectives if they desired, and forbade forcible collectivization. Furthermore, Imre Nagy in his economic planning ignored the grandiose plans of Rakosi and his megalomaniac planners and decreed greater emphasis on consumer goods in the face of demands by the orthodox Communists for continued forced industrialization.

Nagy became the rallying point of all dissident Communists and rebellious non-Communists. His sixtieth birthday, a few days before our meeting at Balaton, had been an occasion of ostentatious homage to the man as a demonstration against the regime. Intellectuals, scientists, artists, and even a large number of Communist functionaries had assembled at Nagy's country home outside Budapest to assure Nagy, who was still in the Communist doghouse, of their loyalty. Government officials, however, remained strictly anti-Nagy.

In this nervous, uncertain atmosphere it was not surprising that my guests, even though willing to defy authorities and spend some time with me, still were somewhat uneasy at the frank exchanges which were taking place. Added to their discomfort was my own bad odor in the nostrils of Hungarian officialdom. I had had several encounters with high-echelon Communists during which I had responded to the smiling opening gambit, "How do you find Hungary?" with a blunt "Rotten to the core," and had continued with a detailed description of case histories of bloodcurdling injustices which I had investigated in 1955. Several heated debates had ensued in various ministries as a result of my caustic criticisms.

Thus, my guests did run a certain risk accepting my invitation even though a number of them were not registered at the hotel, and a few came down in the morning and returned to Budapest at night. During the three days of Balatonfoldvar there were never more than ten persons present at one time. To many, their talks with me represented a part of their rebellion, a daring, hitherto dangerous deviation. It was clear that even the most timid among them was in a state of ferment. A new brew was in the making, and what its effect would be no one could predict, regardless of what the still-faithful Marxists were saying.

Perhaps the most interesting and most thoroughly profitable discussion during the weekend began with an attack on me. I was called upon to defend McCarthyism, the cold war, the unequal status of the Negro, certain FBI practices, loyalty boards, and the like.

I tried to explain that these un-American manifestations at home were reflexes in response to fears engendered by Communist activities in all parts of the world. True, I said, some of our practices and policies were indefensible, but I pointed out that we still were able to speak out strongly against them, even though we might risk stigma, an ugly label, or even the loss of a job. I granted that most of the hysteria in the United States was the result of cheap political trickery, and that we and the Soviet people seem to be in competition to bring out the worst in each other because of our fears. But I argued that, even though we might slip now and then, the sum total of our national and international efforts was concentrated on progressive growth toward greater abundance, greater political liberty, and more humane adjustment between man's freedom and his allegiance to the state.

In no time at all we were in the midst of a discussion of what is the permissible limit which an unwanted and unpopular state machinery may reach in trying to compel its citizens to accept and serve it.

"Did not Lenin enlarge Marx's 'dictatorship of the proletariat' thesis to include the compelling, by whatever means, of the acceptance and maintenance of Bolshevist rule by the people?" I asked.

There were several attempts to hedge the question, but upon repeating it I got the answer from Ivan.

"During the take-over period, dictatorship to control the class enemies of the proletariat is justifiable, but only in case of active civil war or incitement to a civil war."

"But both Lenin and Stalin exceeded these limits," I said.

"Not Lenin," was the reply, "because while Lenin participated in the government there was constant threat of an invasion of the

Soviet Union by armed White terrorists. There were seven groups of military formations armed by the West sent at one time or another against Russia. Stalin's crime was to perpetuate this state of dictatorship unnecessarily and ultimately to employ it against his personal enemies."

"Will someone please describe the operation of the three forces which keep a Soviet citizen in constant terror?" I asked. "I have heard much about their paralyzing effects, and I have a wealth of data about incidents relating to them, but I should like to hear a description of their structures."

The quietest of my guests was Tamas, a civil engineer who was one of six among them who had been imprisoned for three years on a framed charge and had been recently rehabilitated. Having lived through the horror himself, he was persuaded to tell me what I had asked for.

"I am not an expert, despite my experiences," he began, "and all I know is common knowledge. The surveillance begins at home. Your house delegate keeps a record of your comings and goings. He reports to the AVH [State Security Authority], and they keep a dossier on you. Periodically they visit your neighbors and friends, asking about you. Then they encourage anyone who knows something about you to report to them. They will tell you it is your patriotic duty to inform on your friends and neighbors. Anyone, simply anyone, could send an anonymous letter, which goes into your file. That file is called your *kader*; you live and die by it. If you are accused of something, you never have a chance to face your accuser. It is enough that the accusation is in your kader.

"Everyone has a kader. With most youngsters it is begun in the first grade of school. I venture to say that each of us would be terribly shocked if he were permitted to look at his own kader. The shepherd in the hills may have a simple kader: it would show whom he knows, to whom he talks, who his relatives are, and how reliable he has shown himself to the regime. The engineer, however, will have a huge kader.

"Besides all the gossip the investigators can gather about you, your kader also contains a minute description of your work and the evaluation of your work by the kader keeper, who is a representative of the Interior Ministry and of the AVH. Even though what is in your kader is purely malicious gossip, you will never be permitted to prove it to be so. What is in your kader is sacrosanct.

"The kader also accompanies you wherever you go. If you change your home, the new district will get it. If you change your work, a new kader keeper takes charge of it. For better or worse, it is your shadow; and it is a dangerous one because you never know what it contains. Everything you do or want to do depends on your kader. If you want to travel, buy a bicycle, ask for a better apartment, a raise, or a new working opportunity, your kader will be consulted first. It makes it possible for a single mean, unscrupulous person to place a stigma upon you for the rest of your life. *That* is the kader."

Tamas glanced around as if for confirmation, and then continued. "The next set of chains you carry in our system is forged around you at the place of your employment. You also owe absolute, blind obedience to the party secretary at your place of employment. And if the chairman of the UB [Plant Committee] finds fault with you, regardless of how faithfully you peform your work, you are in trouble. But even if you are a paragon, and manage to please everyone, it may still happen that one day you will be selected as the sacrificial goat because the norm was not fulfilled or because of some other displeasing event at your place of work. In that case you are arrested and tried as a saboteur in the pay of Western imperialists. Once you are chosen, nothing will stop them from sending you to jail or hanging you, depending on how vocal you are. If you are quiet and confess, and beat your breast even though you know nothing of the crime you are charged with, you may escape with your life.

"The fear of your kader and the fear of being dragged into something at your place of work which might destroy you are both overshadowed by your fear of the AVH and of the party. The two are the same, because the AVH is the fanatical arm of the party. Nonattendance at political meetings, a misinterpreted word you dropped at a dinner, the letter of complaint you may have written about the plumbing in your apartment—everything comes under the scrutiny of the AVH or a party functionary."

He stopped, trying to think of how to describe the AVH and the party, and finally looked up with a wry smile, and said: "There are

32

no words to tell you of the tens of thousands of ways you may run afoul of the AVH, or of how you must behave to guard against being arrested, because there is no way to be secure in our system. I guess it's a matter of luck or time when and how you will be called to account for something which was deemed unpatriotic. . . ."

There was a depressing silence after Tamas had spoken. Then one by one stories were told to illustrate what Tamas had said. Their suppressed indignation poured forth in dozens of instances of cruelty, callousness, injustice, and degradation. Not impressive, big stories, but tales of pinpricks by arrogant tax collectors, traffic police, minor municipal officials, streetcar conductors, store clerks, inspectors, and waiters. Seemingly everyone who came in contact with the public was affected by the tenor of the regime. To hear these people was like listening to the murmur of an angry sea; to see them was like looking at men and women possessed by a disease which made them claw one another and themselves with sharp, dirty fingernails.

This low-echelon cruelty was not new to me. I had observed it in every type of dictatorship or authoritarian state in Europe and in the Americas. It is an inexorable consequence of tyranny, and it spreads from the top and affects everyone, especially minor officials, permeating the entire socio-political life of the country. The petty Nazis were often crueler and more brutal than their leaders; the same was true of Fascists of all varieties; and the same was apparently true of the Communists.

Here at the Balaton, and during my swing across the country, the dominant refrain was insecurity and the fear which begets it. The Hungarians, always a humorous people, divided themselves into three categories: one, those who had been through prison or penal camp; two, those who were there now; and, three, those who were going to be taken. Another thing I found among them, which seemed typical of totalitarian countries, was that everyone was affected, but the higher the person's position on the social or political ladder, the greater his fears.

Four months later, during the revolution, I was to get an explanation for this fear among the elite from a wounded rebel who was the manager of a large industrial combine.

The feeling of being trapped in a high position was general

among Communist officeholders and functionaries, and even among non-Communist professional men. A dismissal from a position was not only that; it was also a disgrace with serious consequences affecting one's family and friends. There was no quitting, and this alone was one of the most powerful deterrents to rebellion.

There was one distinct difference between the complaints of my guests at Balaton and those of the population in general. It was generally admitted that things had improved politically, economically, and legally during the past few months and that things were on the upgrade. Even to an outsider like myself the changes were visible. For instance, the meeting at Balatonfoldvar could not have occurred the year before because, if for no other reason, very few people would have accepted my invitation. The difference between the intellectuals, engineers, Communist functionaries and professional men on one hand, and the people on the other, was that the former passionately believed that the improvements would continue until a free democratic socialist state was achieved. The people as a whole mistrusted their new-found freedom and were, by and large, uninterested in the struggle that was taking shape. Most of the common people believed it to be futile to fight the regime, whereas the large majority of the country's elite was determined to continue the fight at all costs until final victory. This difference was largely due to the apathy with which the workers and peasants viewed their life and to their hopelessness regarding the future.

Discussion of this difference with my guests produced some disturbing thoughts and a plausible explanation. They foresaw the difficulty in forcing concessions from the regime if the masses were not behind them, for they would thus expose themselves to the charges of bourgeois deviationism and of fomenting insurrection. As for the reason for the indifference of the masses, the consensus diagnosed it as an emotional exhaustion produced by constant fear and deliberately planned browbeating exercised under the name of propaganda.

It occurred to me that this perhaps was the explanation of a puzzling experience I had had in a factory in Budapest, and of later similar encounters in various plants.

The factory was not a large establishment. It had an employment roll of eight hundred, mostly women, sewing pillowcases and other simple household goods. The men, except for the management and drones, known as party functionaries, were truck drivers, mechanics, and maintenance men. I had listened to a long list of complaints concerning various officials at the plant, and when one worker offered me a chance to attend a Party Day meeting, I accepted.

This particular meeting opened with the UB chairman calling on the party secretary for a political report on the country's problems. The secretary read a long-winded, mostly incomprehensible editorial from the *Szabad Nep*, the official Communist organ of Hungary. He took nearly an hour to read it, laboriously wading through the Marxian jargon which was, to all appearances, over his head.

After the reading the chairman asked the audience for their contribution to the lecture. And here is, verbatim, what transpired.

"Comrades," said the chairman, "has anyone anything to say to what Comrade Peter has read?"

Silence.

After a sour look at the audience, the chairman again asked, "Has no one anything at all to say about such important matters?"

Silence.

"It does not speak well for your socialist consciences that you are so little interested in what the comrade secretary was saying." After a long pause he continued, "Now let's go to the second item on the agenda: Suggestions and Complaints."

The silence deepened.

The chairman, now surly, asked, "No one has any complaint?"

The audience continued to sit in rigid silence.

"Comrades!" cried the chairman, "now is the time to open your foul mouths, and not when you are outside. Damn you, talk here and now, and shut up when you leave this hall!"

You could feel the audience stiffening, but not a word was spoken.

Finally the chairman, with a few appropriate curses, closed the meeting.

Outside, I questioned my guide. Why weren't the many complaints aired? I myself knew of at least a dozen serious brutalities and injustices perpetrated against the workers of the factory. Why had not anyone spoken?

"In the first place," said my guide, "it would not have helped. No one would have bothered about correcting anything. In the second place, the complainants usually are called before the disciplinary board. But third, and most important, we are wise to their technique and we know how to defend ourselves. The secretary spoke for nearly an hour. No one, not even himself, understood anything he said. Then why did he speak? Why are we forced two or three times a week to sit through meetings where incomprehensible abracadabra is being said? Do you think that the Communists don't know that it is worthless as far as making us believe in them? They know it. The reason they hold these meetings and try to make us participate in them is to talk us into a stupor. Into deafness. To tire us out. If anyone had spoken we would have been forced to sit there at least another hour, listening to monotonous droning sentences until every bone in our bodies would have been aching and we would have wanted to scream to get out of there."

At that time I believed that my guide spoke out of malice, but I encountered, all over Hungary, the same attitude. (And I might add, in all other Communist countries.) The blazing slogans painted everywhere on shop walls, street corners, public conveyances; the chants Long Live Stalin, Long Live the Five-Year Plan, Long Live Rakosi, repeated over and over, for five, then thirty minutes at a time, with speakers droning away in between—all were incomprehensible and irritating to me and to the Hungarians until I was shown that this was a carefully devised method of emptying the masses of political and social passion.

It came to me that this was what Martin Borman, deputy to Hitler, said before the war, when I asked him about the ridiculousness of the weird chants of the Nazi meeting. What was being done to these people was to put their critical faculties out of commission. They were to leave each of these meetings with a burning desire *not* to discuss politics or anything else. They were to be made in a sense apolitical.

I remember once asking an American Communist, "Why do you keep on repeating yourself and chanting slogans ad nauseum?" and his telling me, quoting Carl Liebknecht, the murdered German socialist, "We are not repeating; we are hitting the head of a nail until it sinks in." I had my doubts of the value of chants, in-cantations, long-winded and jargon-studded speeches as effective propaganda methods. But here, in Hungary, looking at it from below, so to speak, it appeared understandable. It was an anesthesia.

Now my guests supplied the missing link. It was a carefully concocted and deliberately applied anesthesia as far as the masses were concerned, and it was used simply to make them more pliable through a kind of mass hypnosis.

"Were the instruments of this mass hypnosis aware of their role, or were they unconscious of the effect they were made to produce?" I asked.

Undoubtedly, I was told, the very top of the Communist leader-ship knew exactly what was happening and planned it to happen. Hence the deliberate discouragement through intimidation of ordi-nary worker-speakers at such meetings. But many who were privy to higher planning and strategy claimed that the lower echelon Com-munists who were leading and directing these meetings and parades were themselves victims of the fraud. They were sold on the value of "socialist propaganda" by schools they had to attend and by the carefully compiled blueprints on how to conduct such affairs.

It became clear that the interminable propaganda sessions were not designed to convince but to exhaust the listeners, to debilitate their energy. Intelligent young men and women in the higher schools of learning were particularly incensed at these ordeals, which left them limp from sheer nervous exhaustion. They considered the technique an insult, and to escape its effects they took to mockery and parody of the speakers and their rituals.

I had begun to discover the difference in Hungary between the dissatisfaction which was real, and which arose from many sources, and the undeniable economic and social stability of a country on the upgrade.

One factor I had to consider was the disinterestedness and lethargy of the peasantry. This could not be classified as an ex-clusively Communist phenomenon, although it was markedly present in all Communist lands. However, the peasantry in Europe had always been the most conservative class of citizens in any country. Added to their natural disinclination to revolt was the undeniable fact that the lot of the majority of peasants on the lowest economic scale had improved under the Communists. Their lives were still hemmed in and hard; their self-expression was severely circumscribed by the weight of the atmosphere around them. But on the other hand their sons and their daughters were encouraged to study and advance themselves.

The mood of the peasants was bitter and sullen, but they were far from ready to rise wrathfully and join a national uprising. These people had been slaves for centuries, and the habits of the slave were clearly visible in their lack of militancy and in their grumbling acquiescence. The workers, too, appeared to be unready to join in anything more serious than the voicing of criticism and the passing of resolutions.

But were the vocal intellectuals, of whom a good cross-section were my guests at Balatonfoldvar, active revolutionaries? My strongest impression was that if anyone had dropped the word "revolt" among them they would have blanched. What was biting them was the more or less sudden realization that their ideal had collapsed around them and that a chaos was in the making. They were angry, bitter men and women, deeply stirred by the first clear sight of their land and their own activities. That glimpse which showed them from above what it looked like from below sent them scurrying, beating their breasts and looking for scapegoats.

But they were not willing to give up their socialist ideals. What they wanted then, and also four months later during the first part of the revolution, was a house cleaning, a fresh start, a social and political order which would satisfy their essentially humanistic ideals and which, through a confusion of dogma and jargon, they called socialism or Communism. They were not aware then and during the first part of the revolution that what they wanted was neither Communism nor socialism in a rigid Marxian sense, and when it dawned on them that they were in the right pew but the wrong church it was too late to formulate a program. Outdistanced by events, the leadership of the revolution was wrested from them.

4

Reporter in Budapest

On my return from Budapest, the attaché assigned to me by the Foreign Office had a tight schedule ready. I was to visit the newly cleaned-up prisons, attend police line-ups, and see for myself that legality had returned to Hungary.

For twenty-six consecutive hours I went through jails and courts, accompanied police raids, played chess with prison inmates, ate with prosecutors and judges, and discovered with amazement bordering on disbelief the hair-raising degree of juvenile delinquency in Budapest.

My note pad containing the impressions and interviews of that long day is before me now. A sheet attached to the top of the pad bears three words reminding me of its contents: Decay and Decomposition.

I spent the morning hours visiting three prisons, the military and political lockup in Fo ucca, the prison on Margit korut, and time out for chess and lunch at the Gyujtofoghaz. What I was shown looked clean, and the prisoners were reasonably well taken care of. Many responded to my questions freely and seemingly without preparation. They all said that the old practice of beating and torturing them to force confessions had been done away with and that they had access to defense counselors.

At the Fo ucca prison I was not able to talk to any political prisoners because, said the warden, there were none. The military and civilian prisoners were humdrum and two men charged with manslaughter made up the elite.

One disconcerting incident took place during my afternoon visits to court officials. Prosecutor Vago was detailing to me the various safeguards that had been instituted to protect the accused and to ward off miscarriages of justice. He also gave me a detailed account of the machinery employed to review all past cases and to re-habilitate the unjustly convicted.

"Admittedly there were a large number of judicial frame-ups in the past," I said. "You say so, and your government officially admits it. Now, tell me, how many prosecutors and judges have been arrested or tried for being parties to these frame-ups?"

"None as yet," said Vago, "but we are investigating, and a special committee of jurists has been set up to look into this phase of the matter."

"I watched the other day the ceremonial reburial of several rehabilitated corpses. Looking their cases up in old newspapers, I found a number of names of judges and prosecutors who are still functioning in this court, including your own name. Are you people investigating your own misdeeds?"

Vago tried his best to convince me that the fault was not the judges', but that false evidence and forcibly extracted confessions had been presented to them by the police, and they had accepted them in good faith. But his words rang hollow. There was too much evidence to show that prosecutors and judges were not trying cases of accused persons on their merits but were following party orders and were passing predetermined sentences.

As several other court officials joined our discussion, the question of their sincerity arose again and again. Even if it were possible to overlook their past misdeeds, were they sincere in their protestation of wanting to create a law-abiding, independent judicial system? Could they disassociate themselves from political dogma or would they be permitted to do so? They were all emphatic in their resolve never again to be a part of a terror regime of the kind they had served in the past. But despite their words it seemed, on balance, that unless the structure within which they lived and functioned was to be changed radically, they would have to continue to be servants of their political bosses. It was disheartening to watch intelligent and even high-minded men trying to rid themselves of the muck and dirt in which they had lived and with which they were still covered. Later, during the October revolution, the same judges sent a message to the prime minister to say that none of them was willing to preside over proceedings under the martial law which the government had proclaimed against the revolutionaries. This was to be their atonement.

But the real horror of that long June day came in the evening. No one could have spent any time in East Europe without being aware of the enormous proportions which juvenile delinquency had assumed. Budapest after sunset often seemed like a teeming hothouse of young hoodlums and teen-age prostitutes. But the few glimpses I had had previously did not prepare me for the revelations of that night.

The abandoned subway excavations and bombed-out buildings throughout the city were the clubhouses of thousands of youngsters banded together in neighborhood gangs. The gangs were known by the names of their leaders, who, embarrassingly, used "American" names like Tommy, Joey, Frankie, and Johnny, and affected the worst behavior seen on American screens. They were like so many strutting Edward G. Robinsons and George Rafts lording it over their followers and the neighborhood. And they were really bad. They beat up their victims, mugged them in public, and even killed them. The police often had to use tear gas while raiding their clubs to prevent serious resistance. They lived by their own laws and were arrogant, mean, and uncontrollable.

During the night in question we raided four clubs filled with snarling, knife-wielding youths and piled high with their loot. Perhaps nothing could have more simply and effectively shown conditions in Budapest than the spectacle of these hoodlums and their spoils: mostly shabby rags, broken furniture, worn furs, and poor imitation jewelry.

The most shocking of the raids was staged in the city park called Varosliget. A stone's throw from the gaudy Stalin Memorial, the bushes of the park were alive with teen-age girls entertaining their guests. For the equivalent of twenty cents to a dollar they offered themselves for sale, dutifully turning over their earnings after each customer to the nearby lurking young gangsters, their "protectors." These girls ranged in age from twelve to eighteen. More than half of them were diseased and nearly all of them were homeless. Many used flour for face powder, shoe polish on their eyelashes, and brick dust for rouge. Nearly two hundred girls were brought in that night, and they were the most obscene, tragic sight in Hungary.

An angelic, hardly grown thirteen-year-old calmly recounted her nightly chores: between twenty to thirty paying guests plus her protector and his assorted hoodlum friends. At that, she earned in one night fifteen to twenty times more than the daily wage of her father, from whose home she had escaped.

One of the hardened police officials who examined the nightly haul pointed out a girl of sixteen who had been in and out of jails and hospitals since the age of eleven.

These young delinquents were regularly turned out by the police for lack of room in the overflowing jails and hospitals. The more hardened ones were sent to serve for a few weeks in penal institutions, and they regarded this as a mark of distinction. The government was not sufficiently interested in them to arrange for their rehabilitation, and they came out of jail more hardened than ever.

The arrested juveniles were herded together in the courtyard to await the opening of the police court at seven in the morning. They were a gay, noisy, unruly crowd, and the police had to train a fire hose on them to keep them reasonably quiet.

In the morning a sleepy police judge, a female of around fifty, with tired mien, took over. The names of the delinquents were called, the police referee said a few words, the judge glanced at the prisoners, and it was over. By the time I left at nine o'clock, seventy cases had been disposed of. Twenty girls were sent to jail, and the rest were released to pick up where they had left off the night before.

Captain Vamos, commander of district police in the toughest area, called Ferencvaros, was an experienced police official with twenty-five years of service behind him. "I hate to send my men out," he said. "Those kids know we are powerless. They jeer when we arrest them and laugh in our faces when we have to let them go."

"What do you think is the reason for the great increase of juvenile delinquency in Budapest?" I asked.

"It is not only in Budapest," he explained, "but in every city of any size. The reason? The same old reason which was always responsible for it: unhappy homes and poverty. Now we have more unhappy homes and more poverty, so we have more kids rotting on the streets.

"But there is something else," he added: "they are all infected by their parents and other grownups with a feeling of disrespect toward authority. Outwitting the state is not a crime here; it is an act of valor."

The last part of Captain Vamos' statement was the clearest explanation I have heard for the widespread corruption in Hungary. In a country where everything was owned by the state, and where most people regarded the state if not as their enemy at least as a hard taskmaster, no one had the slightest compunction about cheating and robbing the state. Government officials, store managers, clerks, and policemen were for sale, together with great stores of stolen goods from factories, shops, and other state-owned enterprises. Partly for the hell of it, but mostly of genuine need, all those who dared or hoped to get away with it somehow dipped into the state's treasury.

This utter corruption was observable not only in Hungary but in every other Communist country as well. In Poland a high police official in Warsaw defended his corrupt men by saying, "How do you expect them to live on 1500 zlotys a month when a pair of shoes costs twice that much? We crack down on them only if they overdo it."

The corruption and juvenile delinquency which existed in Hungary were two reliable signs that the state structure was in a condition of decay and decomposition. But I was interested to hear a Marxist explanation. Shortly before I left Hungary I had an opportunity to ask my questions, and I received answers couched in scientific jargon meaning—if they had meaning—"The replacement of one social system with another always causes dislocations in moral values; hence there are always people who find it hard to make the necessary adjustment." Of course, this did not take care of the lack of food which drives people to steal and prostitute themselves. But since those phenomena are, according to the Marxists, only observable in bourgeois societies, they had no words with which to explain them when they occur in their society.

Zoltan Kodaly, the world-famous Hungarian musician, was next on my list of "musts." He is addressed by Communists and non-Communists alike as *Meltosagos Ur* (Excellency), and he is the only artist who came through the years of terror unscathed. He laughed at my suggestion that his world-wide popularity protected him from the serious consequences of his many sharp exchanges with the regime.

"No, I just ignored them," he said. "When Zhdanov issued his famous manifesto on how to write music, we decided to let him do it since he seemed to know so much about it, but we went on our way."

Several days before my arrival, Hungarian musicians led by Kodaly had sent a memorandum to the government demanding long-overdue reforms, including the end of their isolation, the removal of governmental controls, freedom to establish relations with Western artists, and the end of government meddling with artistic endeavors. "Something had to be done," said Kodaly. "They were getting in our hair all the time.

"We really are not hankering for the cacophony which passes for music in the West," he said. "We tried and rejected Schoenberg thirty years ago, while in Paris the young are still wrestling with him. To us music has always been a direct emotional language; the more direct, the better. But what we object to is the stultification of artists."

He illustrated on the piano what he meant by playing a few bars of music which was at various times condemned as formalistic

44

and decadent and at others praised as a prime example of socialist music. Kodaly hoped that out of the present ferment an ideal situation would emerge, but he did not underestimate the troubles ahead. He was devoting most of his time to advancing musical education for the young. He had already organized ten elementary schools which devoted six hours every week to music. "When the dust settles and the excitement is over, I will demand thirty schools for my experiment. The thing is to go ahead regardless of who is in the seat of the mighty."

"Do you believe that the excitement will be soon over and the dust settled?" I asked.

Kodaly became thoughtful, then he said: "My inclination from the beginning was to stay out of the fray. But it can't be done. We musicians are not as exposed as are the writers and the journalists. They are in the firing line; they are the most vulnerable of us. We can't let them down. That's why we are going ahead with our organization, protest meetings, and petitions.

"I believe that if the pressure is kept up, we shall win a measure of freedom and then we can go on from there. Step by step we shall reach a decent, free life. Any alternative is unthinkable."

I reminded him that the premier performance of his new choral work, *Talpra, Magyar* (Arise, Hungarians), had been canceled and that its performance was forbidden.

He smiled. "Ah, yes, but you have not heard the latest. The work will be performed in Karolyi Garden, a popular summer outdoor concert garden." And he added: "It makes no difference where it is performed. The point is that it will be performed despite official displeasure. Great wars can be won by small victories."

I asked Kodaly for the names of the writers and journalists with whom I ought to talk, inasmuch as I had been invited to meet with a group on the following evening. He gave me a list of names and said: "They are all in a state of ferment; even the heretofore rabid Stalinists have experienced a moral revolution. They are fine, intelligent young people in search of a better world. It saddens me that you in the West hold them in such contempt because of their politics. They need you and will continue to need you in the times ahead. Ask your Western friends to believe in them and offer them a friendly hand." Kodaly believed that on the Communist intellectuals rested the hope for a better world. "You want to destroy the objectionable parts of Communism," he said, passionately, "with guns. And you will never succeed. But these young men are fighting against them with far more effective weapons. With ideals, moral courage, and a deep belief in humanity. If there is to be a better world, the victory will be theirs and not yours."

The frail old man was deeply moved. After a long silence he said in a quiet voice: "Many of our brave young men are still in a state of shock. I fear them even though I bless them."

At the meeting in Balatonfoldvar I had been told something of the struggle which preceded the partial victory wrung by Hungarian writers from the authorities. One of the milestones of the struggle was a petition signed in the fall of 1955 by fifty-eight writers, demanding freedom of speech and press and the right to maintain connections with the Western world. Elisabeth Andics, the minister of culture, called in the writers and with threats and blandishments succeeded in persuading fifty of them to withdraw their signatures. But eight remained steadfast. They were subsequently tried by the disciplinary committee of the party and were given "last warning"— the final step before expulsion and censorship. Khrushchev's exposure of Stalin and the subsequent relaxation of totalitarianism in Hungary prevented the authorities from proceeding against them, and the rebellious eight were permitted to earn their living as writers again.

During those dark days of the previous December these writers, among them the Kossuth and Stalin prize-winning novelist Tamas Aczel, never slept in the same bed two consecutive nights. They were moving from place to place, always a whisper ahead of the AVH.

Several lesser-known writers had already been arrested or removed from their positions. One well-known editor, Miklos Molnar, whose wife was the daughter of Rudnyanszki, the best known Hungarian Communist theoretician, was called on the telephone by Stalin's own commissar in Hungary, Matyas Rakosi, who demanded that Molnar suppress forthwith a poem by Laszlo Benjamin which was to appear in the next issue of the *Literary Gazette*. Molnar listened to Rakosi in silence and then quietly said: "Comrade Rakosi, I disagree with you. Benjamin's verse is a fine piece of poetry," and hung up. The poem appeared and Molnar was dismissed.

Almost every piece of exposure which appeared in print in Hungary up to the time of my arrival was accompanied by an extraordinary display of courage and bravery on someone's part. These men were literally writing in the shadow of prison bars, if not of the gallows.

I wanted to meet them.

Many things have happened since that evening in Budapest. Most of those whom I shall now call on to speak are in jail. A few have escaped. But the majority felt like Tibor Dery, the most compromised among them, who said in November, 1956, "For me to escape would be to admit that I was wrong and they were right; to escape is to leave the front on which the future of mankind will be fought." He remained in Hungary and, together with more than twenty of his courageous colleagues, was sentenced to a long term in prison. An unknown number of them have been executed.

I have selected brief quotations from them to include in this book with an eye on their public record. What some of them have said to me and what appeared in print in Hungary under their by-line are identical. Therefore my inclusion of their words will not add to their burden. My only regret is that space prevents me from including more in this honor roll of Hungarian intellectuals.

Peter Veres, president of the Writers' Federation: "We shall never again be required to endorse that which we oppose, that which we know to be untrue, that which is inhuman. To force us to write against our own conviction is to degrade us. The writer's natural element is truth, and we resolve never to deviate from it."

Zoltan Zelk, poet and novelist, one of the most talented of the younger writers: "I shall not give up my ideals which led me to embrace the cause of the poor, the oppressed in my youth. Today I know that I gave up my youthful faith when I, too, believed that without humanism, without morality, disregarding our national cultural treasures, a just cause could be served. Never! I committed a horrible wrong against myself and against mankind when I accepted such a monstrous perversion of truth, and my two years of struggle against it is a part of my atonement.

"I would beg the authorities that they should not force us to

47

fight any longer and grant us the right to say the truth as we see it, develop our talents, such as they are, and permit ideals and beliefs to flourish in open competition. . . ."

Gyula Fekete, head of the Committee on Prose of the Writers' Federation, a well known novelist: "We don't want and will not accept a 'permitted' democracy, one which may be stamped 'Good until revoked' and may be taken away. We don't want concessions —for each a handout. We don't want to be the passionate army who takes the fort and a few weeks later must evacuate under orders of the general.

"Our leaders tell us that they have no reason to trust us and must watch and control us. If this is true then the reverse must also be true. We don't trust them; we must watch over them and control them.

"We have justice and honor on our side: we have not been found wanting as they have been. There is only one way out of this impasse. We say to them: Trust us to be honest, to be humane, to be compassionate and to be truthful. Trust us with organizing our lives as we see fit and as it suits us. Then, only then, shall we trust you and believe in your good intentions."

Gyula Hay, the greatest living Hungarian playwright, whose phenomenally successful, biting portrait of a Communist party functionary appeared in the *Literary Gazette* under the title "Why I Don't Like Comrade Kutchera" and contributed largely to the prevailing mood in Hungary, wrote: "For us Communists, self-criticism shall not be like reading prayer beads, not empty *mea culpas*, not a strategic chess move but a way to bring truth and justice to victory. We came out of the soul-searching, searing time of self-criticism with the high resolve: Never, under any circumstances shall we lie to ourselves and to our public."

Lajos Konya, novelist, whose diary was confiscated two days after its publication: "The issue is simple: the injustice, the oppression, the callous disregard of human values affects us only as a part of the people. We cannot fight for our rights, our freedom, our livelihood without fighting for those of the nation! Our wounds were caused by the same instruments of illegality as were the wounds of our brothers and sisters. Either we all win this fight or none."

Geza Kepes, poet and translator whose detailed indictment of the regime was copied by hand and distributed all over the land because the editors were forbidden to print it: "It is too late for this leadership to make amends, to rehabilitate and promise. There will be no peace in this land, no trust in our government, no stopping the avalanche which is threatening to bury us all until all those who were guilty of bringing the horrors on us are punished and we have made very sure that we shall never be victimized again."

Of the genuineness of the moral revulsion which spread through these men there could be no question; some of them earned more than did the prime minister and all of them lived well above the Hungarian living standard. They not only threw away their plush incomes and special privileges, but also risked their freedom and their lives by leading the revolt in Hungary.

For a Westerner it would be hard to imagine what it was like to challenge the relentless power of the Communist oligarchy. A small group of men without the slightest moral restraint, not even such as may be inherent in their professed faith, were slaughtering, robbing, and torturing an entire nation to make it fit into a mold which no human being could endure. And these few men were still in power at the time these brave writers rose determined to stop them. By all measures these were heroes who deserved the respect of their fellow men, and they certainly had mine.

In the early morning hours when we left the palatial house of the federation on Stalin ut, after a night of heady talk and high resolves, Kodaly's bitter words about the Western attitude toward these men came back to me with a new urgency.

But were they mere dissenters or were they hammering away at the foundation of Communism? Could they achieve what they were demanding within the framework of their ideology?

It was time to ask the apostles. I wanted to get answers which, I hoped, would explain some of the things I had heard and seen which seemed so contradictory as to appear irreconcilable. I had heard that Dr. Fogarasi, the vice president of the Hungarian Academy of Science and a leading Marxist theoretician, came out strongly against dogmatism and was echoed by all the top philosophers and scientists of the country, including those who theretofore had been the strongest "scientific" supporters of Stalinism.

But if they have no dogma, what have they? On what do they

base their authority? What gives them the right to rule in the name of Holy Marx and Lenin?

Dr. Gyorgy Lukacs was the Marxist best known throughout the country as the leader of the new approach, and the intellectual circle swore by him.

I went to see him.

"Marxism has never been in such disrepute in our country as it is today," said the professor. "The reason is that during the Stalin period the so-called Marxists exhausted the whole field by finding two or three quotations, mostly taken out of context, with which to justify what they were doing. The same fate is apparently being prepared for Lenin. He too will be quoted to suit expediencies without regard to the basic philosophy of Lenin."

"What you are saying, Professor, is that if Marx and Lenin had not been misquoted and misused, a true path could have been found through their dogmas?" I asked.

"No, no! The Stalinists made dogmas to suit their purposes, but there are no dogmatic absolutes in Marx. In fact there is no such thing as Marxist logic, ethics, ideology, pedagogy, and so on. What we have is a collection of his teaching, out of which, or rather with its help, we of this generation should evolve our disciplines. The same thing applies to the teaching of Lenin. By collecting together what Marx said on ethics, for example, we do not have Marxian ethics; what we have is merely a method of approach to guide us."

"This seems to be getting us far afield," I said. "If there is no Marxist dogma, what is the authority on which these people arrogate to themselves the right to govern and govern according to their own lights?"

"No socialist country should have a government which arrogates to itself the right to govern on dogmatic bases; it must rest its authority on the consent of the workers," replied Dr. Lukacs.

"Fine, but neither Lenin nor his best-loved disciple Stalin, nor Stalin's best-loved disciple in Hungary, Rakosi, has ever consulted the workers. Yet they still maintained an iron rule in the name of Marx and Lenin," I said.

"What you are saying is part of the indictment against them, and history will undoubtedly find them guilty of gross distortions," said Dr. Lukacs.

"But getting back to Lenin," I said. "If what you say is true of Marx and Lenin, then where did Lenin get the notion, which he laid down as party principles for the Communists, that the Communist party was a chosen instrument of Marxism and that only through a correct, single interpretation of Marxism shall Communist countries be governed? Moreover, Lenin seems to have got this idea from Marx, who believed that history could and should be shaped by ascertainable scientific factors. Could you reconcile this view of Marx as applied by Lenin with your own notion of democratic socialism?" I asked.

"The Communist party and its principals can be and ought to be in harmony with the teachings of Marx insofar as they apply to the present situation of society. 'Can' and 'ought' are not the same as 'be' and 'is.' The Communist party can err and get off the track just as anybody can," explained the professor.

"But who is to say when the Communists are on the right track or off the track? It seems to me you are opening the way to the very thing you condemn: an infallible Pope of Communism who by his final judgment of what is or what is not Marxian would, in due course, become a dictator even as Stalin and Rakosi. Thus his own views would become the law of the land and he himself would become the administrative, legislative, and judicial head of the country," I said.

Dr. Lukacs seemed to enjoy the debate. The old man had a youthful gleam in his eyes, and relished every challenge.

"There is where the trouble lies—in godheadism which Lenin never advanced seriously but which Stalin established by misapplying both Marx and Lenin. The supreme court of a socialist country must be a deliberative body of men, elected by the workers, peasants, professionals, intellectuals—in short, all productive people of the country," he said.

"I noticed, Professor, that you said 'must be' and 'ought to be,' but I am talking about what *is*. And what is, is a personal dictatorship or at best a dictatorship of a small inner circle. Now, how do you propose to enforce the 'what ought to be' over the 'what is'?"

51

"There will be no need to enforce what is right in a socialist country," he replied vaguely.

"All right, I am willing to take your word for it," I replied, "just to get on, because my next question will, I hope, bring us nearer to the crux of the matter. Also, to get it out of the way temporarily, I accept Stalin's personal guilt, although it appears to me that the system is even guiltier than Stalin was for tolerating him.

"But having seen dire and wasteful results of scientific socialist planning, and having been convinced that the planners were faithful Marxists of good intentions, how can you justify this regime of economic planning from 'above,' which keeps the country plundered and its people next door to starvation? And the second part of the question: What recourse have the people against twenty-four-carat, faithful dyed-in-the-wool Marxists, who are neither Stalinists nor autocratic, but who believe what they are doing to be good even when it proves not to be good?"

"The answer to that," said the professor, "is simple. We must get better planners and better economists and, incidentally, better human beings."

"Professor, let me first of all apologize for my caustic language, but being a nonscientific person who waded through Marx and Lenin as he tried to understand people's thoughts before and after them, I am trying to get at the basic question involved here as simply as I know how.

"Please tell me what is wrong with this Western view of what goes on here: First, there was the belief of the Communist being the chosen instrument of history. This is what Marx said as interpreted by Lenin. This was Lenin's justification and moral authority for establishing the dictatorship of the proletariat. Lenin also insisted that there was a correct, scientific Marxist line which every Communist was duty bound to follow.

"Now, the question arose: who would determine the correct Marxist line? While Lenin lived, he did. After he died the disciples fell out, and he who had the biggest stick, Stalin, came out as the only correct and true interpreter of Marx. The others had to accept his interpretations—or else.

"Thus was born a hierarchy with the infallible successor of the

Prophet on the top, with the archangels under him, followed by the higher and lower clergy leading the faithful in a crusade to convert the heathens either by preaching or by the sword. The 'liquidation' of heathens became a holy calling, sanctified by the ethical and moral system as promulgated by the Prophet and dutifully accepted by the Synod.

"We in the West think of all this as a fantastic travesty on religious structures—in fact, as a new religion with the brimstone and fire of oldtime witch-burning religionists. And, needless to add, we also think of all this as a tragic and needless waste of human life, endeavor, and happiness."

The professor had an amused smile on his face throughout the last part of my recital.

"I have often heard Marxism compared to religion," he said, "but it is a superficial view. Let me tell you a Hungarian joke.

"The village secretary of the party fell in step one day with the village priest and said to him: 'Father, there is something I don't understand. After all, we are in the same business. How come when you call for a procession everyone in the village falls into line? When you call a meeting, everyone goes there. Now, when I call for a parade, only a few people show up, and when I call a meeting I face an empty hall. Tell me, Father, what is your secret?' The priest smiled, and said: 'Really, it is very simple. No one has ever returned from the Paradise I promise the people. . . .'"

Dr. Lukacs laughed heartily, and continued: "Communism can never be a religion because it is too easy to expose it. We pride ourselves on creating many more scientists than you do, and a scientific mind cannot long be enthralled by unreality. Religions— at least those we are talking about—are based on the unknowable, rest on pure faith, and nothing about them is ascertainable. Hence it is a matter of emotions. But not so Communism. We gave our people the only weapon with which they could defeat necromancy and defend themselves against conjurors—the habit of scientific thinking.

"The pressure in the Soviet Union after Stalin's death and we here in Hungary bear testimony to the fact that even if we tried we would never be able to get away with any kind of orthodoxy which demands the abdication of reason.

"No, we are not wild-eyed believers. What happened under Stalin was—let us not quibble—enforced by terror and was a perversion of Marxism. But we are at the foot of the mountain. As we climb upward we may have to deal with several more Stalins and plug up many more holes through which the future Stalins could crawl in. Isn't your slogan 'Eternal vigilance is the price of freedom'? Well, it applies to us, too.

"Marxism is modern humanism. True, we face different problems today than Marx did in his time. We will not permit Marx to become the Communist Buddha."

"I am grateful to you, Professor," I said in parting, "for your patience and courtesy. But permit me to say that even if all your hopes and ideals come true, the price your people have been paying, and I am afraid will continue to pay, to reach that earthly heaven in which you believe is far too high."

Perhaps my most disappointing encounters in Hungary occurred at the American Legation. While all Hungary seemed on the verge of momentous changes, the legation was frozen in its rigid isolation and the deep prejudice of its views. My reports of events unfolding in the country were met with open and sometimes hostile disbelief. Reds against Reds? Who cares? What did it prove?

The fact that I had established friendly relations with a number of intellectuals was, in the legation's view, prima-facie evidence of my own unreliability. Vainly I argued that we had nothing to fear by meeting with these people in open debate about the merits of our respective views, that, on the contrary, in most cases it was child's play to beat the Communists in their own ideological territory.

The attitude of the legation officials in Budapest was not an isolated instance of Americans operating in foreign countries from insulated ivory towers. Particularly in Communist or neutralist countries, where easy informality and friendly discussions would have done a world of good for both sides, Americans were tightly fenced in and restricted in their contacts to other Western diplomats. The result of this attitude was harmful in many ways. Most importantly, it discouraged a friendly approach to Americans by the natives. The fact that Americans did not care to mix with them singled out those who had the slightest contact with Americans as spies, and these were particularly watched by their political policemen. Hence not being accepted by Americans became a stamp of loyalty, and contact with Americans became suspect. Even though the Communist hierarchy favored this isolation, Americans should have used their best efforts to break through, instead of erecting impenetrable walls around themselves.

My experiences and those of other Western newsmen showed that except in a country which just then was going through a crisis, Communist intellectuals and leaders were eager to meet with Westerners and discuss their problems. Often these discussions were frank, and afforded Westerners penetrating insights into the workings of Communist societies. Unfortunately those among Westerners who, in their fear of breaching protocol, maintained a rigid, formal, and cautious attitude did much to encourage the view that the Western world was not interested in examining the working of a Communist society, but only in its destruction. There was nothing to be gained by erecting a curtain between us, but a great deal to lose.

Our officials in Budapest and elsewhere were not only indoctrinated in the idea of a life-or-death struggle between the East and West, but were also hemmed in by their own fears. Since the destructive raids on the State Department led by Nixon and McCarthy, our Foreign Service has deteriorated noticeably.

I tried to persuade our officials in Budapest to establish contact with the Hungarian revolutionary movement, even though some of its leaders were Communists or former Communists and were not in a position to pass our outlandish security check. My argument was that those intellectuals who were playing leading roles in the movement against their government were once young idealists who joined the Communist party simply because it offered the most radical remedy and contrast to the Fascist horror which, as children, they had learned to hate. "These disillusioned Communists are still not willing to ally themselves to the evils of the past," I said, "but would be willing, nay, eager, to follow a genuinely democratic line. But apart from our view of them, these men are about to lead a revolt. Why not make them our friends now, when they are facing the hostility of the East and the West?"

55

It is a moot question how much of this rigid and unbending attitude among our diplomats was the result of McCarthyism and how much of it reflected their own views. I have known many Foreign Service officers who, in unguarded moments, spoke bitterly about the ideological prison in which they were kept and how ineffective our Foreign Service became because of it. Perhaps the most fantastic part of this setup was the ridiculous fear of contamination of Western people—officials and private citizens—by Communist ideology and practices. The ascertainable results had always been the opposite: Western sympathizers with Communist ideology came away from a visit to their dreamlands partly or wholly disenchanted, while the inroads which Western ideas had made among the Communists were noticeable all along the line from the rarefied atmosphere of the Council of Prophets (Politburo) to the workers and peasants. There were always a few officials in each Communist country who were invulnerable to any ideas outside their own narrow views, but my own experience has always been that the most rigid orthodox Communist supplied the best ideological weapons for Western advocates.

The damage to our cause in Eastern countries caused by our own shortsighted orthodoxy extended beyond the walls of our diplomatic stations. Gimes and Szilagyi, two Hungarian newspapermen executed with Imre Nagy, illustrate this point. Both newspapermen had just before and during the revolution some slight contacts with Westerners. These were innocent enough, since both were convinced socialists of the democratic variety, and their contact with Western diplomats and newspapermen was prompted largely by their fears of the consequences of the impending Hungarian catastrophe. But the fact that their contact included American Legation officials gave the Hungarian Kadar regime a convenient alibi for stamping them as traitors, since, notoriously, Americans were never known to be interested in any kind of Hungarians except the extreme rightist variety.

It has long been known among American newspapermen that the legation in Budapest was in the business of selling its views and interpretation of Hungarian events to visiting reporters. Those who accepted them were favored and much courted; those who insisted on independent investigation were frowned upon, particularly if what they found was not quite what the legation wanted them to find. This situation led to Eric Johnston's amusing experience in Budapest. Johnston, president of the Motion Picture Association of America, Inc., since 1951, arrived in Budapest in the summer of 1956 to negotiate a motion-picture agreement with the Hungarians. As was customary with people of his high standing, the legation wanted to give a cocktail party. Johnston assented, and gave the legation a list of leading Hungarian educators, artists, and officials whom he wanted to invite. The legation officials were shocked. Finally, one of them said, "But, Mr. Johnston, we never meet with these people socially."

The enigma in Hungary was not the thoughts and actions of the Hungarians; those were understandable enough. The enigma was the unreal attitude of the American Legation.

5

Yugoslavia

Viewed from the East, Yugoslavia may appear to be a Communist heaven, from the West a seed which one day may spread poison weed among the Communists. But a closer look reveals it as a hell whose inhabitants have not the vaguest idea why and for how long they must endure it. There is nothing in Yugoslavia to encourage the hopeful Laborites of Britain, the diplomats in Washington, or, for that matter, the Communists of other Eastern lands who often look longingly toward Belgrade.

The last gasoline station on the Austrian side of the border is the exchange office where one can get twice as much for his money as at the official Yugoslav banks. But nothing over a 100-dinar note is ever accepted by the Austrians, for fear of a sudden Yugoslav withdrawal from circulation of the larger notes; thus the changing of one hundred dollars into dinars becomes a major problem.

Yugoslav refugees who steam daily across the border usually bring sackfuls of the money and sell it at any rate the gasoline attendants are willing to give them. The dinar has no international value; except in Switzerland, Yugoslav money can't be given away.

Inasmuch as the border guards of Yugoslavia are more used to seeing foreigners than are the guards of other Communist countries, the Yugoslavs are more relaxed and courteous. Cameras, radios, typewriters, and recording equipment must be carefully registered as in other Communist lands, but the process is seldom grim and the guards often engage the travelers in conversation.

But just as soon as one leaves the friendly camp of the border guards, the picture changes abruptly. Soldiers with fierce dogs patrol the area, and it is not uncommon to hear shooting in the hills above the highway.

The deeper one gets into Yugoslavia, the more confusion one meets. On the lowest level, in the offices of factories, farms, and commercial enterprises, as well as those of municipal and county authorities, political functionaries and government agents all operate on a definite pattern carefully laid out and to be followed to the letter. Narrowed down to the daily task of a factory worker or a village clerk, the pattern is clear and understandable. But only on that level do people know what they are about. The rest is utter confusion held together only by a relentless hierarchy.

On my way to Belgrade I stopped in nine villages, towns, and cities, including Ljubljana and Zagreb. I wanted to collect as many facts as I could before meeting the elite of the country: intellectuals, engineers, managers, political functionaries, and leaders. I wanted to know first of all wherein the Yugoslav brand of Communism differed from the other types and whether what was known as Titoism could successfully meet those problems of Eastern Europe which the other types of Communism were manifestly unable to solve.

As in Hungary, I was interested here in an ant's view rather than in that of a bird. I was familiar with the stock Communist argument that the end justified the means and that all the pain and misery are but antechambers to a better, freer, gayer, and more abundant future. But I wanted to know what happened to the common worker and peasant who were asked to invest their lives and their children's future in an experiment which they neither understood nor wanted. What was the relation between the people under the "brotherhood of Communism"? How did the commissar deal with his people? What was the essence of Titoism, the moral justification for all that the people had to endure?

The ant's view in Yugoslavia is much more difficult to attain than in Hungary, Poland, or Czechoslovakia because Yugoslavia is made up of many nationalities, each with its own culture, and each affected differently by the impact of Communism. For instance, nothing the Communists had said or done was enough to move the Bosnian peasant devoted to his few goats and plum trees, whereas the Slovene peasant obsequiously bows to orders from above; the factory hands in Serbia are slow-moving and resentful; their colleagues in Croatia are alert and political-minded.

But more than anything else in Yugoslavia the question of minorities is every present, and this issue, despite official denial and whitewash, represents a constant irritation.

In Novi Sad I had an opportunity to talk to the cultural leaders of a number of minorities, such as Hungarians, Germans, Swabians, and Slovaks. Between Varazdin and Novi Sad I had been to a number of places and spoken to many people on the subject of the supposed freedom of minorities in Yugoslavia. My impression was that there was a definite effort to discourage the cultural efforts of minorities. In many instances this discouragement amounted to suppression—since in a totalitarian regime no one dares to defy official discouragement.

"Tell me," I asked the editor of the Hungarian-language Communist newspaper, "how do you justify the destruction of Hungarian and German culture in Vojvodina?"

He was horrified. Where did I get that impression? Why he himself was the editor of a minority-language newspaper!

I had to explain to him slowly. Yes, he was the editor of a paper which was a word-for-word translation of *Borba*, the Serbian newspaper, an official organ of the Yugoslav Communist party. I was also aware of the fact that *Borba* appeared in Croatian and other languages. But that did not make him the editor of anything except a group of translators. Then I detailed to him the sad story of the theater in Subotica. Once this old institution had its own group of actors and singers. Its Hungarian repertoire included world classics in drama, opera, and operetta. Today it was dark except for an occasional amateur show. The reason was that at first the Cultural Committee ordered the theater to be bilingual and then cut its budget to such an extent that artists of any standing could not make a living, and thus abandoned the theater. The result was that hundreds of thousands of Germans and Hungarians had no outlet for their cultural striving.

Then I went into the story of the Albanians (called Skiptars in Yugoslavia), the largest minority group in the country. Their suppression was a never-ending source of trouble between Albania and Yugoslavia. And on and on went my report.

After a while the editor admitted that the symptoms were too many and too concentrated to be coincidences, and said: "You do not understand at all. We are going toward a unified Yugoslav culture!"

"What kind of nonsense is that?" I asked. "You people are rich in traditional arts and ways, and now you want to destroy twenty age-old cultures for something as unreal as an artificial Yugoslav culture, a hybrid which, if it ever develops, would mean a new nation."

"But you have just that in America," he said.

"We have nothing of the kind. We have a newly formed culture— that is, we have an evolving culture. But in the process we did not destroy the ingredients from which this culture is evolving. We had nothing to start with, and out of this nothing, by living together, we evolved a tradition. But you are deliberately destroying what is great in your people and trying to force them to adopt something which is alien to them. Apart from being silly, you can't be serious about believing that it would succeed?"

"Spoken like a bourgeois sentimentalist," said the editor. "It is not we who are consciously trying to create a new culture, but the universality of the machine which does. Once we are industrialized and strong, the mechanical age will bring its own culture. We are merely consciously preparing the way."

I would have been inclined to take this as the editor's personal idea, but too many Communist higher-ups held the same view, and were aware of the slow extinction of national cultures, to leave any doubt that it was the official policy of the Yugoslav Communist party.

In Belgrade I confronted Slobodan Kritic and Ljubisa Stojkovic, both of the Executive Council, with the data I had accumulated and asked them to explain the difference between the old ways in which minorities were suppressed in the Yugoslav Kingdom and the Austro-Hungarian Monarchy, and their new approach to the problem. I was given an official Communist pamphlet dealing with the minority problem which, while admitting that Yugoslavia was made up of twenty nationalities, contained so many distortions that it was useless. The suppression of nationalities goes on just as before, except that the Communists are more subtle and manage to describe and explain their actions in a special jargon said to be Marxian.

But there is more to the Communist cultural policy than mere chauvinism. There is an ambivalence which no Communist has been able to explain satisfactorily. On the one hand, Communism encourages nationalism, in fact thrives on it, in Communist countries as well as in non-Communist lands. On the other hand, nationalism, let alone chauvinism, is condemned as a scourge and suppressed with terror. A blatant example of this policy was the hanging of several Communist leaders and intellectuals on the charge of Zionism in the Soviet Union and Czechoslovakia, while Arab nationalism was encouraged and supported with money and arms. Again, in Yugoslavia, Hungarian patriots were jailed as "Fascist chauvinists" while the regime, at least on paper, urged its minorities to keep on with their nationalistic activities.

Examples could be multiplied. "There is a line beyond which nationalism cannot be allowed to go," a member of the Executive Bureau of the Federal Republic explained.

"Who sets the limit and what is it?" I asked.

Several attempts were made to define the limit, but all agreed that the Political Executive Bureau of the Communist party, the Politburo or Presidium, as it is called, sets the limit.

"Suppose I am a Skiptar writer," I said, "how would I know

whether my story of the hero of an earlier Skiptar revolt was within the limit, at the limit, or beyond it? How would I know in advance where to stop and whether I would be published or jailed?"

The Executive Bureau member replied, "If you were a Communist you would know where to stop."

"But that can't be the truth," I argued, "because in all Communist countries, including yours, many writers and others were jailed and executed, although they were ostensibly good Communists, for not observing the borderline or being ignorant of it: to mention two of the most obvious countrymen of yours, Wlado Dedijer and Milovan Djilas. They were surely good-enough Communists, and yet they were jailed for crossing the border into the land of free speech which your constitution guarantees on paper."

I was told that I did not understand the problem. After all, the Communist elite—Tito and his committee—are competent to determine when a political or cultural issue reaches the permissible limit. Djilas and Dedijer were renegades, cosmopolites, bourgeois sentimentalists, deviationists, Trotskyites, anti-Marxists—in short, they were in the Communist doghouse.

When I visited Belgrade I went to see Dedijer, a brilliant historian with a sense of humor. He gave me an explanation which seemed to cover his part in the spectacular Djilas-Dedijer affair.

"I do not agree with many things Milovan had to say. And I still have my reservation about the wisdom of his saying them. But there can be no question about his *right* to say what he honestly believed to be the truth."

Dedijer laughed off his suspended jail sentence but was obviously hurt by the attitude of his former friends and colleagues at the top of the Communist hierarchy: Kidric, Kardelj, Pijade, Tito, Rankovic, and others.

"As a historian," he said, "I can only deplore any deviation from the morality of our revolution. We should be allowed to disagree and should be free to speak our minds, or else we are lost."

His wonderfully loyal wife and his American-born mother were both proud of Dedijer's unyielding fidelity to his ideals.

Dedijer told me the following story of his wife's determination to see him do the right thing. Several Communist leaders visited

Dedijer to urge him to withdraw his support of Djilas' heresies. He was promised party rehabilitation and, what was more important, he was assured that he would get his professorship back at the University of Belgrade where he taught history before his summary dismissal.

His visitors were on their way out when Mrs. Dedijer said, "Wlado, if you accept, I leave you and take the children with me."

Dedijer added, "It made me really proud of her, even though I never for a moment entertained any idea of accepting the offer."

Then we went over the situation as Dedijer saw it from his own position. As the biographer and close friend of Marshal Tito, he believed that Tito was yielding to political pressure in approving his and Djilas' persecution. His calm acceptance of what was in store for him, and Djilas' own declaration that "Truth must be lived to be valid" made me realize that these two Yugoslav revolutionaries were the living refutation of all the sham humanism of the Communist elite.

As in Hungary, where I tried to avoid putting anyone on the spot, I refrained from embarrassing Dedijer. It would have been child's play to point out to him that his disappointment in men merely emphasized the weaknesses of the system, and I was sure his intellectual integrity would not have allowed him to avoid the issue. But this man was too vulnerable for me to badger and perhaps endanger.

The old-fashioned courtesy of the Dedijers was in sharp contrast with the callous indifference to the social graces of other Communists. Soon after my arrival at their home, the Dedijer children were brought in, their mother and grandmother proudly making the introductions. These well-mannered people showed no marks of the vicissitudes which had been visited upon them by their former friends. The children, as well as the grownups, displayed such a heartwarming quiet dignity, friendly good humor, tolerance and compassion toward people and issues that they seemed to represent an oasis in the vast, cruel sand dunes around them.

My next project was to examine how the Workers' Councils, which were supposedly in charge of all industrial and business enterprises, functioned on the lowest level and then to follow the chain of command up, as I had done in Hungary, to the highest economic organs.

I had selected Sarajevo for my study because ever since my kindergarten days it had a special significance for me as the cradle of World War I. It did not take long for me to run into the shade of Gavrilo Princip. Across from his memorial, in a little café, an old waiter told me all about the old conspiracy, the Narodna Obrana, a Serbian nationalistic secret society, the ensuing World War I, and the many hard days which came to Sarajevo after Gavrilo Princip assassinated the archduke. From the way the old waiter spoke, I gathered that Princip and his fellow conspirators were not regarded as heroes, but as tools of power-politicking powers, "fools of which there were and still are many" in the varied lands of Yugoslavia.

The factory I wanted to examine was an electronics plant which manufactured radios, communications equipment, and electronic gadgets. It had a good record for efficiency and performance.

"Spark," as the factory was called, was situated a few miles outside Sarajevo on a lovely hill overlooking neat, orderly meadows, small farms, and housing projects. At the time of my visit it employed nearly four thousand workers. My request to be permitted to visit the plant was enthusiastically granted, and several young men in long white robes, a mark of their station above ordinary workers, offered themselves as guides. They all appeared to be proud of their plant and eager to show me their version of "socialism in action."

By Balkan standards the factory was all that I was told it would be. Spotlessly clean, airy, with a few new, but mostly obsolete machines, it was a cheerful place, and the friendly glances and bantering exchanges between the workers and our group slowly making its way added to the feeling of camaraderie. In no time at all I was regarded as a special representative of the West who had come to admire their glorious experiment in building successful socialism.

My companions were all younger men, technically trained and above average both in intelligence and in skill. I asked them at the beginning to identify their stations at the plant: which of them belonged to the management, which of them were members of the Workers' Council, and which of them were appointed to their jobs by the district or national Economic Council? After each identified himself I explained why I wanted to talk to them: I believed from all that I had seen in other places that there was much ambiguity in the relations among these various elements in each plant, and I needed enlightening.

The description of the function of each group was relatively simple. The Workers' Council had much authority: it could hire and fire the managers; it could set the production quota; it could dispose of a part of the profits and attend to the welfare of the workers. In some instances the council was empowered to make basic investments in facilities and buildings with or without higher approval, depending upon whether it proposed to invest the money from the workers' share of the earnings of the plant or whether it needed outside capital.

The management was nominally under the control of the Workers' Council but operated independently and often against the wishes of the council. The management consisted of technicians—who, as it developed, had to be diplomats as well, in their dealings with the council.

The District Economic Council representatives (or representatives of the state, depending upon whether the plant was originally conceived and financed by the state or by the district) were there to help run the plant, but in effect they had veto power over both the council and the management. However, this veto power was used only regarding policy decisions which would affect the entire economic structure of the country or district. These representatives were also entrusted with policing the activities of the plant from the standpoint of over-all national needs both in regard to domestic markets and the export-import trade.

Each plant operated much as a capitalistic enterprise would; it had to show profit. The distribution of the profit also followed capitalistic lines: first the state claimed part of the profit; next, the State Bank (for capital investment), then came a scale of bonuses for executives and special workers. The rest of the profit went back to the plant to be distributed or reinvested under orders of the Workers' Council. If the plant did not operate profitably the District Economic Council (or that of the state) would step in and take over. Financing of a plant was carried through by various stages. A local (community) council could decide to start a needed enterprise and apply to the District Bank for endorsement and money. If the coun-

66

cil was turned down, the Community could appeal to the District Council, and finally, if the project was big enough, to the State Council. A project might also originate in district or state planning agencies, in which case the organization of it would remain in the hands of higher economic bodies. But, regardless of where an enterprise originated, the economic hierarchy controlled it at various levels, leaving to the Workers' Council a purely nominal control.

For the sake of clarifying the problem I proposed to examine a fictitious project. "Suppose," I said, "Stefan is the owner of a small farm near the city. Now, while digging in his garden he discovers a well of fabulous mineral value. What does he do?"

I followed the explanations in detail. Stefan could go to the Community Council and propose a bottling plant. Will it be his? No. Will he be the manager? That depends upon whether the Workers' Council would elect him. What, then, would be his incentive to report such a discovery and exploit it? Only that the possibility of getting a job appeared to be pretty good.

"Now what happens if the Community Council turns down his proposal or has no money to build a plant?"

"If Stefan is turned down he could go to the District Bank. If the District Bank refuses to advance the money, the council may go to the State Planning Board and to the State Bank."

"How does a bank decide whether to advance money for a project?" I asked.

"How does your bank decide whether to finance a factory in America?" countered a young engineer.

"Well, it would examine whether the project was feasible and whether it was profitable and finally whether or not the men proposing it had the necessary qualifications," I said.

"Exactly," said the engineer. "We do it the same way."

"Oh, no, not quite." I said. "We reward the promoters of new projects or inventions and thereby give them the incentive to dream up newer and better projects. But what happens to Stefan?"

From then on we got into the pointless argument about the idealism which was supposed to supply the motive force in Communist societies and the greed for profit which, in their minds, was the sole criterion of industry and commerce of the West. We followed the respective careers of their Stefan and my Joe Doaks, but we got nowhere since Stefan was operating in an economy which was radically different from the one in which Joe Doaks sought his fortune. Soon we were using words which lost their meaning. It became obvious that there could be no comparison between the respective economies of Eastern and Western lands; even the labels and political or economic terms with which we tried to express our thoughts and ideas acquired Eastern and Western meanings in their use. We did agree, however, on one major premise: that economy which served the people best was the economy which appeared to be most desirable.

"That being the case," I said, "let's talk about razor blades." Everyone stared at me. "We agreed," I continued, "to take the measure of your economy in its operation, so let's talk about the razor blades."

For some time there was an embarrassed silence until I assured them that I knew all about the nearly one and one half billion dinars which were lost in a harebrained attempt to manufacture razor blades at their plant.

"Please correct me if I am wrong," I said. "My information is that the Workers' Council decided to manufacture razor blades against the advice of the management. The council raised half the money by using the accumulated funds of the plant treasury and by cutting wages and bonuses. The other half came from the District Bank. After buying German equipment and Belgian steel, you began manufacturing razor blades. But they were of such bad quality that the state stores could not sell them; in fact, you had to buy many of them back, and after a while you stopped the experiment altogether. My information is that you spent two and a half million dollars for buying eighty German electrical band sharpeners and Belgian steel tapes. Now, what I would like to know —if my information is correct—how did this transaction develop and who was responsible for it?"

The management representative said: "The information you received is by and large correct. We warned the Workers' Council that machinery would not be enough and that the manufacture of razor blades called for skilled mechanics, but we were overruled."

The engineer who had previously defended Stefan's socialistic enterprise again took up the defense. "To begin with," he said, "the idea of manufacturing razor blades was a good one and still is. The country needs it. Perhaps the comrades acted too precipitately, but the experience taught the council a lesson and it is not likely to happen again."

"Who pays for the losses?" I asked.

"It will be paid for over a period of years out of the profits of the plant," said the engineer. What this "over a period of years" meant on closer examination was a considerably reduced living standard for the workers.

Just then G.R., the director of the plant, the highest executive officer, joined our group and took a sharply differing view on the subject. His point was that while Workers' Councils were good insofar as welfare matters were concerned, they should not be permitted to make policy decisions or issue management directives. He cited one instance after another to show how the efficiency of the plant had suffered throughout the years from amateur meddling and unscientific direction.

"The mere fact that I can be fired," said G.R. "for opposing some crazy, unscientific proposal is enough to make me less eager for innovations, no matter how desirable. Instead of running the plant as it should be run, most of the time I am playing politics, wasting my time in receiving committees, sitting in on discussions which get nowhere, explaining, defending, and cajoling people who in most cases do not know what they are talking about."

I noticed the outspokenness of G.R. and marveled at his courage. My neighbor, one of his assistants, whispered that he had several important offers from outside Yugoslavia from capitalistic enterprises at much higher pay and that he was pretty independent because of his managerial talents.

I asked G.R. why did he not leave the place if he thought that he was ignored or that he could not operate it satisfactorily.

"Oh, you misunderstand me." G.R. smiled. "I am a socialist and I do believe in what we are doing. My complaint is that we could do these things more efficiently and with much greater benefit to the Republic if some of the useless political frills were cut off. I also believe that the Workers' Council is needed here if for no other reason than to keep discipline among the workers and make their sacrifices palatable. For, unquestionably, they are earn-

69

ing, even at the present rate, much less than their production warrants simply because we are principally working for foreign exchange and not for what a socialist economy should ultimately work for. We need foreign exchange currency for further investments, and of course the money must come out of our hides."

We carried the argument late into the evening and continued it after dinner. My point was that socialist enterprise claims to be more efficient than capitalistic enterprise, but by their own testimony that was not true; I also said that Workers' Councils and all other political claptrap were dishonest because the economy of the country was directed from above and not, as it was claimed, by the workers.

As a single issue the razor-blade episode could have been written off as a mistake, but the same situation existed with slight variations in many others plants. The Workers' Councils, even in their limited sphere, were not an improvement, but a handicap to modern production.

Others around the table recounted many instances of conflicts, inefficiencies, and heavy losses arising from divided authority. All agreed that in every case the State or District Council had the last word, and banks often used their veto power over farmers and workers. There was hardly a question as to the lack of economic value of the Workers' Councils, but nearly all agreed that they make the situation in Yugoslavia more tolerable for the workers.

"Is not the price too high?" I asked. "Would not greater efficiency bring higher rewards and greater contentment than the fictitious belief that the workers own their own factories and in fact are their own masters?"

Late into the night we argued and debated. There was certainly a difference between the Yugoslav exponents of Communism and the Hungarian. Even of those who disapproved of one or several aspects of their systems, the Yugoslavs as a whole were enthusiastic and optimistic, whereas in Hungary the dominant note was indifference and resignation. In Sarajevo as well as elsewhere the Yugoslavs seemed to believe that somehow everything would work out all right.

Perhaps this emotional loyalty was the difference between Titoism and Stalinism. Examined piece by piece, Titoism had very little to recommend it above Communist practices in other countries, yet undeniably there was a great difference in the people's acceptance of it. Whether this difference was due to the worship of Tito or to something else remained to be seen. The defense of Tito even by such a deeply offended person as Dedijer was an eloquent mark of the esteem with which the people, both high and low, regarded their leader.

Dedijer had given me a copy of his biography of Tito which carried Tito's own endorsement and modest disclaimer. Every night on the road I read parts of the heavy volume to familiarize myself with the background of the revolutionary leaders of Yugoslavia, inasmuch as I had an interview with Mose Pijade as the next major item on my schedule. Measured with Western eyes, it seemed to me that in any free election Tito would win an overwhelming majority. The question which was not easy to answer was: What after Tito? Did the whole structure rest on his personal popularity, or was there a more solid base to Yugoslav Communism?

6

Pijade, Titoism, ana Neutrality

Mose Pijade, next to Tito, was the most beloved person in Yugoslavia. The higher one went among the Yugoslav Communists, the more often one came across Pijade worship, which, I was told, extended to Tito himself. "Uncle Yanko," as he was affectionately called, was the outstanding theoretician of the Yugoslav Communist party.

A frail, unassuming little man, Pijade went through the Second World War as a trusted confidant of the partisan high command and was the first victim of Soviet treachery as he waited in vain for months in bitter cold in 1943 at Durmitor for promised Soviet supplies which were never sent. At the fateful meeting of the Yugoslav Communist party of April 12, 1948, when it was decided to break with Stalin, Pijade spoke bitterly against Stalin and denounced the Soviet dictator as a traitor to socialism.

Now, at sixty-seven, with a lifetime of struggle behind him, Mose Pijade was the president of the Skuptstina (Congress) and vice president of the Federated States of Yugoslavia.

His office in the Parliament Building, a stone's throw from the party headquarters, was in keeping with the man: quiet and tasteful. His ready smile and quick wit often saved us from embarrassment during the major part of three days I spent with him. Many of the things said at these meetings were off the record, and my dispatches to the North American Newspaper Alliance were replete with references to "Communist insiders" and "well informed persons." Most of the time "their" name was Mose Pijade.

Our first discussion revolved around the baleful consequences of the cold war for all concerned. Pijade pointed out that the cold war froze everyone and delayed much-needed progress in the world's economy and social institutions. "If this freeze continues much longer," he said, "the world will explode and the consequences will be incalculable."

He distributed the blame for the present situation equally between the East and the West, and added, "You are much less justified in your fears than the Soviet Union; what you really are afraid of is yourself."

I pointed out to him how ludicrous it is to imagine for a minute that Communism could gain a serious foothold in America, saying that in our country there just does not exist the soil in which Communism could grow. Pijade agreed, and went on to say that that was why the American strategy of the cold war was nefarious because it was a sham for expansionist policies. While accepting the unreality of the Red scare in the United States, I had to point out to him that many Soviet moves after the war were such as to give at least a semblance of a foundation to our fear.

"I hold no brief for nearly all of Stalin's policies following World War II," he replied, "but if Stalin had an anti-Western phobia he had at least some real grounds for it. You Americans and British began the cold war, and that is an undeniable historical fact."

I asked Pijade to explain.

"Nearly everything you did while the war was going on was knowingly or unknowingly designed to scare the Soviet Union as well as non-Communist revolutionaries in Europe. Long before a single Soviet soldier crossed the border of his homeland you were busily engaged in re-creating the prewar status quo."

Pijade recounted the history of the revolutionary movements operating behind the Nazi-Fascist forces: how thousands of patriotic people in all occupied lands had given their lives for a freer, better future, while in "London and Washington their former tormentors, the ex-majesties and excellencies," were organized for a triumphal return to their homelands. He mentioned North Africa where the Allied forces tried to install pro-Nazis like Darlan, Pucheu, Peyrouton, and others, into power, ignoring the revolutionary anti-Fascists, most of whom became Communists because of their disillusionment with the political policies of the Allies. He mentioned the Allied decisions in Italy to recognize and deal with Badoglio and the king, while the republican forces were disbanded and scattered; in Greece, where the Allies wantonly broke their pledge not to permit the return of the king and his British-organized army until after a plebiscite and to maintain the military and political status quo until then. He explained some of the troubles the Yugoslavs had with Washington and London about King Peter and his assorted excellencies trying to foist themselves on a hostile country. He went into great detail explaining the inside story of the Polish government-in-exile, its aims and membership and the Allied insistence on handing Poland back to that group of cruel feudalist gentry.

"If the Russians feared that you were trying to reestablish an impossible order of things in Europe which could not help leading to World War III," he continued, "we were scared too. Stalin, for all his cruelties and megalomania, tried his best to stop the spread of Communism during the war and immediately after it, in order to placate the Allies. He nearly smothered us here in Yugoslavia, and in Poland, Hungary, Czechoslovakia, and Romania he maintained a coalition government as long as possible. But you were politically insatiable, and once the die was cast Stalin moved ruthlessly, crushing every opposition to his will except here in Yugoslavia. You can check dates and facts, and you will see that the chronology of events will condemn you as the initiator of the cold war."

Pijade's exposition of Allied political mistakes was not new to me.

In Greece, in the fall of 1944, I had watched the British maneuvers which resulted in the Civil War and which led to the control of the EAM (National Liberation Front) by the Communists, a consultative political body which until the deliberately provoked internecine war was the most democratic institution Greece ever experienced. I also remembered Eduard Benes' bitter words in 1946 after the Byrnes speech in Stuttgart, saying, "You are forcing Central Europe into the arms of Moscow." And Jan Masaryk's unprintable language concerning American decisions to rebuild the economic might of Germany at the expense of the Allies.

What Mose Pijade did was to detail the order of events and show justification for the subsequent Soviet behavior. "You were all out," he said, "to re-create European Fascism, and the Soviets in retaliation tightened their grip on Central Europe."

Pijade was willing to grant that America was not motivated by a conscious desire to re-create an intolerable status quo in Europe. "It was your ignorance of European history," he said, "and your predelection for dealing with 'respectable' people—bankers, industrialists, bishops and clerics, officers and aristocrats—the traditional enemies of European progress. You never understood, and I am afraid you still don't, that there was no Middle in Europe—only Left or Right. The masses of Europe had had a thousand-year experience with the cruel exploitation of the Right, and by insisting on dealing with the Right America forced them toward the extreme Left."

The old man several times lost his quiet, detached manner during the discussion, particularly when we came to the question of whose mistakes were greater and more grievous, those of the Western nations or those of the Communists. My point was that even if I were to accept everything Pijade said, and undeniably there were strong arguments on his side, nevertheless, the subsequent behavior of the Communists toward their own people was indefensible. "Why was it necessary to take out your fears of the West on your own people?" I asked. "If, as you say, your people were ready to revolt against Allied determination to re-create the status quo, why completely blanket all freedoms?"

In answer Mose Pijade vehemently denied that what they were

75

doing amounted to a complete suppression of freedom. He called it "reeducation," the short cut to the twenty-first century, the painful experience which comes from forced growth.

Later the talk drifted toward more immediate problems. I asked him whether it was true that Tito believed that both the Warsaw pact and NATO were useless and wasteful, and hence opposed them.

At first Pijade was unwilling to talk about Tito's military views, but after I gave him in detail certain information I had received from a military personality close to Tito, he became more open. He said, however, that Tito represented so much the thinking of all Yugoslavs that, "When you say Tito thinks this or that, you are saying the Yugoslavs think this or that." I accepted this qualification because obviously Pijade wanted to hedge and was trying to avoid quoting Tito; nevertheless he wanted me to know that the prevailing military thinking was Tito's.

"Yes, we want to remain neutrals. If there is no general war, then both military camps needlessly restrict the economies of the participating countries; if there should be a general war both organizations would fall apart at the first explosion of a bomb."

He went on to analyze the situation much along the line I had heard from my military informant. Accordingly, I gathered that Tito (or, as Pijade insisted, the Yugoslavs) believed that the moment America and the Soviet Union began fighting, Europe would revolt and proclaim its independence. Thus, while the United States and the Soviet Union were busy exterminating each other, the European nations would quickly rise against their governments which might want to lead them into the war on one side or the other. That would be the time for Yugoslavia to emerge as the leader of Europe: first, because Yugoslavia would be a rallying point of neutralism; second, because Yugoslavia would show the way to socialism; and, third, because Yugoslavia would have an independent and intact army, capable of restoring order.

This, according to Pijade, explained two seemingly conflicting actions of the Yugoslav government: the maintenance of an expensive, strong, and well-equipped army, and Yugoslavia's refusal to join either camp. He readily agreed that there was little likelihood that the Soviet Union or her satellites would attack Yugoslavia, the official reason for the maintenance of the Yugoslav army. However, he added, should there be a general conflagration among a number of the satellites, which was not out of the realm of possibility, the Yugoslav army might be called upon to play an important role.

"What role?" I asked.

"Keep war away from our border, protect a sanctuary for refugees, and be ready for whatever aid we could render after such a conflict."

"Would Yugoslavia intervene in a civil war between native Titoists and Kremlinists among her neighbors?" I asked.

"No, never. No, no!" said Pijade.

I asked him why Tito believed so strongly in the military uselessness of NATO. He gave me two cogent reasons: one, because no one in Europe believed in the cause of America strongly enough to fight for it, and, two, because in a few minutes' time all NATO bases would be wiped out by present Soviet intermediate ballistic missiles, and this was a fact known by all military and political leaders of Europe. He added a number of other reasons to show that NATO was a military and political monstrosity, and said, "But all the reasons I gave you, except the existence of ballistic missiles, applies to the Warsaw Pact Alliance too."

"Do you believe that an American-Soviet war is possible or likely?"

"Possible, yes, likely, no," he replied. He went on to say that at this state of "weapons development," despite what the generals and admirals on both sides say, "A major war between America and the Soviet Union would surely be tantamount to mutual extermination. That, however, he said, does not exclude the possibility of stumbling into such a war or accidentally precipitating one. He also said that it was his firm belief that neither America nor the Soviet Union was plotting such a war: "The object of a war is to gain advantage over the enemy. And that is not possible today."

It is hard to reproduce from notes, even though some of them are direct quotes, the flavor of Mose Pijade. Our discussion ranged over all aspects of Communist thinking. He appeared alternately as a fiery spokesman and as a detached observer, but throughout he maintained a magisterial pose exuding certainty and conviction. He managed to clothe even his hesitations with a judiciousness which hid his own disquiet. For Pijade, despite a lifetime devoted to Communist theology, was far from as sure as he wanted to make me believe. There were times when he came perilously close to heresy and to questioning the wisdom of his own beliefs. A significant exchange occurred during the second session between us.

I had questioned him closely about the loss of human values in a Communist civilization and the likelihood of permanent damage arising from forcing man back to his prethinking, preexpressive, submission-to-absolute stage. I drew a parallel between the all-encompassing theology of the Middle Ages, its retrogressive effect extending over several centuries, and the heavy-handed orthodoxy demanded and enforced by the Communist hierarchy in matters most important to man's growth. I demanded an answer to the key question: Is what you are doing to man's spirit worth the material advancement which you promise in exchange, even assuming but not admitting that you will be able to fulfill your promise? Again, assuming your essentially humanistic impulse, could you not serve man in his search for a more abundant future without damaging his self-respect, his pride, his basic freedom? And, finally, when Pijade remained silent, I asked him, Do you believe you can undo the harm to man, once this forced industrialization ends?

He answered quietly, "I hope so."

Again we reverted to more immediate problems. Is a synthesis possible between the East and the West? I reminded him of Litvinov's famous remark to Roosevelt: "After the war you will be a little less capitalistic and we will be a little less Communistic, and we shall meet somewhere in the middle."

"There are two answers to the question," he replied. "One, the immediate one, is No. The other one is the long-range answer: It will come not by design but by daily living together and by the accommodation of one another to the exigencies of our daily mutual problems."

"Does this mean that you believed Anthony Eden's solution: Attack small problems one by one as they arise, and the larger problems will solve themselves?" I asked.

"Something like that" Pijade replied. "You Americans want everything in black or white; we Europeans have learned long, long ago to mistrust 'absolute solution.' We believe people accommodating themselves to their daily needs will find ways to cope with them. This is one reason why the present vogue of name calling and insults seems to us so childish and harmful."

When questioned as to the direction this "accommodation" should take, he replied unhesitatingly: "Economic adjustments which undoubtedly would benefit you as well as us. The cold war has erected such economic barriers that unless they are removed we shall all retrogress."

I called his attention to the new economic phenomenon in Yugoslavia, the international trade banks. I told him the story of one deal that I investigated which showed that in order to conclude a trade agreement with Holland, the Yugoslav bank went out on the world market and bought at high prices Yugoslav copper which was originally delivered pursuant to a previous agreement to Britain. The loss to Yugoslavia was tremendous, but at the same time there was no other way to conclude the agreement with Holland for needed machinery and raw materials. Would Pijade care to explain this new approach to international trade?

"It is a part of the same picture. The economic barriers— political as well as economic—which exist today are such that we had to resort to wasteful practices in order to be able to trade with the West. In fact, in most cases we are held up by extortionist prices and conditions because we have no ready access to Western markets. I should really say 'American markets,' because America dictates the economic conditions of the West."

Later it was Pijade's turn to question me. He wanted to know about John Foster Dulles and what made the man so almighty righteous, even when he was "wholly and destructively wrong." Nothing I said would satisfy Pijade. He was genuinely puzzled by Dulles. He could not believe that Dulles was not aware of his own, in Pijade's words, "fundamentally hypocritical" approach to East-West problems. No matter how convincingly I tried to show him that Dulles did believe the things he was saying, Pijade shook his head in disbelief. "If he knows so many wrong things," he asked, "how could he possibly be your Secretary of State?"

Then the conversation drifted toward Hungary. He listened carefully while I recounted signs of the outraged conscience which was compelling the Hungarian Communists to oppose militantly the present regime. He listened attentively while I read to him a report I had just sent to The Reporter entitled "Budapest: Rehabilitated Corpses and Guilty Consciences." He agreed that unless major

79

reforms were instituted in Hungary the situation might get out of hand at any time. We both agreed that the Rakosi-Gero regime must and undoubtedly would go, little dreaming that a few months later I would be sitting in my car at the Parliament Square in Budapest listening to the arrogant voice of Gero rejecting the demands for overdue reforms and denouncing the demonstrators in a speech that led directly to the Hungarian Revolution.

I asked Pijade to explain the basic difference between what they were doing in Yugoslavia and what the other Communist countries were doing.

"Perhaps the most important difference, apart from our independence in foreign affairs, is the fact that our system is not directed centrally. The parliamentary committees are constantly working on legislation; they hold open hearings and generally ascertain that a proposed law would meet the needs of our society."

"Do party members vote according to directives from the party?" I asked.

"Yes, of course. But the party directives are not issued arbitrarily; they are products of deliberation," Pijade explained. "Also, we have no censorship, no party propaganda; artists may create freely," he continued, and, seeing a smile on my face, added, "Of course, people must be responsible for what they write or say; irresponsible troublemakers cannot be tolerated. There is a basic difference between freedom to express oneself and license to try to destroy or damage our society."

"Let me ask you then, if I as a writer and political commentator could not find a market for my articles in the official publications—and there does not seem to be any other kind around here—how would I go about starting a publication of my own?"

Pijade, with a gleam in his eye, said, "Well, if you have the money and find a printer, you can start any kind of publication."

We both laughed, and that seemed to dispose of the no-censorship issue.

"There are further differences in the structure of our Workers' Councils and their rights. Our agricultural system is different in that peasants are free to join cooperatives, state farms, or remain independent."

"Provided their holdings do not exceed roughly the plot a man can cultivate with his family—twenty-five acres," I interjected.

Further questions elucidated the fact that all peasants, independent or no, marketed their produce through a marketing organization controlled by the state and that that marketing organization determined the prices the peasants received for their products. Pijade tried to make clear that the marketing organization established its daily quotations for produce according to the prevailing prices at the retail outlets, but he could not clearly state just how this mechanism worked since the retail prices were also set by state-controlled stores.

Going over the structural differences between Titoism and the other kind of Communism, we always came back to the point that Yugoslavia insisted on an independent foreign policy. This was well enough established, but what I was unable to get from Pijade was a categorical statement as to why this was necessary as long as the systems of Communist practices, even though with variations, seemed basically to be the same. Was it national pride? Tito's ambitions to become the prophet of Communism? The interesting possibility of having commercial ties with both worlds? The fear of war? Finally I asked Pijade point-blank: "If, despite Tito's views on an East-West war, a prolonged struggle ensued between them in which the stake obviously would be which of the two systems would prevail, would Yugoslavia still remain neutral even though, if the East lost the war, Communism as a political and economic system would lose its roots?"

"No, I don't think we could or would remain neutral. But your question was unreal. That's your American black or white. Socialism would never lose its roots because its roots are in the very existence of man. By any other name, cooperative social effort is the law of mankind."

Leaving Pijade for the last time, I tried to sum up my impression of the man, and wrote in my diary: "The old man hates to part with his life dream, even though his wise eyes know better."

After the Hungarian Revolution, in the spring of 1957, I was once again in Yugoslavia, impatiently awaiting Pijade's return from abroad to continue our discussion on Hungary and the factors

81

responsible for the collapse of the revolution. Pijade was due back in a few days when the news was broadcast on Belgrade Radio that he had died suddenly in Paris.

While waiting for him, I had been reading excerpts of a manuscript by Djilas, which later appeared in the West under the title *The New Class*, and I had prepared a number of quotations from it for Mose Pijade to answer. Walking in his funeral cortege, among thousands of genuinely grief-stricken people, I could not help thinking of the painful circle which so many intellectuals must travel these days to arrive somewhere near the truth. Pijade and Djilas, like the Hungarian intellectuals, rose against the extreme cruelties of their time and youth with weapons equally cruel and extreme, and only through long years of painful soul searching were they able to free themselves from both and to strike out for themselves. The first unlearning process was easy: violence for violence, an eye for an eye; the second, the awakening and maturing of their moral concept which led them to turn against all of their past, involved intellectual and emotional agony. I believe that Mose Pijade, at the time of his death, was at the end of his second unlearning process.

Living standards in Yugoslavia, much to my surprise, were lower than in Hungary, somewhat on a par with Poland, and a notch higher than in Romania.

This is not altogether the regime's fault, although with Western trade and large American credits Yugoslavia by then should have been a happier place to live were it not for the incredible waste at every stage of the economy. The unevenness of Yugoslav economy was an inheritance from previous regimes. Parts of the Federated State which were under permanent Austro-Hungarian rule were better developed economically and culturally, and the living standard was higher in those parts. Slovenia, Croatia, and the Vojvodina were comparatively better off than Serbia, Montenegro, Bosnia-Herzegovina, and the Dalmatian parts where the Skiptars lived.

The differences were comparative because poverty was universal. While the Slovian peasant would have a cow, it would also be his plow beast, his source of food, and occasionally the cow would be used to drag his wagon. It was not uncommon to see a horse and a cow hitched to a heavily laden cart in Croatia or Slovenia. In the more primitive parts of the country motive power for cultivation and transport was still largely supplied by human muscles.

Industrial workers were paid a bare minimum for subsistence. In some newly developed housing projects workers' families had slightly better facilities than those living in old sections of industrial cities, but new or old, an average Yugoslav room still housed from three to six people crammed together in tight proximity.

Theoretically, the Communist regime of Yugoslavia was devoted to the full development of Yugoslavia's human and material resources. Practically, however, this was far from true. The economy was saturated with political and military considerations. From the crazy restrictions that a village machine repair shop, which can have only one helper, must become communized as soon as another pair of hands was needed, to the poor imitations of Western industry, which in some cases were undisguised military establishments and in many others top-heavy and indifferent drains on the country's economy—all contributed to Yugoslav poverty.

The fanaticism with which Communists defended the system of state ownership from the smallest to the largest shops was one of their most glaring blind spots. The idea was sacred, and nothing one could say against it would make the slightest difference to an orthodox Marxist. Even when it was demonstrated to them that the system caused untold damage to them and was likely to wreck or at least retard their own socialistic program, they stubbornly defended it. To a set of facts I had presented to them, they gave the stock answer: "Well, even so, we may get there slower this way, but we'll get there."

As in other Communist countries, in Yugoslavia, too, the hope for some alleviation of the rigors of the narrow confines in which the people live came from the Communist elite, the intellectuals, artists and educators. One of the strictest of orthodox Communist taboos was being violated those days at the University of Belgrade: social sciences were getting out of the narrow Marxist groove, and Western ideas and discoveries were slowly beginning to modify what Professor Lukacs of Hungary called "tape-recorded Marxism."

It was still called "Marxist education," for everything had to have the imprimatur of Apostolate, but the fact that social sciences were taught at all—and soon would become compulsory—was in itself a major heresy. Social anthropology, psychology, humanism, and the evolutionary sciences were suspect sciences in Communist countries, suppressed or at best modified and distorted to meet the restrictions of the hierarchy. Every fact, discovery, theory, or experiment which had been in conflict with the Marxian concept of man and his history had been relentlessly suppressed by the Holy Inquisition and were listed among the deadly sins.

Dr. Boza Djordjevic, deputy-rector of Belgrade University, was one of the many educators trying to improve the scientific standards of Yugoslavia, especially in the field of social sciences. "Patterns must be avoided in Marxist education," he said, "and abstract and dogmatic approaches to it made impossible." What he meant was that the new social sciences, which he called Marxist, should be made to fit existing circumstances—flexible and dynamic. He freely admitted that one of the most important problems Yugoslav education faced was the preparation of students to accept social realities both in the field of national endeavor and in the interrelation of races. After much prompting, in less polite language all this narrowed down to making the students accept a compromise between Marxist theology and its contradictions and immoralities, and at the same time sell the idea of a multiracial national existence with somewhat greater success than was heretofore possible. The good rector and some of his colleagues whom I subsequently met were less sure of themselves than the cocky members of the Communist party elite; the educators seemed to have a foreboding that the younger generation would be less amenable to eternal verities handed down by the presidium of the party than were their fathers. More than that, a large proportion of the students were frankly caustic about some of the ideologies they were ordered to absorb and applaud.

The apprehensiveness of Yugoslavia's top educators was matched by the foreboding of the educators in other Communist countries, with one major difference: the Yugoslavs were able at least to present their views to their betters, whereas in other countries, with a small degree of exception in Poland, educators were watching the slow rise of intellectual and moral discontent among their students and faculties in enforced silence. I do not wish to convey the idea that there was anything remotely like intellectual freedom in Yugo-slavia. No, the Yugoslav *Gleichschaltung* was all-pervasive; however, windows were not so tightly sealed as in the other "People's Democracies." One could, with enough courage and trouble, climb out of the ideological prison—provided one did not stray too far.

The best one can say about Yugoslavia's neutralism is that for Yugoslavia it is an economic and political asset. The people are intensely antiwar, and American military assistance bolstered the Yugoslav economy. But this neutrality is merely on the surface: in a major European war Yugoslavia would not be able to stand aside. This is the unanimous opinion of every Yugoslav leader with whom I discussed this problem.

Yugoslavian military experts are less worried about a world war than about a localized European war or, if a world war becomes inevitable, the aftermath of such a war. As they see it Yugoslavia would not have a major role to play in the first phase of a major war. The two giants, the U.S.A. and the U.S.S.R., would paralyze each other within a few days after the outbreak of the war. In the ensuing general melee Yugoslavia would be able to give a good account of herself, especially since her opponents would most likely be members of the "socialist camp" whose military morale and loyalty to the U.S.S.R. would be very low.

The Yugoslav view was that to avoid such a war with Communist countries would call for Yugoslavia's entrance into the Warsaw Pact. For several reasons, including that of safety, Yugoslavia considered this for some time but came to the conclusion that the Warsaw Pact would not stand up under war conditions and that its members would needlessly expose themselves to Western retaliation. Neither were the Yugoslavs overly trustful of NATO, which they also considered a weak structure whose role would be played after the major powers had disposed of one another. Taken one by one, the NATO countries, according to the Yugoslav view, would have their hands full as the heirs of a conflict between America and the U.S.S.R. and a devastated world, and would scarcely be able to help Yugoslavia.

Neutrality pleases neither Washington nor Moscow. But Washing-ton is more tolerant, and recognizes the value of Yugoslavia's stand to the extent of several hundred million dollars' worth of military and economic aid. Moscow periodically tries to steamroll Yugoslavia into the "socialist camp," but there is very little chance of that. On the contrary, every attempt leaves severe bruises on Yugoslavia's pride.

The weakest link in the neutrality chain is Yugoslavia's military equipment. Her heavy weapons and air arms are of Western manufacture. There is no certainty of continued American military aid, and in a war replacement would become impossible. Therefore, the first military fact the Yugoslav army leadership must consider is the short-lived quality of the heavy arms. A considerable part of Yugoslav military opinion holds that in a major war NATO and Warsaw Pact countries would be in the same predicament; the United States and the Soviet Union would not be in a position to keep their allies supplied with adequate replacements.

The Yugoslavs are manufacturing small- and medium-sized arms in nearly enough quantity. Both quantity and quality are being constantly improved, and army experts hope that in the foreseeable future the country will become self-sufficient in infantry and medium artillery equipment except for anti-aircraft weapons. The Yugoslav terrain favors nonmechanized warfare, and the high command of the army is composed of veterans of the last war in which the Yugoslav partisan army successfully battled with small arms against thirty superbly equipped German divisions.

The patriotic morale of the Yugoslav army is probably the best in Europe, but its willingness to fight for socialism is less certain than its eagerness to fight for Yugoslavia. Although the ritual, as with everything else in Yugoslavia, is Communist, the Yugoslav soldier's first love is his country, in which he has a ferocious pride. Communism will always be a second thought with him. Much of the Yugoslav army's high morale stems from its heroic deeds during World War II, and it seems to be a thing apart from the general morale of the country.

For all their cocksureness, Yugoslav military leaders are aware of their equivocal position, and dream of a solution which, in their view, would bring safety to all Balkan countries. They say that a Balkan federation composed of Yugoslavia, Romania, Bulgaria, and possibly the two non-Communist countries of Greece and Turkey would be the perfect answer to all their problems. This Yugoslav dream has dominated much of Tito's political thinking in recent years. The Yugoslavs say the first step was the loosening of their ideological ties to Moscow, to be followed by a successful example of building socialism in Yugoslavia which may in time become attractive to other satellite countries. Some Yugoslavs even think in terms of a federation which would extend from the Sea of Marmara to the Baltic.

As the Yugoslavs see it, such a federation would not be hostile either to the Soviet Union or to the United States. Somewhat naïvely, they postulate a world within which countries would be free to develop, and power politics would be a thing of the past. They argue that a Balkan federation would not be merely a military blessing but a perfect economic unit, each part complementing the other, that large-scale industrialism could only be successful in large economic units, and that the tremendous riches of the Balkan and Central European area, if properly exploited, would bring abundance to all.

The Yugoslavs know that this idea of a federation of the Danubian nations has been popular with the helplessly intermingled races and nations of the area for centuries and that it has a hold on the imagination of the people. To enlarge this imagery is Yugoslavia's present military and political aim.

The Yugoslavs uneasily realize that they do represent a menace to the Kremlin. And because they know this, they fear the wrath of Soviet leadership. As a high government functionary put it: "They have thrown everything at us and we have survived, stronger than ever. But the war is far from over. . . ."

On the surface the quarrel between the two countries revolves around Yugoslavia's reluctance to join the "socialist camp," meaning the Warsaw Pact. The hard feeling engendered by Yugoslavia's categoric refusal to join the socialist camp is a convenient camouflage to hide Soviet chagrin over Yugoslav insistence on following a new path toward socialism and their comparative success. The Kremlin, according to the Yugoslavs, believes that its own leadership is in danger and that something will have to give. The price Khrushchev paid for Tito's friendship was the fatal "there are many ways to socialism" line which, according to Yugoslav and Soviet experts, is the constant menace with which Tito's independence threatens the Soviet bloc.

Even though the Yugoslav leadership would be inclined to accept Soviet friendship uncritically, the people are not. The vicious Soviet propaganda against Tito and Yugoslavia's leadership left a deep mark on the people. The Yugoslavs may joke about and even curse Tito, but he is Mohammed, the true prophet, nevertheless.

The most interesting aspect of Yugoslavia is one which the Yugoslavs accept because they live with it and have been conscious of it for many centuries, but which for a foreigner is hard to understand—namely, the many different standards which are applied in various parts of the country. Except for a thin veneer of Marxism which covers the country as a whole, Yugoslavia might very well be six different countries, each with differing and often clashing standards, attitudes, cultures, and racial temperaments. Perhaps this is the real reason behind the frantic Communist efforts to smother national cultures and develop a Yugoslav monoculture. Something is not jelling in Yugoslavia, and Marxism, the dedicated religion which is counted on by the Communists to do the job, is much too obscure to command true devotion.

As long as the revolutionary fervor which carried over from the bitter years of the war is still alive and Tito's personal magic remains potent, the deep contradictions in the Yugoslav state remain dormant. But the war is receding; the heroic legends of the partisan days are beginning to fade; and Tito is not immortal.

A few of the less fanatical devotees of Marx are beginning to see the need for modification of their practices; they also realize that this need will surely become urgent. Uneasily, they hope that when the time comes to carry through basic changes they will be up to the task and that the next transition period can be kept bloodless.

PART TWO

The Hungarian Revolution

7

Paris Prelude

When I returned to Paris in the summer of 1956, I found a message
from the editor of *The Reporter* saying that my report on Hungary
would be published late in September and asking me to consider
bringing it up to date. I reread the piece in the light of what I had
learned in Yugoslavia and it seemed to me that the warning, "The
roof is shaking above their heads," was still valid and indeed that
the situation had deteriorated in the meantime. I looked up copies
of my dispatches to NANA, one of which ended: "However, it is
a less intriguing question as why these things have taken place than
is the seemingly unanswerable: Where will it all lead? Even though
no one is able to make a prediction, one thing appears certain—
the old-style Communist state is going, and if anyone should try to
impose it again the situation would explode in a revolution.
Curiously, those who are certain of this are the elite of the Com-

munists, who with one voice are saying that they would not permit anyone to enslave them again."

In saying this I had in mind Imre Nagy, who, during our brief and largely fruitless conversation, stubbornly maintained that "decent" application of Communist principles would bring salvation to Hungary, and who went to all sorts of lengths to ignore or camouflage the larger issues. His insistence on decency in the application of Communist principles showed either an unbelievable naïveté in a man so experienced in statecraft or a disguise for something else which Nagy did not dare to name.

From Paris, during July and August, it looked as though the situation in Hungary would, after all, explode in a revolution.

Matyas Rakosi, the hated head of the Hungarian Communist party, had finally been removed from office, but his successor, Erno Gero, brought no solace to the disgusted Hungarians. Gero, a dour, brusque, dry, inhuman person, was thoroughly disliked by everyone, including his colleagues in the party. His appointment was considered an insult and was greatly resented.

The second sign of increasing tension came toward the end of July when the Central Committee of the party issued a reprimand and a warning against too much criticism and called upon party and nonparty Hungarians to hew the official line lest sharp measures be taken against "deviationists."

Soon after, an order was issued to DISZ (Democratic Youth Federation) to cease holding meetings and to curb the dissatisfied element within its ranks. DISZ officials fell in with the order and stopped the Petofi Circle, which was a creature of DISZ, from holding public forums on current issues.

But the pious statements issued by the leaders of DISZ only further enraged its membership. This membership was largely made up of students of higher educational institutions, with other elements, mostly young intellectuals in various trades and arts, joining "to develop Socialist consciousness." The dissatisfaction of DISZ membership with its leadership was the fuse which ignited the revolution in October.

September was quiet, but the silence was ominous. The ceremonial reburial of rehabilitated corpses continued, and the macabre spectacle of the bones of hanged Communists being dragged through the

streets of Budapest accompanied by the breast-beating of party poten-
tates broke down whatever respect Hungarians may still have had for
the regime. After all, except for the belated departure of Rakosi, nothing really had changed. The Presidium was still loaded with Rakosi-
Stalinists, and Gero himself, the new first secretary, was a faithful
Stalinist.

The crisis centered more and more upon Imre Nagy. His recall
as premier during the summer would have eased the tension sufficiently to enable Hungarian Communists to clean house if they so
desired. But Nagy was kept from the helm, and the highest party
organ was still heavily loaded with his enemies. By the end of
September it was clear that a showdown between the regime and
the dissatisfied elements was in the making.

My decision in early October to return to Budapest in anticipation
of a major crisis was subsequently challenged by two widely differing sources. Hungarian officials after the revolution claimed I had
foreknowledge of the coming revolution. Otherwise how did it happen that I was the only Western newspaperman to enter Hungary
on October 19th—such a conspicuous date? I could never convince
them that my decision was the result of a simple calculation based
on my earlier observations. They were convinced that I must have
been part of that nebulous Western conspiracy which they claimed
had fomented the revolt in Hungary.

On the other hand, a husband-wife team of Hungarian-born
Western correspondents stationed in Budapest attacked me in a
letter to one of my editors saying in effect that the Hungarian revolt
was unpredictable. Since this also happened to be the official view
of the American Legation in Budapest, it was obvious that the
attackers were trying to defend the general Western ignorance concerning matters in Hungary.

At any rate, I drove to Budapest on October 19th and arrived at
the hotel in the afternoon. There I found a message from an official
of the Foreign Office asking me to call on him.

On the phone he said that my arrival was opportune, and suggested that I drive to Szeged, where interesting events were in the
making. Budapest seemed quiet during the few hours I drove through
the city, and I wondered whether I had not let my own wishful
thinking run away with my judgment. I called a few of my con-

93

tacts on the phone and noticed that they were deliberately non-committal. With cautious phrases, which were in sharp contrast to their earlier willingness to talk, they seemed to say that they were still hoping that the situation would ease. But their opinions were vague and largely pessimistic. Much later I found out that they were afraid to talk. Earlier that afternoon word had come from Warsaw that things were moving there and that the political police in Hungary had been alerted.

8

The Conflict Begins

I met the Hungarian Revolution on Sunday, October 21, 1956, in Szeged, the second largest city in Hungary.

As I write, three years have passed since that sunny afternoon when students streamed toward the Ady Square, but their glowing faces, shining eyes, and excited voices are still with me. Gay, self-confident, in holiday mood they were streaming along the shores of the Tisza, from the Szechenyi Square, from the students' quarters around the Dom toward the university where a meeting was to take place with a single point on the agenda: "Dissolving our ties with DISZ, it is resolved that we proclaim the foundation of an organization to be called MEFESZ (Hungarian University and High School Student Federation) wholly independent of all previous ties and devoted to the political action of the Hungarian students."

It was an impatient crowd. They knew exactly what they wanted and how they intended to accomplish it. The great hall of the university was packed with smiling, cheerful, lighthearted twenty-year-olds. They were ready to cheer everyone, their rector, Baroti, as he took his elevated chair, the young student Andras Lejtenyi, who was to read the resolution, the sunny day, the blue sky, the autumn smell in the air, the whole big world which looked to them that afternoon like a wondrous miracle which they were ready to adore. It was as unlike a political meeting as anything ever staged anywhere. These young people were in love with life, themselves, their courage, their confidence, the future; they even showed good-natured tolerance toward the few dissenters among them.

No one was angry that afternoon in Szeged. Professors and students beamed alike when young Lejtenyi read: "Our aim is the freeing of spirit, of thought . . . the throwing off of the spiritual shackles with which Stalin and Rakosi have kept us in bondage. . . ."

It was a deeply moving sight. The spirit of youth clashing with the dark forces of totalitarianism, unmindful of danger, gaily challenging the powers, and demanding their right to be heard and to be masters of their souls.

Compared to the list of demands which was to be advanced a few days later in Budapest, the students of Szeged were modest and cautious in theirs. Dean of the Law School Joseph Perbiro, the chairman of the meeting, was full of praise for the restraint the students showed, and was confident that the anxiety with which Budapest authorities were following the meeting through a telephone hookup was groundless.

The faculty, to a man, endorsed the resolution of the meeting. Afterward we gathered in the faculty room, where Professor Fedor, an obviously devoted Communist, argued that the anti-Rakosi, anti-Stalin, antiregime flavor of some of the points was in keeping with the mood of the country and the line of the Communist party itself. "We do want a house cleaning, and the students were right to take the lead," he asserted.

Thus the avalanche began. Looking back over the years, I am still impressed with the naturalness of the events which followed Szeged. There was not a voice of dissent. In the streets, at party meetings and factory councils, among student bodies, state employees, organizations, professional clubs, and throughout all Hungary, to the very inner core of the Communist hierarchy, the feeling was unanimous. A basic change had to come, and it came. When the news flashes from Warsaw announced the peaceful change-over from the Stalinists to the Gomulkaites, all doubt disappeared from the minds of the Hungarians that the changes would not be carried through speedily, thoroughly, and efficiently.

What went wrong? Many things, as I shall recount. One thing must be said at the outset: No event in recent history has been so much lied about, distorted, and besmirched as the Hungarian Revolution. Greece in 1944 comes to mind as a comparison. But there the lies were all one-sided. The Hungarian Revolution was distorted on both sides of the East-West fence. The real tragedy lies in the fact that the essential beauty and greatness of that gallant uprising have been buried by ignorant partisan interpreters and observers, by cheap political trickery and wishful thinking; but, above all, they were buried by the concerted action of government agencies on both sides.

For had the spirit of that revolution been permitted to live, even after its defeat, it would have given an important clue to both Communists and Western democracies as to which way this world was tending. Perhaps to bury that clue was the real reason that almost instinctively and certainly instantaneously the propaganda machinery on both sides shifted into high gear to smother the basic issue of the Hungarian Revolution. If there has been one recent historic event in which the essential morality of man shone with greater clarity and brilliance, I have not seen it or read about it.

Lest some may read into the preceding paragraphs a personal complaint, let me state that I have none; editors with whom I have dealt have all given me the widest latitude and consideration. I do not know whether John Hunt of the North American Newspaper Alliance, Gardner Cowles and Daniel Mich of Look, or Philip Horton and Max Ascoli of The Reporter agreed with what I wrote for them, but I do know that they faithfully published my dispatches and articles. In one instance, an editor went so far as to print an article knowing that for diplomatic and political reasons I had changed the time and locality of an interview. Nor do I intend to blame editors of other publications or of the radio and television. The atmosphere within which we all worked was largely responsi-

ble for the distorted picture Western people received from Hungary
—that, and the unholy blindness which prevailed in our official and
semiofficial propaganda agencies, diplomatic and government circles.
We seemed to be accepting eagerly any and all lies and distortions
without a moment's hesitation or regard for their sources, so long
as they were anti-Communist. But the truth would have hurt the
basic structure of Communism far more. We were after sensational
stories, heroic "freedom fighters" who pledged to die fighting and
who never existed except on Western radios. We hailed 200,000
escapees as heroic resistance fighters, while at no time were there
more than 5,000 Hungarians actively engaged in fighting the Russians.

I have read nearly everything that was printed in the West since
Szeged, and except for Emil Lengyel's book I have found nowhere
a true picture of what happened and why, in Hungary during those
fateful days. Among others, I read a book by a "student leader" who
did not have a single fact straight and who, if he was actually in
Budapest, certainly did not read the newspapers which mushroomed
immediately after the revolution began. Neither have I found in the
United Nations report, Section II, which recounted the revolutionary
events, very much that corresponded with the events as four of my
assistants and I observed them. Some quickly written books published in Vienna and London had parts of the picture, and Melvin
Lasky's compilation had some noteworthy reports; but on the whole
they reflected the distorted view which was so eagerly accepted by
the West.

Throughout the months following the Hungarian Revolution I
tried to understand the phenomenon. I have known some Hungarian
refugees of unquestioned integrity and honesty before and during
the revolution, yet when I read their accounts it seemed to me they
missed the point altogether. Much later it dawned on me that what
had happened was that each had seen a fragment and interpreted it
according to his own involvement in the events. Partly that, and
partly because once in the West they quickly understood what was
"salable," and conformed. I shall return to this subject in greater
detail.

As for Western reporting, it was haphazard because not until the
fourth day, after some fatal mistakes and crude terrorism had already

launched the revolution on its downward track, had Western news-papermen arrived in numbers, and they in haste accepted anyone's story, filing them immediately as eyewitness accounts. The results were fantastic. On Sunday, October 28th, on the sixth day of the revolution, I made a quick trip to Vienna to file stories, and of course bought every newspaper I could find on the stands. I found among others a hair-raising, eyewitness account of the uprising by a distinguished British journalist who was not even in Budapest to witness the events he described so dramatically and with such gusto. In fact, after his belated arrival he was by far the laziest among us, never leaving his hotel unless to stroll over to the British Embassy.

During the first days of the revolution there were three Western newspapermen in Budapest: John MacCormac of the *New York Times*, Endre Marton, a native Hungarian who filed for AP and also for UP, substituting for his wife, Ilona Nyilas, the regular UP correspondent who was then in Vienna, and myself. Late Thursday evening, October 25th, Seymour Freidin of the *New York Post*, and his wife, together with Gordon Shepherd of the *London Daily Telegraph*, arrived and, thereafter, first in driblets and later in droves all sorts of press representatives flooded Budapest. In fact, during the checkout at the Hungarian Foreign Ministry on November 10th we found that more than half of the people for whom we were asking safe conduct out of the city were not representing anyone but their adventurous selves. Outside the Hungarian border there were a number of newspapermen and agency representatives who bought up anything anyone was willing to sell to them, greatly contributing to the chaos which grew to awesome proportions as the days wore on.

There were three important factors, all of them ignored by the West and certainly suppressed by the East, which would have given an accurate picture of the Hungarian situation and enabled Western governments to render whatever service they could have rendered to the Hungarians.

First in importance was the chronology of events. Had this been correctly understood, I still believe that the Hungarian Revolution could have been saved or that at least the West, particularly America, would not have contributed so heavily to its downfall.

Second in importance was the makeup of the demonstrators and fighters. As the revolution changed, so did the nature of the armies in the field change. There were five clearly delineated changes in the composition of the revolutionary masses.

Third were the "outside" influences, which at first slowly but later with increased tempo, tried, but never succeeded, in preempting the revolution.

There were three points at which the revolution could have been brought to a successful stop. The first was on October 23rd, shortly after midnight, during the session of the Politburo of the Communist party following the outbreak of hostilities at Radio House. The second time was Thursday morning, October 25th, when fighting had nearly come to a halt in all respects. The final opportunity was on Sunday, October 28th, when the Russians offered to evacuate Budapest after Imre Nagy's ultimatum was accepted by the Politburo and the Hungarian Workers' (Communist) party itself was dissolved.

Upon my return from Szeged, on Monday the 22nd, I drove the two university delegates who hitched rides with me to the Student Council at Serb ucca where everything was in ferment. Messengers were coming in and leaving for various schools; copies of resolutions were brought from student bodies and forwarded to others. Toward evening, when all the student bodies expressed themselves in favor of a demonstration of Polish-Hungarian solidarity on the following day, the Executive Committee of DISZ decided to call an emergency meeting for noon of Tuesday, the 23rd.

While there I met several writers and journalists whom I had known from my previous visits. One of them had participated at my weekend at the Balaton. From what I had heard from them and from the students it was clear that the Hungarians wanted and were confident of getting a "Polish deal," with Imre Nagy playing the part of Wladyslaw Gomulka. However, comparing the resolutions of the various schools and intellectual groups, it seemed to me that the Hungarians wanted to go further in cleaning their ranks. Prominent among the political demands were: the return of Matyas Rakosi from the Soviet Union for a trial on his abuse of power, together with his henchmen, among whom was, though unmentioned, Erno Gero, still first secretary of the party; the revision of trade treaties, including the Uranium Concessions between the Soviet Union and Hungary which were considered unfavorable to Hungary; something called "socialist equality" among Peoples' Democracies, which was a euphemism for Hungarian independence; a wider democratic base for the political structure of the country; and, lastly, the curbing of police power in Hungary.

The overconfident atmosphere at the Student Council left me with an unidentifiable unease. All logic, reason, justice, morality, and plain common sense were on their side. Even from a strictly Marxian point of view they seemed to be on solid ground. The signs were all favorable for their movement to succeed: Nagy had two weeks earlier been readmitted to the party; political denunciations were at a minimum and were not taken seriously any more; the State Security Authority itself was affected by the virus of reformism; and the fact that these meetings which a year ago would have been considered treasonous were tolerated at all pointed to the fact that the higher ups had seen the handwriting and were prepared to abide by it.

I tried to analyze my disquiet, and came upon its source. From what I had seen and heard there did not seem to be sufficient cohesion to hold the thing together. My fear was that it would fall apart unless Nagy took hold of it. But would he? I did not know enough about the man, and what I knew was not exactly reassuring. I understood Nagy to be a warmhearted, easygoing man with a wealth of knowledge, great and true sympathies for his people and their suffering—in short, a humanist who, if things went wrong, would be called upon to become an iron-fisted leader. Could he do it?

To find the answer I went to the clubhouse of the Writers' Federation and sought out a few acquaintances. Late into the night we discussed Nagy's qualifications. Finally I was convinced that my informants were certain that if Imre Nagy could not measure up to the task, there were enough good men around him to carry the program to a successful conclusion, with Imre Nagy supplying the moral prestige.

Curiously, there was more excitement at the club over the impending first performance of Gyula Hay's long-suppressed play *The Profession of Gaspar Varro*, which was scheduled for Thursday the 25th, than over the events which were about to unfold. The disappearance of the old Rakosi-Stalin clique from the helm of Hungary was a foregone conclusion. Gero and the rest were sure to be pitched out tomorrow or the next day. Had not the Russians agreed in Poland that the old days were over?

Hay, who was sitting at the table next to ours, joined the discussion, and when I told him that the Foreign Office was unable to get me tickets for the premiere, he handed over two of his own. Hay, a veteran revolutionary was perhaps less cocksure than any of the others. I had heard him speak on several occasions against the immoralities of the regime and demanding freedom and decency for his country, and I had read many of his articles. But on this night he was pensive and spoke little. What he did say was that precipitate action must be avoided at all cost lest the Stalinists find an excuse to crush the opposition. Compared to Hay, the frail old Tibor Dery, whom many regarded as the center of the revolt, was as excited and confident as a young student. Any reference to the possibility of the revolt getting out of hand met with flashing indignation from Dery. He considered it a personal insult to question the sincerity and integrity and, above all, the socialist patriotism of the movement.

This was the night before the tragic day, Tuesday, October 23, 1956. During the following night I spent a short time again at the club, but by then a new epoch was in full swing and all the certainties, as well as the doubts of the night before, were swept away by the dynamics of events.

9

Victorious Rebels

There is no important difference between the Eastern and Western versions of what happened on October 23rd until 8:00 P.M. The Polish-Hungarian solidarity demonstration by students was first permitted, later canceled, and then permitted again when it became clear that the students would march anyway. It began on schedule at 2:00 P.M. at the Petofi statue, from which the students in orderly fashion marched to Buda, to the statue of the Polish hero of the Hungarian revolt of 1848, General Jozsef Bem. Around 5:00 P.M. the demonstrators began to drift across the city, and all gravitated toward the Parliament Building to await Erno Gero's speech, announced for 8:00 P.M.

With Ildiko, my Hungarian secretary who was with me constantly until her death barely forty-eight hours later, I circled Kossuth Square outside the Parliament until Gero began to speak. We parked at the corner of the square at Alkotmany ucca and turned on the radio. Soon we were surrounded by a dozen Budapest policemen all wanting to hear Gero. When the first secretary of the Hungarian Workers' party began to speak, the nearest policeman said, with loathing, "He lies with every breath he takes." The other policemen took the remark as a matter of course.

Gero's incredibly stupid speech truly created the mood for outbursts of violence. It was not so much what he said, although his references to the demonstrators as "enemies of our people" and his remark that "there are people who try to create a conflict" went over badly; but the cold, inhuman, arrogant manner in which the man spoke to nearly two hundred thousand people in the throes of high emotional tension, dismissing the whole movement to bring decency, justice, and a measure of relief from poverty as a mere ideological aberration, visibly transformed the crowd. Until Gero spoke the massed humanity on the square was in holiday mood. Although purposeful and serious, boys and girls from universities, colleges, and high schools were laughing, and singing gaily between impromptu speeches and the reading of resolutions. There was no anger in them—only a stubborn determination to get what they wanted.

Gero's speech changed all that. Student leaders and intellectuals on the upper tier of the Parliament steps, sensing the changing mood of the crowd, became panicky. Announcements were broadcast through loudspeakers that Imre Nagy was on his way and would address the crowd. A few minutes later Nagy arrived, and though to this day it is not quite clear what frightened him, he obviously was deeply worried.

In a two-minute speech he said that he had no authority and could do nothing, but should the party entrust him with power to restore the June, 1953, program, he could be relied upon. "You know I keep my word, and I say to you that should I be called to serve, I will restore our program." Then he begged the crowd to disperse, saying that he would appear before the Politburo to plead their cause.

In itself the speech would have had the desired effect had not Gero preceded it with his disastrous challenge and had Nagy been surer of himself. Of course, the man had just escaped from the stigma of counterrevolution and the Politburo still had a clear Rakosi-Gero majority dead set against Nagy's policies. The man's nervousness was understandable. But the effect of his appearance before the crowd deepened the pessimism and sullenness of the young people, who a short while ago had been all aglow with hope and certainty.

Although the mood hardened and the anger of the crowd deepened, no one really expected the fury and violence which erupted during the next few hours. There can be no question of Gero's responsibility for the incendiary atmosphere, but to assign responsibility for the first bloodshed is, although implicit in the situation, still not easy.

Leaving the Parliament after the speech, Ildiko and I drove directly to Radio House on Brody Sandor ucca. We left the car two blocks away and walked through the Museum Garden to the studio building. The main gate was closed, and a large crowd of young boys and girls milled around in the narrow street. Suddenly a fire hose began to spray water from a hydrant on the corner. Boys immediately attacked the wielders of the hose and cut it into ribbons with their jackknives. The water was turned off.

I was told that a delegation of three students was inside, demanding that the resolution passed by the combined student councils be read on the air. As time passed, shouts were heard demanding the return of the delegation. Someone on the balcony of Radio House began to speak, but we could not hear him. Pots and pans were brought from a neighboring tavern and thrown by the students to reinforce their demand that the delegation be freed. From some upper windows tear gas bombs were dropped, and the stinging acid filled the air. A block away an AVH uniformed detachment arrived in a truck. With fixed bayonets they marched into the radio building.

Now the demonstrators brought coal, china, bricks, anything movable, and began to hurl them at the windows, chanting their demands.

Shots were heard from the upper windows of the radio building, accompanied by flashes of what were obviously blanks.

Up to this point no serious damage had been incurred on either side. From here on, all accounts I have read—the detailed description of the siege in the Hungarian Nepszabadsag, as well as Western accounts, differ considerably from what Ildiko and I actually saw.

The shots were blanks; the crowd was unarmed. Then a tear-gas bomb exploded in the face of an army captain who was part of the demonstrating crowd. His face was torn, and he died instantly. His body was lifted up, and people began to scream. Just then at the Boulevard, a long block away, an AVH truck was overturned by the students. The uniformed AVH men, eight of them, began to threaten the boys, who argued with them. I heard part of the argument. The boys said, "Comrades, you are not going to fight for Rakosi and Gero against us?" The AVH men, all young, replied: "Of course not," saying that they had come to restore order. Slowly the students convinced the AVH men, who peacefully handed over their rifles. A few of them joined the students, racing toward Radio House with the rifles.

By now a number of demonstrators were injured, some by flying debris, some by exploding gas-bomb fragments, and it was hard to tell what was going on because the firing from the Radio House windows was continuous. I saw a number of flashes which looked like blanks, but now there were real bullets fired also. Then the boys with their AVH weapons began to fire at the windows. And the battle was on.

Some time after nine o'clock I left the Radio House, where the situation had hardened into a siege, although there weren't enough guns in the hands of the demonstrators to do a great deal about their avowed intention of liberating the delegation. By the time I returned, a little after 11:00 P.M., the battle was about to take on a different complexion altogether.

Leaving the Radio House, we drove to the Stalin Memorial, where a great number of people were assembled to watch the toppling of the huge Stalin figure. Acetylene torches were cutting off the iron legs, and heavy ropes were tied to the figure. The crowd seemed in a holiday mood, and quite a few city policemen among them were enjoying themselves.

Following a truckload of students who were going to the ammunition depot at Soroksari ut, we noticed hundreds of people clustered on street corners and in front of tenements discussing events. There was a slight resistance at the plant; the students loaded into their truck a number of cases containing rifles and ammunition. Two boxes of Tommy guns were also among the loot.

Back at Radio House we found seven Hungarian tanks drawn up alongside the studio, with a colonel in charge. By then the sniping from the windows and from the students below was going on in dead seriousness. The colonel assured the students that he, too, was a worker and had no intention of bringing about a massacre. He proposed, and the students quickly agreed, that he would take over Radio House, evacuate the AVH, and restore order. He ordered a major to enter the radio building. The major marched up to the main entrance to the building and was promptly shot down by the AVH.

This was the turning point in the battle. The army, led by the colonel himself, joined the demonstrators. Weapons were distributed among the students, and with the reinforcement just then arriving from the ammunition depot there were several hundred weapons in the hands of the investing force. The tanks used their cannons against the doors and windows of the building, and the AVH began to shoot back with heavy-caliber machine guns.

I was on top of the iron fence which was embedded in a stone parapet alongside the radio building, trying to identify the shots crisscrossing the black night, when the battle began in earnest. Below me, people threw themselves behind the stone parapet because the shooting had become wild and indiscriminate. It was just midnight.

At this point it seems worth mentioning that the radio never did broadcast the students' demands, which would have stopped the fighting immediately. Members of the student delegation did escape during the night, and subsequently I checked with my assistant, who sat during the night in my car listening to the radio, and he confirmed their story. The radio was violently partisan and pro-Gero until it was silenced.

To preserve strict continuity of events I have omitted a number of pertinent observations and encounters which will be related in due course. Suffice to say that at midnight, when I left Radio House and drove around the city in a roundabout way to the Federation of Writers' Club, the situation, while bad, was far from hopeless.

What was needed was quick and decisive moves on the part of the authorities. I mention here three which would have ended the revolt by morning: permission to broadcast the student demands, an announcement of the appointment of Imre Nagy as prime minister, and the resignation of Erno Gero and a resolution of the Politburo to accept the demands of the students and intellectuals. The reason I believe that the situation could have been saved was that at midnight the student organizations still had control of the demonstrators, and their leaders would have been obeyed.

It was not only I who held this opinion. At the club where we had a hasty meal, since none of us had had anything to eat since morning, most of those who were out with the demonstrators held the same view. In fact, the writers just then had sent a delegation of three to the Central Committee's building in Academia ucca to plead with the Politburo to act quickly.

During the hour we spent at the club, the situation deteriorated on the streets. A few scattered truckloads of workers from the suburbs were coming in, and more small-arms fire was heard all over the city. Interestingly enough, there was no resistance anywhere to the demonstrators except at the Radio House and except for a very brief skirmish at the ammunition depot.

The shooting was more in celebration, aimed at Communist emblems, Russian signs and memorials and carved slogans on buildings, than at an enemy who had not materialized in any number. AVH was the enemy, but there were no AVH detachments anywhere—on the contrary, a number of AVH uniformed men were among the demonstrators. The city police joined the rebellion immediately. Army men in uniform were also among the demonstrators, and except for the tank detail at the Radio House, which was actively fighting, there were no army units on the streets. Close to 1:00 A.M., on my way to the telegraph office, held open by a kind lady for me even though she had orders to stop after midnight, we met a large army truck on the Kossuth Lajos ucca heavily laden with weapons and ammunition which were being distributed to all comers. All one had to do was to step up to receive a Tommy gun or a rifle with several hundred rounds of ammunition.

Some time after 1:00 A.M. the iron Stalin was dragged through Rakoczi ut toward the National Theater, where the offices and printing plant of *Szabad Nep*, the party organ, were also located. By then wild tales concerning the battle of Radio House had infuriated the mobs, and corpses of fallen demonstrators were being carried through the streets. The last two items the printing presses ran off before they were damaged by the mob were an extra edition condemning the AVH for its stand at the Radio House, and brief leaflet announcing that the Plant Committee of *Szabad Nep* had decided in an extraordinary meeting to stop publication of the paper until the just demands of the students and the intellectuals were granted.

It had become increasingly dangerous to drive in the city in an automobile. Least of the hazards was confiscation by the revolutionaries, but since only the Communist elite had automobiles in Budapest, a shiny foreign car became a natural target. Although I had a French license plate, my car had several close calls; therefore we drove into a courtyard across from the hotel and locked the gates. My secretary and I then set out to visit the headquarters of the Central Committee where, I was told, the Politburo was in session and momentous decisions were to be expected.

We walked through the dark streets paralleling the Danube and found the streets leading to the party building occupied by entrenched AVH troops with machine-gun nests behind hastily thrown-up barricades. We were challenged several times, and at the last corner I had a heated exchange with the major in command. Our voices rose and were heard by the man in charge, who turned out to be Colonel Varsanyi in civilian clothes, a man with whom I had had a run-in at the Foreign Office earlier. He took us in charge.

Just as we entered the building two young men came in excitedly describing the burning of the *Szabad Nep* office and bitterly demanding troops to save what could be saved. They were told that no troops could or would be sent. They were cut off with a gruff, "Comrades, you just have to wait."

On the second floor I met Imre Nagy. He was seated in a high-backed chair flanked by two AVH officers, and no one was permitted to speak to him. When he heard my demand to be permitted to talk to him, he looked up and shook his head. Janossi, his son-in-law, came up the stairs and we walked away to a corner.

He told me that Nagy was not under arrest but that he was not permitted to communicate with anyone and that he had thus far been twice closeted with the Politburo. Janossi also told me that Soviet troops were on their way and that Nagy was outraged at the idea of assuming power under such circumstances.

I asked another official whom I recognized whether it was true that Soviet troops were coming in. He said Yes, by morning everything would be over. That was why Nagy's conditions had not been accepted by the Politburo.

A well known Hungarian radio commentator was standing by with a recording outfit to relay whatever decision was to be made behind the high oak doors of the council room. He promised to call me at the hotel whenever the announcement was ready.

Ildiko and I left the Central Committee building a few minutes after 3:30 A.M. on Wednesday, October 24th. As we approached Molotov Square, which opened on the Danube, we heard the heavy rumbling of approaching tanks. On the quay there were tramway tracks, and on those tracks fast-moving Soviet tanks were racing toward the north. We stopped to count them, but the line seemed interminable. Sandwiched between tanks were a number of armored vehicles crammed with troops holding their guns ready. I knew that they were coming, but no one had indicated that they were already in Budapest. My encounter with them occurred in the center of the city, and the time was 3:45 A.M.

By the time we reached the hotel the heavy booming of Soviet cannon intermingled with sporadic rifle fire was heard from the city. The Hungarian Revolution had entered its second phase.

Much that went wrong with the Hungarian Revolution revolved around this point. Subsequently, after Nagy assumed the premiership, he was violently and incessantly attacked by foreign radios, principally by Radio Free Europe and the Voice of America, as having brought in the Russians. Inasmuch as nearly all radios in Budapest were tuned to Munich senders during the days to follow, the effect of this calumny was tremendous, and contributed most importantly to the inability of Nagy to control events and thus avert the major catastrophe of November 4th.

Executives of Radio Free Europe and the Voice of America defended themselves later by pleading ignorance. This simply cannot be true. Elementary arithmetic should have shown them, if they had cared to find out, that Nagy could not have brought in the Russians.

The generally accepted time of the Russian entry into Budapest was 4 A.M. The tanks came from Szekesfehervar, a town five hours away; thus, calculating the speed of the tread belts of the tanks, they had left at 11:00 P.M. the night before. But before they left they needed at least one hour, if not more, to load supplies and fuel. That brought the timetable down to 10:00 P.M. Obviously the Russian commander had to get his orders from Moscow, and in Moscow some consultation must have taken place before the order was issued to the Soviet commander in Hungary. Calculating an unheard-of speed, and taking into consideration, too, the time the Hungarians needed to make such an important decision, the request could not have left Budapest later than between 6:00 and 7:00 P.M., at a time when the Hungarians were in a gay mood, awaiting the surely expected change in their government.

On the face of it, the explanations as to why Hungary was flooded with false accusations against Imre Nagy by Western agencies do not stand up. Much more plausible was the assumption that the Hungarian *émigrés* of the Nyilas and Horthy regimes entrenched in Munich were deliberately trying to wreck the Hungarian Revolution and steer it into a Fascist counterrevolution.

As a matter of fact, I learned from Soviet officers that tanks were sent from Temesvar (Romania) as early as Sunday the 21st, at the time of the Szeged meeting. I have also spoken to Soviet tank troops who came from the Soviet Union and who left there four days before the revolution began in Hungary. But the crucial point during the following days was this: Did or did not Nagy send for the Russians? The West hurled a deafening Yes, and a very large part of the population believed it. It took a week for the Hungarian revolutionary authorities to make a dent in this wall of hate which the West erected around Nagy.

It was also true that on the following morning, at 8:15, the Hungarian Radio announced that the "Central Committee recommends that the Presidential Council of the People's Republic elect Comrade Imre Nagy as Chairman of the Council of Ministers." Western receivers heard this first mention of Nagy just as well as the Hungarians, and by then Budapest was flooded with Soviet troops and tanks. At this time Nagy still was not the prime minister of Hungary. In fact, at noon he was "persuaded" to record in advance a broadcast asking for a cease-fire which was put on the air nearly ten hours before Nagy accepted the premiership. At 6:00 P.M. on Wednesday, October 24th, I spoke to Nagy, and he exclaimed in despair, "How can I assume responsibility for this without authority?" What he meant was that the Politburo was still heavily stacked against him and that what his comrades wanted was a figurehead. Not until a little after 9:00 P.M. on the same day, when the reports of the fighting had grown to ominous proportions, was Nagy given conditional power to deal with the situation. As Nagy said later, he could no longer hold out and watch the city being destroyed in a senseless massacre.

Those who called in the Soviet troops must have been astonished by the reaction of the Hungarians. The Russians were equally nonplused, if not more so, by the resistance and hostility they met everywhere. Wednesday, the 24th of October, showed this so clearly that the Russians were in constant touch with Moscow about the matter, and it resulted in Mikoyan and Suslov leaving Moscow immediately for Budapest. The effect of Wednesday's fighting on the Russian soldiers was deeply etched. Whenever they had an opportunity, they explained that they had come to deal with the "Nemetzki fastzisti," the German Fascists who, they were told, were trying to take Budapest away from the Hungarian workers.

During the morning hours of the 24th I went to the American Legation and after a brief discussion of the situation was given a flag to protect my car. Thus, with the Stars and Stripes flying from my radio antenna, I toured the city most of the day.

There was fighting everywhere. Rather, there was gun play everywhere, and there was large-scale damage. But as to fighting, it was of a curious, haphazard kind. Soviet tanks and armored cars raced up and down the streets seeking the revolutionary army. But there was no army. There were almost everywhere a few armed people grouped together sniping at the Russians. These small, independent bands roamed the streets and fought impromptu engagements with the Soviet troops. A few hard points developed. One was the Kilian Armory and the other the Corvin Arcade. When I first stopped at the Kilian barracks I learned that two battalions of labor troops made up of politically unreliable Hungarians had been given arms from the magazines and were holding the huge square building. Five months later I learned from my housekeeper in Vienna, who had been trapped in the cellar of the barracks during the entire period of the revolution, what really went on in there. Maria was working at the barracks as an employee of the Ministry of Buildings. On Wednesday morning she had gone to work as usual. She did not get out until the Russians left Budapest on the 30th of October.

Pal Maleter's presence at the Kilian barracks is still an unexplained mystery; however, in the light of subsequent events, it became clear that among the few who had plans for the revolution Maleter was one and that his taking command of the two battalions was not a coincidence.

My contacts during the day among the intellectuals and student leaders revealed to me the real damage the entry of the Soviet Army caused in Hungary. Communist and non-Communist alike were all for a fight to the bitter end against the "Russkies." In this atmosphere the Hungarian Revolution became a bitter civil war with incalculable consequences.

Thus the day passed in turmoil, fighting, and uncertainty spiced by wild rumors coming over Western radios. The whole movement fell into small fragments, with each operating on its own. This was the very last minute when disaster could have been avoided. Curiously, the Soviet command was alert enough to see and to understand that fact. At nightfall on Wednesday the Soviet troops received strict orders not to shoot unless attacked first. At about the same hour Mikoyan and Suslov boarded their plane with orders to remove Erno Gero from the helm of the Hungarian Communists and appoint an acceptable first secretary. The Soviet anger at Gero equaled the Hungarians', to whom Gero had always been a conspicuously loathsome object. It did not take long for the Soviet commanders to realize that Gero had dragged them into a quagmire from which the Soviets could not extricate themselves easily.

The night passed in comparative quiet. An occasional sporadic shot was heard, but Soviet troops were not sent out on patrol. Thus dawned Thursday, October 25th. During the morning hours the complexion of the revolution changed once more, and by noon the third and bloodiest phase had begun.

I had had a rough night. I had left Ildiko, my secretary, with strict orders not to leave the room and to listen to the radio, make notes, and watch the three visible bridges from the window. When I returned late in the evening I found her nerve shaken, and when I spoke to her she broke down completely. I gathered between her hysterical outbursts that heavy fighting had occurred in the street where lived her widowed mother from whom she had been cut off by the entrance of the Soviet troops the previous night. She sobbed for hours, and only toward morning fell asleep in my arms. I was to hold her bullet-ridden corpse barely twelve hours later.

A few hours of sleep restored Ildiko's resilient youth, and I went down to make a quick trip through the heart of the city. On my return the manager of the hotel, a sober and reliable man, came to me and said that the manager of the Astoria Hotel had called a few minutes earlier to say that Soviet troops had joined the revolution. He wanted to know whether this was true. "No, of course not," I replied. "What a crazy idea!" A few minutes later he came back, saying that he had called his colleague at the Astoria and that it was true: the Russians had joined the revolution.

During my quick trip I had seen great numbers of people on the street. It was a sunny, joyous morning, and some Soviet troops on street corners were amiably talking to Hungarians. It appeared that the people's passion had spent itself during the previous day's bitter fighting and that there was a good chance the revolution could be brought to a successful end, provided Nagy could persuade the Russians to leave. Perhaps widespread reforms would be announced immediately. Everything I had seen that morning confirmed this feeling of an approaching end. But, even so, the manager's report sounded incredible, and I would have dismissed it completely were it not for his reliability as a source of information. I decided to drive over to the Astoria to see for myself. By going, I became an eyewitness to the greatest tragedy to befall the Hungarian Revolution.

At the corner of Kossuth Lajos ucca and the Boulevard, where the Astoria was located, I met hundreds of laughing, gay Hungarians who kept repeating, "The Russians are with us!" There were three

Soviet tanks parked there, decorated with flowers and Hungarian flags. Girls were kissing Soviet soldiers, and men were shaking their hands. It was the most joyous fraternization between a populace and foreign troops I had ever seen, including the reception received by American liberating troops in Paris.

I wormed my way close to the lead tank and listened while a Soviet lieutenant explained that they had made a mistake: he said that their mission was not to shoot Hungarians but German Fascists and that they would never shoot again. Gaily he began to distribute bullets from the ammunition belts of the heavy machine guns to show that he meant what he said.

The jubilation was so great and so contagious that it soon seemed that an alliance had been formed between Soviet soldiers and the Hungarian people against the AVH and anyone else who would thwart the revolution. No wonder the manager of the Astoria was taken in, as he watched what was happening. But what he did not know was that basically nothing had changed; the Soviet soldiers merely had followed and gaily improved on the previous night's order not to shoot unless attacked. They repeated this over and over again—within my hearing—but the Hungarians understood it as they wanted to understand it: the Russians would not shoot if the Hungarians went about cleaning their own house. Which was, after all, true.

Sometime after 10:00 A.M. the Soviet crews of the tanks were persuaded to lead a triumphant "friendship" demonstration to the Kossuth Square, outside the Parliament. Hungarians waving flags and flowers seated themselves on the tanks, and the procession began. Thousands of people poured from their houses beside the long route through Bajcsi Zsilinszky ucca, happily joining the parade. I drove quickly ahead of the column, stopped at the American Legation where I left a message of the developments, and circled back toward the slowly advancing column. By the time the flower- and flag-bedecked tanks turned into the broad street leading to the square, I estimated the crowd at around ten thousand.

It was close to 11:00 A.M., just about the time when Mikoyan and Suslov alighted from their plane at Ferihegy Airport.

The roofs and upper windows of the ministry buildings around the square were dotted with machine-gun nests occupied by the

AVH. To the left of the square, in the direction of the narrow streets leading to the courthouse on Marko ucca, was the tank station of the Soviet armed forces. Two unmanned tanks were on the square.

The three tanks leading the parade entered the square surrounded by thousands of flag-waving Hungarians. The AVH on the rooftops had no way of knowing what was going on, or, if they knew, they did not care. What they saw was three tanks and thousands of revolutionaries pouring into the square. Possibly they assumed that the tanks had been captured by the revolutionaries; possibly they simply panicked. No sooner had the procession entered the square than from several rooftops the AVH began to fire.

The Soviet crews in the tanks stopped their vehicles in amazement which quickly turned into anger. They were being shot at! They, too, panicked. Their orders were to shoot back. They began to revolve their tanks on their pivots to throw off the people precariously perched on them. Then they began to shoot back at the rooftops occupied by the AVH.

Having emptied their machine guns, the Russians used their cannons indiscriminately. It was not quite clear to them what was happening; they simply knew that they were being attacked. So the slaughter began which was to turn the nearly victorious revolution into a carnage.

Since that Thursday morning I have read many versions of what happened there, and while I have found fragments which fitted into the whole story, nowhere have I read a full record of that massacre. John MacCormac's account, in the *New York Times* of October 27th, 1956, came closest.

Within a few minutes the square was littered with dead and dying men, women, and children. Among them were the subchancellor of the University of Budapest and the young man whose athletic picture adorned the twenty-forint bank note of the Hungarian Treasury.

Just as the exaggerated story of the Russians joining the revolution had swept across the city a few hours earlier, so now a more sinister story began to spread. "They have betrayed us!" "They led us into a slaughterhouse!" "The Russians made us believe they were with us and led ten thousand people into a massacre!" Like a black whirlwind descending out of the sunny skies that morning, an incredible revulsion and a feverish desire for revenge enveloped everyone. People poured out of their homes, and marchers formed columns in every part of the city. Black flags were broken out in thousands. Black flags and the Hungarian tricolor were everywhere. Solemn, angry-faced men began to march. Weapons appeared. "The murderers must be exterminated!" These were no more laughing revolutionaries; these were people going to war.

Thus the revolution became a blind, merciless war between half-armed people and the Soviet Army. The AVH was temporarily forgotten. This was a war between Hungarians and Russians.

It mattered little that at 2:00 P.M. Erno Gero was removed as first secretary of the Communist party and Janos Kadar was named in his place. Who cared about that? There was a war on. In that war I lost Ildiko—but of her death later.

On Friday, the 26th, the fourth day of the revolution, a new government took over. It included the reconstituted parties of the Social Democrats and the Small Holders. The beloved Bela Kovacs was named minister of agriculture, although, as he later told me, he was included in the ministerial list without his knowledge or consent. He was sick in bed in Pecs. However, he understood the necessity for using his name, as things were getting rapidly out of hand in Budapest.

Friday and Saturday saw the heaviest fighting of the revolution. Several strong points of resistance were established by the Hungarians, and the Russians paid dearly for every victory they achieved. For just as soon as they wiped out one pocket, another sprang up in its stead.

On Saturday, Imre Nagy realized how hopeless his position was. The canard of his having brought the Russians in would not be downed. The Politburo was heavily stacked against him, although Gero was gone. Foreign radios kept pumping cheering messages into Hungary, promising "All-out aid" and dramatically repeating Ambassador Lodge's statement before the United Nations—"We shall not fail them!" There was nothing for Nagy to do but to keep ahead of the revolution and thus try to halt it or to resign. He found himself in a position with which fire-fighters are familiar: he had to start a wall of fire ahead of the flames to save the forest. The

Thursday massacre and the Hungarian reaction to it made it impossible for him to continue without immediate Russian withdrawal. But, above all, he needed authority. The price of peace had gone so high that he knew there was no chance of a compromise. Hadn't the Western radios promised everything to the Hungarians if they would only hold out?

Thus his four-point ultimatum to the Politburo was born. I heard about it on Saturday, October 27th, at noon, and Nagy announced that he would resign on the following day, Sunday, unless he received all he asked for.

The four demands were: that the Hungarian Workers' party, with its Central Committee and Politburo, give up its authority and transfer all its powers to a five-man committee; that the revolution be regarded as a patriotic uprising, with amnesty to be proclaimed for all; that Soviet forces must be withdrawn immediately from Budapest and negotiations opened under the Warsaw Pact for their withdrawal from Hungary; and, fourth and last, that there be freedom for the political parties, press, and assembly to operate unhindered and that Nagy be empowered to negotiate for a national government with leaders of the newly restored parties.

While these events were taking place, the battle for Budapest convinced the Russian high command that something drastic needed to be done. The Soviet leadership savagely resented Gero's blunder in having brought them, through a series of false alarms and precipitated events, into a situation from which the Soviets could not possibly withdraw beaten. But, strictly from a military standpoint, that defeat which the high command could not countenance was lurking just around the corner. The Russian troops were exhausted and their equipment badly mangled. They had been using second-rate material up to this time, and the treads of their tanks were breaking down. More than fifty tanks had been destroyed or damaged. Thus, when Nagy presented his ultimatum on Saturday, the Soviet representative quickly agreed to meet his demands.

On Sunday, October 28th, the sixth day of the revolt, I was preparing to make a quick dash to Vienna to carry out the dispatches of several of my colleagues and the first batch of photographs taken during the fighting.

At ten o'clock an informant called me to say that all was well and that Nagy's ultimatum had been accepted by the Soviets as well as by the Hungarian Communists. This, in essence, meant that the Hungarian Revolution was over, won by the incredibly gallant Hungarians. Heavy fighting was raging in all parts of the city when I began my journey, but I expected that as soon as the developments were published fighting would subside and the revolution would enter its fourth phase. It had indeed changed complexion by the time I returned one and a half days later from Vienna, but, unfortunately, not in the way that had seemed so certain at the time of my departure.

Shortly after ten, two cars left the center of the city. The first car was mine, flying the Stars and Stripes, and behind me came another Anglo-American flag-bedecked car, driven by John Mac-Cormac of the *New York Times*. With him were Seymour Freidin of the *New York Post* and Endre Marton of A.P. and U.P. The idea of the escort through warring Budapest to the first Soviet block outside of the city came from MacCormac, who wanted to make sure that nothing would happen to me inside the city. The others joined him loyally.

We skirted battle areas to reach the Vienna road across the hills of Buda. At Szena Ter a furious battle was raging. Soviet tanks were relentlessly attacking Hungarians entrenched behind over-turned railroad cars used as barricades. As we turned into a side street immediately adjacent to Szena Ter, we passed a church where Sunday mass was being held before a huge throng.

We drove through the narrow, winding streets of the villa district, where Russian tanks were guarding the homes of Soviet officials and military commanders. Through the back streets of Buda we reached the main Budapest-Vienna highway, and the first Soviet road block was ahead of us. This was the first attempt to break through since the fighting had become general on Thursday, and we did not know what to expect. I was allowed to pass without objection, however. Shortly below Budapest I picked up a colonel of the Hungarian Army who wanted to join his unit below Gyor. He had been a delegate to a meeting in Budapest where the problems of the revolution were discussed. The colonel had a clear perspective on the revolution, and well understood the implications of the events. He gave me such a lucid analysis of the situation that he stands out in my memory among all the political, intellectual, and military leaders I had talked to as the soberest of them all. This middle-aged professional soldier knew all the alternatives his country faced and was prepared to play his role whatever came. He also confirmed my disquiet about Maleter's equivocal position.

The Hungarian road blocks respected the flag I was flying, and waved me on. The Russians often were uncertain as to the best way to deal with this apparently imperious American. I had learned long before meeting them how to handle unsure subordinates, and I managed to clear eight road blocks between Budapest and the Austrian border.

The last Hungarian town before the border was Mosonmagyarovar, where two days before my arrival, on Friday, October 26th, the only true massacre of the Hungarian Revolution occurred. It was a horrible demonstration of what the Stalinist type of Communism stood for, and by contrast enhanced the gallantry, bravery, and devotion of the revolutionists. Into a group of singing, marching, and totally unarmed townspeople the AVH opened machine-gun fire and within four minutes killed 87 men, women, and children and wounded more than 160 others. There had been no attack on the AVH detachment stationed there, no battle, no order to disperse—not even a warning.

Townspeople, their faces contorted with pain, were huddled on street corners waiting for the funeral procession to begin when I drove through Mosonmagyarovar. A soberer reminder of what the Hungarian Revolution was about could hardly be imagined for the traveler leaving Hungary. Exactly one week later, the tragedy of Mosonmagyarovar, the transformation of joyous, happy people into grief-stricken solemn fighters, was to be repeated throughout Hungary.

I drove swiftly on. By two-thirty that afternoon I was at Radio Austria filing American and British dispatches by the yard. The lone Austrian receiving clerk enlisted my help to clear the material through, and this was the first time I had an opportunity to read the observations and interpretations of some of my American and British colleagues.

I quickly added a note to my own editors saying that the Hungarian Revolution had been won and that if nothing went wrong the far-reaching concessions to be wrung from the Communists of Hungary would assure the restoration of democratic processes in that country.

10

The Revolution Transformed

Even though I was wrong, the revolution did come to a successful end that Sunday morning when my informant told me that Nagy's ultimatum had been accepted. To understand how it was destroyed it is necessary at this point to examine two other factors: the make-up of the demonstrators and fighters, as well as their political aims, and the "outside" influences.

The first army which took the field against the regime was made up exclusively of those whom the regime favored most: writers, journalists, engineers, athletes, students, and artists. Ninety per cent of the thousands who marched on the first afternoon and evening and stayed to fight at Radio House were paid to go to school and were hand picked from families of workers, peasants, and Communist party officials. Their demands were "moral" demands: the restoration of justice, decency, and humaneness in

Hungary. They wanted to put an end to arbitrary oppression and they wanted to see the guilty punished.

During the first night—at least until after midnight—the groups on the streets were easily identifiable and were in touch with their leaders who controlled them. After the blood bath at Radio House lines tended to become confused. But even so, the streets were ruled by the students.

Late in the evening younger people, nonstudents, many of them members of the huge delinquent population of Budapest, joined in. When they were too boisterous or stepped too much out of line, they were swiftly dealt with. Three brief incidents illustrate this.

After 11:00 P.M., across from the Museum Garden, some hoodlums were breaking open cases of hard liquor and passing the bottles around. A group of students came up, confiscated the loot, broke the bottles, and chased the hoodlums away. The Boulevard was alive with small groups of people discussing events. Ildiko and I joined many of these to listen to their grievances. In one group a loudmouth began to orate, shouting: "The Jews were responsible for all this! Rakosi, Gero, Farkas—all Jews—brought the Russians, and whom have they murdered? Rajk, Pallfy, Szalai—non-Jews!" Before he finished his last sentence a young man next to him hit the speaker with such force that he fell on his face. The reaction of the crowd was interesting. All cursed the fallen man for his words and his crude effort to incite anti-Semitism, which had always been virulent and politically useful in Hungary. At the time when I was stuck at the top of the iron fence surrounding the radio building, while below me the AVH sprayed the ground with machine guns, a young man jumped up and pulled me down behind the stone parapet. Two days later I identified him as a young actor from the National Theater. These were the kind of people abroad at the very beginning of the revolution.

There was greater variety among the people at the Stalin monument. Groups from sections beyond the park, workers and their families, streamed in to watch the fun. When the students were unable to pull the statue down, three workers appeared with acetylene torches to cut down the figure. But there, too, the dominant group was made up of students who came from the earlier demonstration before the Parliament.

123

Almost all accounts in the West tried to say that workers joined the revolution immediately. This was not true. Intellectuals and students rode all night into factory districts to rally the workers, because there was a real fear that the revolution would peter out for lack of mass support and that the students would be left alone.

Small groups of workers in trucks came in during the later part of the evening, but there was no large-scale movement among them to support the revolt until after the arrival of the Russians.

Thus, the second army was born next day. It consisted largely of students, many of them now armed, and several truckloads of younger workers who came in response to the call to arms during the night. These groups grew, as Wednesday wore on, to include many who simply attached themselves to bands and procured arms either from army arsenals or from city police. There were no commanders of this second army, which by late afternoon of the second day outnumbered the students. He who spoke loudest and made most sense was obeyed. Strategy was developed on the spot. Thus many strong points were established by the necessity of dodging oncoming Soviet tanks and armored cars.

The third army, which was the largest and which sprang up after the Thursday massacre before the Parliament, cut across all lines and included all Hungarians, high and low, educated and illiterate. Anger transformed the city into a heaving, tumultuous mass of humanity, and this was the army which really won the Hungarian Revolution. The incredible bravery of unarmed people walking toward blazing guns with measured steps was a sight hard to credit even for the eyes that saw it. And this was the army which nailed down a plank in the platform of the revolution that caused so much trouble after all other demands were granted. That plank was the immediate withdrawal of the Soviet forces from all Hungary, a demand which could not have been granted without an agreement of the Warsaw Pact nations, lest it look as though the Red Army had been thrown out by a small, insignificant country. Out of Budapest, yes, *that* was accepted and fulfilled; and an agreement to arrange for the withdrawal from all of Hungary was also granted by Moscow. But for Russian troops to get out, and get out immediately, was out of the question.

On Tuesday morning, October 30th, I came back from Vienna,

and it did not take long to discover that the fourth phase of the revolution had produced a fourth army. The students and the workers, the organized forces which had fought the revolution to its successful conclusion, had retired. In their place nondescript groups of Tommy-gun-wielding "heroes" appeared. They were "hunting" AVH personnel. I came under their fire as I drove across Buda to deliver some food I had brought from Vienna. I met them in the lobby of my hotel frisking guests in search of AVH men. Bands of them roamed the streets. There were both men and women, some equipped with newly devised identification cards attesting their membership in something called "National Guards." For two days I watched their activities, including the execution of some AVH personnel, and vainly tried to reach their headquarters or someone who would acknowledge their command. They were, as they said, "Maleter's men." Maleter had by then become the undersecretary of defense and advanced to the rank of general, and soon was to become the secretary of defense and commander of all armed forces of Hungary.

Not until several days had elapsed did I realize that those roving bands were left alone for some purpose which was not quite apparent. Certainly the government was in a strong position by then. Nagy went further than he had originally proposed; he promised free elections in January even though, as he admitted to me, he never expected the combined Left to draw more than 30 per cent of the votes and the reconstituted Communist party more than 5 per cent. Free press was flourishing; the Russians had withdrawn from Budapest; and the official Kremlin announcement said that the Soviet Union was willing to start negotiations to rewrite the Warsaw Pact and allow the withdrawal of Soviet forces from Hungary altogether. Commercial treaties and concessions between Hungary and the Soviet Union were also to be renegotiated. Cardinal Mindszenty appeared in Budapest, and Imre Nagy himself went on the radio to say that the Council of Ministers had annulled the trial of the cardinal and that he was a free man.

Yet no government forces appeared to check the roving bands. A painstaking inquiry by myself and my assistants brought forth this analysis of the armed civilians: less than half of them were intransigent nationalists, Hungarian patriots of the Horthy-Nyilas era—the rest were dubious characters recruited mostly from the dregs of Budapest. Characteristically, the famous picture which appeared in Western magazines showing the execution of surrendering AVH men enabled authorities to identify a number of the prominent "freedom fighters" as known criminals and ex-convicts. The more respectable members of these bands were aware of the type of people their movement attracted, however, and did try to isolate the more conspicuous fakes.

This fourth army was used as an alibi by the Russians for their return to Budapest to crush the revolt. The fact of the matter was that this fourth army was never a real menace and could have been dealt with easily by the Hungarian authorities, even though Maleter began to use it for his own purposes. Stopping them was no problem, and that Nagy and Losonczi, with whom I discussed this problem on Thursday morning, November 1st, did not take energetic steps against them (except to instruct Maleter, whom they trusted, to deal with the problem) was entirely due to the fact that Nagy and his ministers believed that the activities of these bands had been exaggerated out of proportion. There were a few railroad robberies; some relief trucks from the West were emptied; some thirty to forty AVH men had been killed in Budapest. In view of what the AVH had meant to the Hungarians throughout eight horrible years, it was a marvel of restraint with which the revolutionaries met the new day. The danger in the situation was that this nondescript army was conspicuous and noisy and that it took it upon itself to carry out some measures which the government should have undertaken under the due process of the law. But for political reasons they were tolerated and encouraged by nefarious interests which I propose to describe presently.

The fifth and final phase of the revolution began at dawn on November 4th, when the return of the Soviet forces to Budapest again produced a truly national army such as sprang up after the Bloody Thursday of the revolution. Communist and non-Communist, Hungarians all, threw themselves into the fight against hopeless odds and with unbelievable courage. This was the army which was finally beaten and which withered away under weeks of relentless police pressure.

I still do not understand how Janos Kadar could have underestimated so dismally the reaction of the Hungarians to the reentry of the Soviet forces and how he could have hoped to "marry" the Nagy revolution with Soviet shotguns. But that was what he hoped for and that was what he tried to do.

Some of the phases delineated here are simplifications, and I do not mean to suggest that the lines were as sharp as I have drawn them. Forces and political demands often overlapped, but the essential steps as I have described them were clearly discernible.

Budapest was Hungary during the revolt—not merely because significant events occurred there, but because nothing of great importance happened elsewhere. Actions at Miskolc, Pecs, Szeged, Debrecen, Gyor, and in smaller towns were faint echoes of events in Budapest. Here and there brief skirmishes occurred, revolutionary councils were formed, and one or two conspicuously barbaric AVH were hunted down and killed. The country, by and large, remained passive although tense. In industrial or mining centers, such as Tatabanya and Stalinvaros, a revolutionary atmosphere was developing, but it lagged behind Budapest. The reason for this was the curious behavior of the peasantry.

The peasants of Hungary had been full of woes and bitterness and were amoral. They were beaten people, and remained so throughout the revolution. There were no peasant armies marching against the foe; there were no peasant-led guerrillas in action against Soviet troops; no peasant leaders appeared throughout the harrowing days to help plan a new Hungary, except the old leadership of the Small Holders' party. During the height of the revolution trucks laden with fruits and vegetables from nearby agricultural centers appeared in Budapest, and often the drivers from cooperatives and state farms distributed the produce on street corners free. There were no markets in Budapest during those days, and the produce would have spoiled anyway, but the psychological lift of these free distributions of fruits and vegetables was tremendous. It reminded the fighting people of Budapest of the country's solidarity.

Lest the preceding be taken as peasant loyalty to Communism, let me make clear that it was not. But the peasants had many problems and, naturally distrustful and conservative, they feared any sudden change. For one thing, the reestablishment of prewar estates would have reduced the majority of the peasants to landlessness.

For another, whatever movements developed in villages and estates were organized by former gendarmery officers, village notaries, landlords—in short, by the former village elite. This made the peasantry even more distrustful. In vain Imre Nagy and his associates tried to assure them that the former exploitation of the peasantry would not be permitted. What rumor there was among them came from foreign radios discrediting Nagy and from the evidence of their eyes, watching their former masters establishing themselves in revolutionary councils. The confusion in Budapest reacted on the peasantry by making them even more mistrustful and conservative. Had a large-scale revolutionary peasant movement developed during the first days, Soviet commanders, always respectful toward the art of guerrilla warfare, would not have been so sure that the revolution could be suppressed. The resistance which met them disconcerted them enough, but with the help of the peasants the Soviets would have faced a larger decision: all-out war or a quick settlement, largely on Hungarian terms.

Much has been made of foreign interference in the Hungarian revolt. Understandably, the Communists wanted to paint a picture of peaceful demonstrations turned into a counterrevolution by foreign agents. This was as silly as it was harmful to the Communists. For no one knew better than the Hungarians themselves why they rose against the regime and who participated. But why the West encouraged this view remains a mystery. Whether because cloak-and-dagger outfits wanted to justify their existence, or because émigré Fascists living on Western bounty tried to take credit and assure themselves of continued fat living, or because Americans accustomed to black-or-white views could not imagine anything else, the fact remains that the West contributed a great deal to the collapse of the Hungarian Revolution by making it appear as a reactionary movement.

To understand this we must now examine so-called "foreign influences" which appeared during the fighting days and during the victorious days.

For want of a better word I shall use "Fascist" loosely to include all of the following: White terrorists of the Horthy regime; the supporters of the regime which between the First and Second World Wars used concentration camps; special assassin outfits led by

Father Bangha, Hejas, Pronay, and many others called the Awakening Magyars; the intransigent Nem-Nem-Soha patriots who constantly plotted the reconquest of lost territories; the clergy, which by a large majority sided with the Horthy regime (although I have known priests, ministers, and rabbis who were shaken to the depths of their souls by the outrages committed by Horthyists); reactionary bankers and industrialists; the landlords and former gentry and aristocracy of Hungary, who were still thinking in terms of the eighteenth century and who hoped to reverse the clock; and, finally, the followers of Szallasi, leader of the Nyilas (Crossbow) party who were out and out Nazis—the anti-Semitic Hungarians who since time immemorial used their hatred of Jews for political purposes and relentlessly oppressed the Jews.

Hungarians of these groups always had a respectable lobby in Western countries, particularly in America, and were financed after the Second World War largely by American funds. They had agents and sympathizers in Hungary, but the centers of their activities were New York, Washington, and Munich. They infiltrated the Voice of America, Radio Free Europe, and the Central Intelligence Agency, and were used as screening agents after the war. Nearly all American propaganda agencies were shot through with these worthless and harmful people, and one needed merely to listen to "American" broadcasts and propaganda media to recognize the guiding spirit of their efforts. Bela Kovacs, the courageous peasant leader of Hungary who had endured eight years of unspeakable horrors in Soviet prisons, said to me sadly during the night we were hiding together in a cellar after the return of the Russians to Budapest: "No one in Hungary cares for those who fled to the West after their own corrupt terror regime was finished—and then got their financing from the West. . . . I wish you could convince the West and make them keep their reactionaries out of our hair. Many of the exiles America is backing are men who are marked because of their war crimes. Some of the voices that come to us over Radio Free Europe in particular are not welcome here. As long as the West continues to maintain ties with Hungarian feudalists and Fascists, we are handicapped in our effort to seek ties with you."

Thus, when I say Fascist, I shall mean all predatory elements of Hungary, regardless of their motivation.

129

Fascism appeared on the streets of Budapest a few hours after the fighting began. First were demagogues who swiftly received their comeuppance from the demonstrators and fighters. Their number increased during the days which followed the fighting at Radio House, and they expressed themselves largely by using anti-Semitic slogans against the regime. The Rakosi-Gero clique did contain a majority of Jews, and it was fairly easy to equate the "Rakosi bunch" with the "Jewish bunch." Furthermore, it seemed that no sooner would a group form on a street corner or in a hall than one or two Fascist agitators would try to infuse the group with distrust toward the revolutionary leaders and their motives. These agitators, isolated at first, became more conspicuous as the fighting increased, but their greatest help came from the West. At first the radios in Germany beaming their wave lengths toward Hungary did their level best to discredit Imre Nagy, and at the same time encouraged Hungarians to keep on demanding and fighting because the West was behind them, even when further demands and fighting were manifestly destructive.

During the night of Thursday, October 25th, the Russians clamped down a rigorous curfew between 6:00 P.M. and 6:00 A.M. That night I set out to find the high command of an organization which called itself "National Committee," whose agents I had encountered and whose activities smacked of Fascism. Until dawn, when I found myself cornered between two Soviet patrols and had to take refuge in a house, I visited four addresses given to me by various people. The best I could find was a shadowy group of people who spoke from one corner of their mouths of "liberating Hungary from the Soviet yoke," which was by then a national slogan enthusiastically approved by all, while from the other corner of their mouths came demands for a "Christian Hungary." Several days later I removed from a wall one of their first placards, which is now before me. It says, "God, Nation, Family!" and in small letters at the bottom, "United Christian Parties."

Western readers unfamiliar with Central European politics may not know that parties and movements of this kind have always been extremely reactionary, and in fact forerunners of Fascism. But to alert Hungarians they foreshadowed an anti-democratic, illiberal Hungary of the Horthy type.

By coincidence, the family I took refuge with that night was a Jewish family, feverishly preparing to flee Hungary. I listened to them in great astonishment, since I could not understand how in such a short time, and with so few indications, the Jews of Budapest could have panicked. Then I received a quick lesson in recent Hungarian history.

After the Second World War nearly all former Hungarian office-holders were compromised by their Fascist-Nazi ties. There was a great shortage of managers, engineers, doctors, government officials —people who could read and write and keep records—and the few returning or surviving Jews were enlisted almost to a man. The anti-Fascist regimes under Russian-occupied Hungary found the Jews obviously reliable, since they had suffered most from the Nazis and were eager to help rebuild the country. Furthermore, a good many young Jewish boys and girls, to escape the gas chambers of Buchenwald, had taken to the country and become guerrilla fighters against the Germans, greatly assisting the advancing Soviet forces. These youngsters grew up as disciplined members of the guerrilla forces, which came under Communist domination and were an important segment of the Communist party. Hence the vulnerability of the Jews in the present struggle. It mattered little that nearly 80 per cent of the intellectual leaders, writers, and artists who inspired the revolution, among them prominently Gyula Hay, Tibor Dery, Tamas Aczel, Tibor Tardos, Laszlo Benjamin, Pal Ignotus, and many others were Jews. The Jews of Budapest knew beyond reason or logic that if the revolution were to get out of hand, and if the reactionary elements were to prevail, widespread pogroms would follow. This was Hungary, they said, and that's how things were in Hungary.

Thus the first signs of outside influence consisted entirely of radio broadcasts and marginal characters on the streets of Budapest. Subsequently, I tried to run down every lead to find solid evidence of outside intervention. The ultimate in absurdity along these lines occurred when I myself was accused in a note to the American government of having interfered with the Hungarian Revolution and was later accused by Hungarian Embassy officials in Vienna of having lied in my stories. When I challenged them to prove it, they pointed to half a sentence in *The Reporter* which was written on

November 4th in Budapest, in which I said that several members of Nagy's government were in custody. The fact was that on that day, and for several days thereafter, we did receive reports that members of Nagy's cabinet were in custody. Only because we could find no competent Hungarian officials with whom to check the story did we use it at all.

Without the slightest doubt in my mind, I can say that, until the victorious conclusion of the revolution on October 30th, there was no sign of outside intervention at all and that the few émigré Hungarians who infiltrated the country from Germany were ineffective and largely isolated by their own confederates in Hungary. There just wasn't any room for Fascism in Hungary then.

Nevertheless, rumors spread throughout Hungary of mysterious arms shipments, the arrival of "detachments," and momentarily impending Western military assistance. Many Western correspondents, I am sorry to say, believed these rumors and helped to spread them. One incident will illustrate.

Late at night on October 30th I came back to my hotel, where an American agency correspondent gleefully told me that he had a "hell of a story." It developed that he had met a ragged young girl with a gun slung from her shoulder and a bandage on her head. He interviewed her, and she told him that one day, when she was fighting at Corvin Arcade, a mysterious stranger, a Hungarian with an "American accent," said to her that there were several boxes of canned goods upstairs and that she should go up to get some but to be sure to open them carefully. When she went up and the boxes were opened, they were found to be filled with "American hand grenades." I was appalled. My friend assured me that he had sent the story and that the girl's story was translated for him by a reliable American correspondent of Hungarian birth. Later I learned that people in Vienna had the good sense to kill the story. Nevertheless, I came across it several times in various foreign publications.

But the best proof that there never was significant foreign intervention came from Janos Kadar's own propaganda office. This office issued two White Books on the "counterrevolution," as the Hungarian revolt became known among Communists. The books showed photographs of a few foreign-made arms, German and American, which may have been smuggled in small quantities by adventurous

Whites who had rushed into Hungary. But there was never any need for foreign arms. The Hungarian arsenals, military and police, supplied more guns than there were hands to take them. Small arms were never in short supply. What the revolutionaries needed against the Soviet tanks were heavy cannon and armor-piercing shells. In fact, I doubt very much that even if such weapons had been forthcoming they would have done the Hungarians any good. The result would have been more Soviet tanks destroyed and more Hungarians killed; but the revolution was lost the moment the decision was made to remove Imre Nagy's government.

The claims of the White Books can be summed up with a sentence from the second volume: "In evaluating the demands we must take into account also the fact that in this period even the American propaganda center, which directed the entire counter-revolutionary movement, gave the tactical instructions *not yet* to reclaim the factories, mines, and landed estates on behalf of their proprietors." In proof of this contention that the American propaganda center, meaning Radio Free Europe, directed the so-called "counterrevolution," the White Books quote a number of broadcasts by the agency's military analyst, a Colonel Bell, and others.

I have had a number of run-ins in print and in private with Radio Free Europe because of its irresponsible handling of Hungarian affairs, as I shall relate hereafter. But every Hungarian who participated in the revolution can testify to the falseness of the charge. So can I—with authority. For I had Radio Free Europe, and other Western stations broadcasting in the Hungarian language during the time I was in Budapest, monitored by responsible people. I later investigated RFE's role in great detail and I am still of the same mind: Hungarians with special interests, employed by Radio Free Europe, lost their sense of proportion and responsibility and conveyed far more to the Hungarian people by way of encouragement and extravagant promises than they should have, and certainly far more than the situation warranted. The RFE could reasonably argue that they were merely echoing politicians in Washington whose irresponsible statements, year in and year out, had flooded eastern Europe.

There were no shipments of arms into Hungary, no invading armies, and no GHQ directing the revolt from foreign soil. But there was a dangerously rising tide of extreme nationalism of the Fascist kind, beginning at the crucial moment when the revolution was all but won. That these native Fascists and semi-Fascists had ideological brothers scattered throughout the West goes without saying, but just how many "directives" and "couriers" reached them is debatable. My guess is very few; and the fact that the present Hungarian government, with all its police power, could not produce any evidence to contradict my own observations is sufficient proof for me.

Up to the final abdication from power of the Hungarian Communists, which came in response to Nagy's ultimatum, the political progression of the revolution was admirably responsive to the various phases of the revolution.

The demonstrations for a new deal brought, albeit belatedly, Imre Nagy into power. One of the first demands he made of the Politburo was authority to establish Workers' Councils on the Yugoslav pattern, but with wider legislative power. In addition, he wanted two of his trusted lieutenants on the Politburo. Next, Erno Gero was thrown out of office as much by the aroused Soviet executives as by popular demand.

In a dispatch to NANA I described parts of the conversation of October 25th which occurred between Mikoyan and Suslov, on one hand, and Erno Gero, and which led to Gero's dismissal. My informant was with them during the ride from the airport and during the first interchange between the Soviet delegates and the Hungarian leader. On the way in from the airport the Russians were told about the fatal turn of events earlier that morning in front of the Parliament. Suslov said to Gero: "Comrade Gero, we feel that your present position makes any peaceful settlement impossible, and my suggestion is that you resign at once."

Gero blanched, and pleaded with the Russians. He reminded them that during recent negotiations, both in Moscow and with Marshal Tito in Belgrade, it had been agreed that his direction of the party in Hungary was necessary and that without him the party would fall apart.

"The party has already fallen apart, thanks to your incredible blunders," Mikoyan retorted angrily, and continued to berate Gero for having "stampeded" Moscow into sending troops to Hungary.

There was no question in anyone's mind, listening to the exchange, that the Russians felt badly about the turn of events in Hungary. They rapidly agreed to widespread concessions, including the withdrawal of Soviet troops from Budapest just as soon as it became feasible. They ordered Karoly Kiss, a veteran member of the Politburo and chairman of the Control Committee, to present to the Central Committee a resolution calling for the removal of Gero and the appointment of Janos Kadar.

This was the first major political break. Nagy immediately called for a general amnesty and cease-fire. In quick succession he agreed to major economic reforms, the widening of the cabinet to include leaders of two extinct parties, the Social Democrats and the Small Holders. Janos Kadar, as the new first secretary, issued a statement agreeing to the changes.

However, after Thursday, October 25th, the price of peace went up. The immediate dissolution of the AVH was among the new demands. Imre Nagy agreed, and ordered the secret police to cease all activity. After the Saturday ultimatum the Communist party itself withdrew from power, voting itself out of existence.

There were no Communists in the old sense to be found in all Hungary after the fourth day.

The quick metamorphosis of the Hungarian Communists was a wonder to behold. I attended several meetings of intellectuals at which the future structure of the country was being debated. On the night of the fourth day, just before an important policy meeting of the leaders of the revolutionary groups began, a professor of the University of Budapest told me: "We are desperately worried about where all this will lead. There is nothing left of the things in which we believed only a few months ago. We tested the planks of our political and economic structure and found them hollow. But what are we going to replace them with? We can't go back to the semifeudal and semi-Fascist state which existed here before the war."

With guns sounding outside, the rebels sat up all night and laboriously hammered out their program. They called for free elections and an economy divided between public, cooperative, and private ownership. Out went "scientific socialist planning" along with practically every vestige of Marxism. By daybreak these leaders had agreed on combined features of Swedish, British, and American democracy. Incongruously, throughout the debate they called each other "Comrade," as all were members of the Communist party.

The majority of the fighters on the streets and in meeting halls still called one another "Comrade." Professors, engineers, writers, intellectuals, and artists, alternately haranguing in tightly packed meetings and fighting on the streets, were comrades in whatever was considered by them as the cause. Bela Kovacs, speaking of the Imre Nagy of those days, said, "My fondest memory of Nagy will always be his transformation from an easygoing, jolly, studious professor into a flaming revolutionary." This was true of nearly everyone I met during the glorious days of the revolution when the elite of a nation rose in mighty moral revulsion and destroyed every vestige of the obscene past. Driven by conscience, their fervor touched everyone who came in contact with them. This was an auto da fé at which the inquisitors were the penitents, and their act of faith was the destruction of the faith which had betrayed them.

11

Days of Glory

What was it really like?

Since the dawn of their history Magyars had never loved each other so much as they did during the first joyous days of the revolution. An old lady said, with wonder, "It is like the glorious Christmas of a happy child." Smiles, happiness, joyous laughter intermingled with the grim business of fighting the hated enemies, the AVH and the Russians. But even in their curses there was an overtone of happiness; they cursed and fought their enemies with laughter in their hearts. Hungarians discovered one another, the pleasure in one another's company; and they shared their brimming hearts, their joys and their sorrows, with one another. Strangers embraced as brothers, and the light in their eyes spoke of hope, happiness, and great love.

If a window was occupied by stern-faced sharpshooters, their comrades behind them were as likely as not laughing, their happy voices mingling with the whine of the rifles and the explosion of shrapnel. And if all this sounds paradoxical, so it is; but the paradox was in the Hungarians; my eyes and ears merely recorded it.

Watching them milling in the streets, quickly taking refuge at the approach of Soviet tanks or armored cars, and re-forming again in gay groups of chattering people did something unforgettable to the observer. I have never been so conscious of my shortcomings as a reporter than when I tried to convey the scenes before me in the reduced form of cable-ese, the peculiar language of newspapers. How could I convey in telegram style the true flavor of this little incident: across from the Franciscan Church Russian soldiers looted the largest delicatessen and liquor store in Budapest. After they left, a laughing group of people fastened a large placard on the entrance: "This operation was bravely carried out by our glorious Russian allies. We shall not forget their heroic deed!" It was fun composing and painting the sign, a triumph to get it up, and a happy task to man the neighboring windows with guns to drive away anyone who tried to dislodge the placard. Of course, they were fighting for their freedom against a hitherto invincible enemy, but there was no hate or vindictiveness about them, only an irrepressible spirit of joy.

There is a Hungarian phrase, *unnep ronto*, literally translated as "despoiler of holiday"; but the meaning goes deeper than that. Somehow it conveys the idea of taking candy from a baby, throwing mud on a beautiful, laughing child, making people cry when they are happy. *Unnep ronto* was the phrase Hungarians used against the few who tried to sound discordant notes during their first few happy days of fighting for their liberty. Perhaps psychologists could explain the phenonenon of oppressed, angry, and humiliated people suddenly turning against their tormentors with laughter and joy. To me it was a manifestation of man's spirit, his innate greatness, his unquenchable resilience. The Magyars of those few days were truly fit to inherit the earth.

Looking down on Budapest from a great height during its days of travail and glory, one would not have seen and understood the heroic proportions of the struggle. One would have seen a big old city with smoke curling from dozens of buildings, armored cars racing hither and yon, small knots of people scurrying to safety, tanks with their machine guns and cannon spouting fire and spraying the streets, raking the houses, and racing on. Occasionally, from buildings, concentrated rifle or machine-gun fire met the enemy; sometimes exploding gasoline bombs enveloped a tank; and dust rose everywhere from demolished buildings. Broken window glass, ankle deep, covered nearly all the main streets; streetcar wires twisted crazily around corners and along sections of the boulevards. But the overwhelming impression was that of a continuous chase: heavy armor pursuing small groups of lightly armed people, and the people impudently chasing or challenging Soviet units. Through hundreds of streets, squares, and up and down the boulevards the antagonists pursued one another until the city resembled a monstrous bull ring where hundreds of crazy bulls were never permitted to rest but were constantly prodded until in blind fury one or several of them were pinned down for the kill, after which the toreadors circled the arena before a cheering, joyous, proud audience, only to jump back into the ring at any time, anywhere, to go after more bulls until nightfall brought a breathing space before next day's *corrida*.

This picture from the heights would have been interesting enough, but it would not have shown the gallantry which was destined to pass into the folklore of all mankind.

There was, for instance, on Moricz Zsigmond Square, a statue of St. Imre, the patron saint of Hungarian youth. Thirty-two students barricaded themselves around the base of the statue. The square faced an important highway entrance to Budapest, and the thirty-two took upon themselves the task of denying entrance to Soviet armor. With small arms and a few gasoline-filled tin cans they were defenseless facing the enemy. All died, but while they lived through eight feverish hours they held up two Soviet columns and accounted for five tanks, and a glow was still visible on their faces when their corpses were reverently placed in a dirty old truck.

On Rakoczy ut a Soviet tank bore down on a group of people, who tried to hide behind a heavy gate. A few reached safety, but a number of them were still outside when the chattering machine gun began to spray the street. A middle-aged man who had a hand grenade knelt on the pavement and threw the grenade toward the turret of the tank. At that moment the cannon of the tank fired at point-blank range. The pressure from the shell and grenade was so great that a row of store windows was blown out. The tank raced on and the people emerged from behind the gate. One of the demolished stores was a candy shop, and boxes and tins of candy littered the street; another store was a flower shop. All those who had been caught outside the gate were dead. While some of the survivors collected the candy boxes and tins and replaced them in the broken window, a few others gathered up the flowers that had been hurled into the street and covered their fallen comrades. No one spoke until a large crowd had gathered; a passing truck was then commandeered to remove the bodies. Quietly a man said, "Let's go," and another army was born.

On Karacsnyi Sandor ucca a stray bullet from a slowly passing armored car killed a little boy not more than five or six. The mother caught up her bleeding child and ran toward the house. Several bullets were fired at her, and she screamed in pain. The house door opened, and about twenty men and women surged out toward the armored car. Some of the attackers had rifles and revolvers, but most of them had only sticks and stones. It was a horrifyingly uneven battle, but the people's anger had no bounds. When it was all over, eight Soviet soldiers were dead or wounded, their car had been overturned, and the rest had fled. Only three of the attackers remained unhurt.

To describe the hundreds of such incidents I have seen or investigated after they happened would still give only part of the picture. The sight of men, women, and children making the most of unexpected opportunities, and shining for a few seconds or minutes in the fiery red light of heroism can be appreciated only as part of an endless chain linking a million tired, shabby, drab individuals into a single-minded mass of humanity on the march. My notes and those of my assistants are now before me, and as I read the stories we gathered I am struck both by the singularity of each and by the fact that each is meaningless without the others.

Perhaps a visit to a hospital a few blocks from the Kilian barracks will help to show what it was like in Budapest during those days.

Istvan Korhaz was a hospital rich in tradition, but with all its meager resources almost exhausted. I had to circle nearly all of

Budapest to get there because the neighboring streets on Ulloi ut were heavily invested by Soviet troops and armor. I went there to investigate a report which showed a much higher ratio of dead to the number of wounded than I had ever heard of in this or in any other war or revolution.

The explanation was that the hospital was able to minister to a mere fraction of the wounded because Soviet forces shot at ambulances at the very gate of the hospital, and a hastily recruited stretcher-bearer force of twenty-four volunteers had been cut down to a single survivor. Wounded were bleeding to death outside the gates, and there was no way to reach them.

Dr. I. K., medical director of the hospital, said: "Modern history has no equal to the barbarity committed here. Soviet troops have killed or wounded half of our personnel."

Then he described what happened to the ambulances and stretcher-bearers, saying, "Dr. A. G., our chief surgeon, suffered a nervous breakdown upon seeing the wounded on the streets around us without being able to help."

The night before I went there, Soviet troops actually occupied the main wing of the hospital for a few hours. But the doctors and nurses got out and organized a large force of freedom fighters. They sent an ultimatum to the Soviet forces: "Unless you leave within an hour, or if one shot is fired from the hospital building, we will exterminate all of you." The ultimatum was obeyed and the Soviet forces withdrew, but only to occupy neighboring buildings, from which they trained their guns on the streets surrounding the hospital. A doctor who was in constant attendance for thirty-six hours estimated that during that time seven hundred wounded Hungarians died for lack of medical attention.

The hospital was jammed with wounded fighters. Here are a few of my random notes, transcribed verbatim, that I made there that day:

"Livia Czudarhelyi, nineteen, asked an AVH truck for a lift home because she was carrying a heavy sack of food. She was shot.

"So was Zsigmond Kruker, who said he stepped from the doorway of his home to pull his daughter off the street and was hit by a secret-police sharpshooter.

"Jozsef Mikori, seventeen, was one of many crushed against

141

a wall by a Soviet tank. He was among the lucky ones, however. He lived. Scores of wounded and dying were caught unarmed as they stood harmlessly in food lines.

"Lajos Hajdu responded to a promise of amnesty by surrendering with twelve others. All were shot. Four were left wounded but alive.

"Wendel Markus, an elderly janitor much loved by his tenants, lay dying as I spoke to him. The seventy-two-year-old man was shot because he helped a woman carry potatoes and bread though a gate.

"Ferencz Burucz, an AVH man, died, shot by his own officer, because he refused to fire into a milling crowd of his own countrymen.

"Age made no difference: Sandor Ronay, seventy-six, was shot as he inserted the key into the door of his second-floor apartment, Prater ucca fourteen. He was shot four times by AVH and Soviet troops who occupied the apartment while he was away.

"Maria Szobolai peeked out curiously. She was hit by a Soviet sharpshooter.

"Zoltan Szucs, a theology student, rigged up a barrel in the middle of a boulevard. Soviet tank drivers, afraid the barrel contained explosives, drove around it, and came too close to the houses lining the street. The tanks were then within easy reach of Molotov cocktails thrown by Szucs' pals.

"Laszlo Orban, sixteen, was in charge of acquiring guns from policemen. He sneaked up behind them, grabbed their guns, and told them, 'Now you can go home to the wife and children.'

"In an adjoining bed was Peter Boldizsar, fifteen. He had rigged up antitank mines on strings and, with a friend on the other side of the street, tugged at the strings until the tank hit the mine."

Then the women of Budapest! It is impossible to convey the calm bravery, contempt for terror, and moral courage with which they shamed their tormentors.

There was no common determinant or single reason which induced the women of Hungary to revolt; they came from everywhere, each bringing her outraged life and throwing it into the fight wherever events demanded her services. The rebelling women of Hungary were not enlisted or organized, and there was no special appeal to them to come out and fight; they came when the hour struck, singly or in small groups, to join the milling, marching, singing, shouting people on the street, and stayed on when the battle was joined between the revolutionaries and the Soviet troops.

The circumstances of my encounter with the five whose stories I am about to record were as random as their selection. The revolution brought to the surface such a variety of the pain, suffering, and outrage inherent in the Communist system that it was impossible to select anyone as typical of the revolution. These five were typical only as representing a deeply humiliated womenfolk who, against overwhelming odds, arose to say, No more—ever!

I met Ildiko on the afternoon of the 23rd of October, five hours before the first shot was fired in the Hungarian Revolution. She was reading from a crumpled paper to a group of unbelieving citizens: " 'We demand the departure of the Soviet troops from Hungary. . . . We demand the dismissal of Rakosi, Gero, and we demand their public trial . . .' and so on, through the historic twenty-eight points adopted that afternoon by the University of Agronomy, to the last one: " 'We demand that compulsory Russian-language courses be abolished forthwith.' "

The wind blew her long golden blond hair into her face, and she impatiently pushed it back into a sagging bun. Her face was glowing, and her willowly body swayed as she emphasized each demand. She looked like a shabbily dressed, outraged spirit of youth. Her soft melodious voice acquired overtones of harshness as she read the stern paragraphs.

Since she had no second copy of the demands, she readily agreed to accompany me to the telegraph office where I wanted to incorporate some of them into a dispatch I was about to send. On the way over she told me something about herself.

She wanted to become a veterinary physician, following in the footsteps of her deceased father; she lived with her invalid mother who worked at home to augment Ildiko's stipend from school. Though she had no personal grievance, she was burning with indignation at what she called the "relentless oppression" of functionaries at school, at the tenement where she lived, and at the national leaders who arbitrarily held everyone's life and safety in their hands.

For the next forty-eight hours Ildiko was my secretary, friend, and guide. She introduced me to student leaders, dutifully copied proclamations and speeches, served as my courier and, when bullets began to fly, identified for me the protagonists. We carried wounded to hospitals, dodged all kinds of missiles, and finally, around 2:00 A.M. the next morning, were arrested by the AVH while trying to enter the building of the Central Committee of the Communist party.

Ildiko was cheerful, enthusiastic, and incredibly brave. Glowingly she explained that now she would do something for the revolution by helping to inform the West through me.

Her end came on that Thursday afternoon, the 25th of October.

We were watching, through an upper window, a group of about seventy young men and a dozen or so girls armed with machine guns and rifles approach a heavily defended bridge. We knew that Soviet troops had built camouflaged machine-gun nests all around the square, but apparently the revolutionaires did not. With bated breath we watched them coming around the last corner leading to the square before them. When the first tattoo of fire was heard, Ildiko could stand it no longer. "No . . . no! They will be slaughtered. . . . I have to warn them!" she cried.

She raced through the door, ignoring my plea not to enter the square. "They don't know about the trap!" she cried, and was gone.

Later, when trucks came to pick up the dead and wounded from the square, I found Ildiko. Her blue eyes stared vacantly into the setting sun, and her golden hair was splattered with dried blood. She had died in a hail of bullets from machine guns hidden behind the lion that guarded the bridge.

Tired and shaken from an all-day and all-night visit with freedom fighters entrenched in various parts of the city, I went to the clubhouse of the Federation of Hungarian Writers. Klari, a well-known novelist, called out to me. She was surrounded by mountains of papers, drafts of manifestoes, revolutionary declarations, and calls for determined resistance. Her job was to coordinate the activities of the members of the Revolutionary Committee, a group of well-known writers who had been largely responsible for the creation of the revolutionary atmosphere in Hungary by relentlessly exposing the misdeeds of the mighty and by demanding thoroughgoing reforms. Klari asked me for news of the fighting. She had been at her improvised desk in the hall since the beginning of the revolution, now in its third day.

My dreary recital of small victories at the price of large casualties depressed her terribly. She covered her tired face for a moment; then, indicating the papers on her desk, she asked, "Are we really right?" She found her own answer. "Yes, yes," she said with emphasis, "we are right, and we must go on until we are sure that what has been happening here throughout the years shall never happen again."

The time and the mood were right, and I asked her: "Klari, you and your colleagues are intelligent, talented people. For years you have supported this horror. Tell me, how could you have believed in them so long?"

"We are now atoning for what we have done," she said. "For over a year we have been investigating, exposing, searching for the very thing you are asking: How could we have been so blind, so naïve, so believing? Every new facet of this terrorist system that we have discovered and exposed has renewed our determination to end it once for all.

"I know it is hard for you to believe that we were duped, but it is the literal truth. We are all driven by a feeling of terrible guilt. Truly, we intellectuals have been the white-haired children of this regime. Many of us earned far more than did the prime minister. Villas, autos, unobtainable luxuries were at our disposal, but we realize now that those were bribes with which these evil people tried to blind us."

Around Klari and me the best of Hungary's intellectual life was working, debating, directing in excited confusion. Their ferment was real, their enthusiasm contagious. Klari, with a diffident gesture toward them, said: "I am proud of my brothers and sisters. They have given back to me what I now realize I most missed all these years: my faith in the integrity and morality of our people."

On Ulloi ut, near the Kilian barracks, where some of the heaviest fighting in Budapest took place, a point-blank blast from a Russian JS3 tank had blown in the second floor of a shabby old tenement. Where the walls and windows had been, a dark, gaping hole remained. Some of the furniture from destroyed apartments was still visible in a crazy pattern, as if suspended in air by ghostly wires.

At the edge of the hole, partly covered by the remnants of the wall, sat an elderly woman with a rifle across her knees.

Panni, gaunt-faced, tall, bony, and sixty-two years old, was waiting for her personal enemies, the Russians. She peered up and down the street, clutching her rifle. Some of her neighbors tried to persuade her to take cover, but she stubbornly refused to move from her exposed perch.

Resistance around the neighborhood was under the command of a university student who had placed machine guns on roofs and behind stone parapets. But Panni refused to conform. There was something extraordinarily purposeful in her behavior, and the commander let her alone.

During a brief skirmish that afternoon between the freedom fighters and the AVH, Panni took a few shots, but she was not really interested. The police retreated, and a Soviet tank lumbered across the street. Panni at once became all afire. She blazed away, trying to hit the tank's periscope. From a house across the street a Molotov cocktail was thrown at the tank, and in a few seconds Russian soldiers were leaping out of the flames. With nonchalant, deadly aim, Panni brought one of them down.

Later in the evening, when the fighting had ended for the day, I met Panni, still sitting on the stoop in front of her house. After a while, brusquely, she spoke of her abiding hatred of the Russians.

"They took everything I ever had," she said, "everything I ever cared for. In 1916 they killed my husband, a prisoner of war in Russia. My son fell three blocks away from here under Russian fire in 1945. My grandson will be deported because he foolishly surrendered three days ago when they promised amnesty. And that" —pointing to the black hole above our heads—"was my home since I was a child. There is nothing left for them to take from me."

After the return of the Soviet Army to Budapest one afternoon, the square below my window was deserted. A strict curfew was in effect. No one was permitted outside except the military. Civilians were shot on sight. For one hour a day people were permitted to move around and draw food from the rapidly dwindling supply of the city. The hour was never long enough for more than a fraction of the shoppers to fulfill their needs, and the reimposition of the

146

curfew was often accompanied by severe fighting between the people and the militia.

A heavy truck loaded with 1,600 loaves of bread arrived at the square too late; a machine gun opened up to spray the ground around it; and the people fled into the houses.

But not Agatha.

Agatha was a very old, bent woman, a stranger to the neighborhood. She had fled into the heart of the city when her own street was gutted by fire, and now she stood hidden behind a doorway, watching the truckload of bread, and murmuring imprecations. Her simple soul rebelled against what she saw: food for hungry mouths abandoned and useless. Why? Because those accursed profligates thought nothing of wasting God's gracious gift in such a shameful manner.

Slowly, not looking to right or left, Agatha crossed to the truck. Laboriously she lifted two of the five-pound loaves, and turned. There was a warning shout from a group of guards stationed at the statue dominating the square. Agatha gave no sign of having heard it. She turned back to the doorway with the loaves. There she gave them into eager hands and started back again.

This time a warning shot was fired at her. The white-haired old lady continued unperturbed, and once again reached the truck. She lifted two more loaves and returned with her booty to the doorway. By then a large group of tenement dwellers was awaiting her. She handed over the loaves amidst the cheers of the people and once more made her journey back to the truck.

Now several shots were fired over her head, while innumerable persons watched from windows and doorways Agatha's defiance of the armored might of the Soviet Union. The people responded to the firing with a roar of curses, catcalls, and jeers. Old Agatha calmly continued her trips to the truck and back to the house, oblivious of the tense drama developing around her. Occasionally she stopped to catch her breath, and gradually her gait became slower. But doggedly she kept to her self-appointed task of feeding the neighborhood. After twenty round trips she changed to the next tenement.

A Russian officer with a Hungarian interpreter approached her. The officer peremptorily told Agatha that she must stop defying the curfew. The old woman looked at the two men in uniform before her and said: "You ought to go down on your bended knees and pray to God for forgiveness for your sins. Maybe He, in His infinite mercy, will forgive you for keeping our people hungry, killing them for trying to get food for their children. Maybe He will forgive you. But I will pray that He may not grant your plea." And with that Agatha turned away and resumed her journey toward the truck.

All through the afternoon and evening Agatha distributed bread around the square. When anyone tried to help her the Russians began to shoot, so Agatha remained alone with the slowly dwindling mountain of bread. Stubbornly she fought the Russians, her own overwhelming fatigue, and the oncoming darkness. Pale lights from the windows lit up her path, the beams of flashlights whose power was too slight to do more than bathe Agatha in an eerie illumination.

It was nearly nine o'clock when, with only a few hundred loaves still on the truck, Agatha collapsed. The bread fell from her hands and she sank to the ground. From a nearby Soviet tank a soldier ran toward Agatha. He tried to help her up, and when it was clear that she could not stand even with the soldier's help the Russian gently lifted the frail old woman into his arms. The Soviet officer in command of the tanks shouted a staccato order. The soldier hesitated, then responded slowly, saying something in a deep strong voice, deliberately walking with Agatha in his arms to the doorway from which the old woman had started out. There he banged away on the door until it was opened. Handing Agatha over, the soldier quickly returned to his tank.

Szena Ter is a wide, spacious square in Buda, on the right bank of the Danube, below the Royal Fort. Several battles had been fought there, and the square was a tangle of overturned streetcars, fallen wires, burned-out tanks and combat vehicles, piles of cobblestones, and improvised barricades. The square had been intermittently defended, abandoned, and reoccupied by freedom fighters throughout the previous days. I met Anna at the Szena Ter during the quiet period. Everyone called her Nusi, and she seemed to be a respected member of the freedom fighters who had entrenched themselves behind strong points. She was a well-dressed, quiet woman in her late thirties, although her hair was gray and her face was heavily lined. Something in her prematurely grave face and burning eyes spoke of depth and passion. She was armed with an automatic rifle. Conversation was desultory between us until we came to the subject of the revolution and its moral significance. Instantly she came alive.

"What is your stake?" I asked her.

"If I tell you that I have no feeling of revenge," she replied, "for what they have done to me, you would not believe it. But I think it is important for you as a Westerner to know what we are fighting for."

In quiet, carefully chosen words she told me her story. She was a civil engineer, and had been a member of the Communist party since 1938. She joined the Young Communist Federation because she was then convinced that there was no way out of a Hitler-created Europe except for the way shown by the Soviet Union. Her intense hatred for the obscenities and cruelties of the Nyilas drove her into the arms of the Communists, who, according to Nusi, at that time were a closely knit revolutionary group held together not only by politics but by sincere friendships, mutual respect, and helpfulness.

During the war she had married another civil engineer, also a Communist, and a boy was born to them in 1947. About this time they both began to notice that the party they had joined was no longer the same. Once in power, it had turned into a cold, inhuman tyrant, demanding blind obedience. Sensitive and idealistic people like Nusi and her husband felt uncomfortable. But Nusi still believed that harsh methods were needed to extirpate all the vestiges of the old order, and she obeyed her party leaders implicitly.

In the spring of 1952 her husband suddenly disappeared. Months of frantic search and incessant questioning of officials finally brought word that her husband had been arrested and sentenced to twenty years of imprisonment as a saboteur in pay of Western imperialists. She was stunned. She could not believe it. She thought she knew her husband, and although he had been lukewarm toward the party in late years, he could not be a traitor. She felt that had her husband wanted to rebel, he would have done so openly.

She went to a high party official, a former friend of theirs. Though he was sympathetic, he told her sternly that there could be no question of her husband's guilt and that as a Communist she could not remain married to him. The party would take care of a quick divorce.

149

For a year Nusi resisted. Her superiors were constantly after her: she would fail in her loyalty to the party if she remained married to a traitor. There was no way in which Nusi could communicate with her husband; she was never told where he was being held. Slowly, insidiously, the poison worked. She began to waver. Perhaps her husband did do the things with which he was charged. She could not believe that such a gigantic frame-up could be conceived by her comrades. Finally, in the summer of 1953, she gave in and accepted a divorce.

She threw herself with renewed vigor into her work. She wanted to find peace and an escape from constantly nagging doubts. She accepted the courtship of a party official, and her life slowly began to reshape itself.

Just as precipitately as he was arrested, Nusi's husband was released, with an apology, in the fall of 1955, after three and one half years of imprisonment. It was late in the evening when he reached Budapest. Not wanting to shock his wife, he called her sister to prepare Nusi for his imminent arrival.

The reunion and the days which followed were nightmarish for both. Nusi, smitten by a guilty conscience, said and did the wrong things. Her husband, under the shock of finding his wife divorced, could not understand how she could have believed him to be so devoid of feeling for her as to do something behind her back which would jeopardize her safety. Everything they said and did during those days was wrong. Even their son contributed to their misery by revealing that he, too, had believed his father guilty.

Although deeply in love with each other, Nusi and her husband separated, and the breach finally became irreparable. Since then, Nusi has changed completely.

"This immoral system we have been trapped in must go forever," she said. "Since my own tragedy I have spent all my time investigating what we have done to our country and our people and I have come to this firm conclusion: They"—meaning the Communists—"must go, peacefully, if possible. But if not, they must be destroyed."

Her last words were spoken in haste because Soviet tanks were coming down the hill toward us. As they lumbered forward, Nusi carefully checked her gun and placed some hand grenades on the parapet.

Those five brief portraits could easily be extended to include hundreds, even thousands, of women as well as men and children. The first memorable character I met during actual fighting was a man, high in the Communist hierarchy, whom I called Sandor in a story I wrote about him to protect his family after his death on the second day of the revolt.

When I met him the flickering light from blazing guns around him occasionally lit up his determined face. He was watching the upper windows of the Radio House on Brody Sandor ucca. Unarmed students bustling around turned to him for orders, which he gave in a calm, unhurried voice. He appeared to be in command, although he did not issue orders voluntarily; he merely responded to questions. His chief occupation seemed to be to scare the AVH away from the windows by intermittent drum fire from the submachine gun he was clutching tightly to his hip. This was the first night of the Hungarian Revolution. By then the narrow streets around Radio House were littered with dead and wounded students caught by the murderous fire of the AVH from the upper windows.

No one seemed to know him. The milling students instinctively turned to him because he appeared calm and because what he said made good sense. I made many inquiries before I could identify him, and by then he was on a stretcher ready to be taken out of the battle. While he waited for a harassed doctor to attend to his torn shoulder, we fell to talking.

"What made you, of all people, join the revolution?" I asked. He seemed to search for an answer, then said, "I had more reasons than the students—far more."

As I now know, he was an important Communist official: general director of one of the largest industrial combines in Hungary; one of the upper-echelon Communists with his own villa, servants, and limousine, whose word was law, whose every want was readily satisfied, whose health was guarded by a corps of highly trained and well paid physicians, and who commanded privileges nearly equal to those of ancient satraps.

The story of Sandor represented an important aspect of the

151

disintegration of Communism. Sandor was more than a man with a submachine gun hunting for Red terrorists. He was a symbol of the moral revulsion which swept through Hungary. His story has a classic simplicity which helps to illustrate the ideological confusion of the Hungarian rebellion.

Sandor had been a simple house painter, looked upon by his fellows in the trade union as a dependable, honest, level-headed, and modest man with a passion for helping the underdog. Before the war his rebellion against Fascism carried him to the Social-Democratic youth organization; after the war, as a demobilized soldier, he returned to his home, in a suburb of Budapest, to resume his trade. His monthly income in 1948, when the Communists took over Hungary, was around 800 forints, which at that time was equal in purchasing power to $30. His wife, who also worked, earned between 400 and 500 forints a month. They lived frugally and managed to make both ends meet with a little left over for those who sought their help. Sandor was the kind of socialist, common in Europe, who knew little about Marxism and nothing about scientific socialism but who believed in a set of humanitarian principles which the old-time European socialist espoused.

In 1948, because of his popularity and dependability, he was elected as a "functionary" by his union and sent to the Central Workers' Council. His income skyrocketed to 1,800 forints a month. In the council he distinguished himself and soon attracted the attention of party bosses. Sandor was talked into joining the Communist party, and because he was found to be an honest, hard-working, good man—the kind of front man the Communists sorely needed—he became in a short period of time a leading figure in Hungary's economic structure.

By 1954 he had reached the exalted position he occupied at the outbreak of the revolution.

"The higher I got, the deeper I sank in the morass," he said. "I knew how terribly wrong it was for me to carry out decisions such as cutting the pitifully low wages of the workers, increasing back-breaking 'norms,' and reducing manpower to squeeze out more from fewer men, but what was I to do? Resign? Return to where I came from? It was impossible."

"I compromised again and again," he said bitterly, "trying to lie to myself, but it was no good. I knew all along that I could not return to house painting, give up my position, home, automobile, the things to which my wife and I had become accustomed. Where could I go if I resigned? Besides, they would never have let me make a full confession to my people. I was trapped, and I could not see my way out of it until the first report of fighting outside Radio House reached me. Then, suddenly, I knew where I belonged."

And thus the second hour of the revolution found Sandor outside Radio House with a submachine gun directing the siege.

The memory of the people I met during the gallant days of the revolution is one of the reasons I resented the fakes who flooded the West as refugees, telling spurious heroic tales. There was no need to contrive and lie; there were truer and greater stories to be told of that brief flash that lit up the Communist skies, revealing the true degradation of the people and the wrath with which they tried to shake themselves free.

Most serious of all, however, were the distortions that tried to cover up the scum that appeared on the periphery of the revolution. To deny that Fascists, anti-Semitic, predatory people tried to steal the revolution would not make it greater; it only covered up an important lesson which the West as well as the Communists ought to have learned. For by supporting these people throughout the years, the West cut itself off from the main stream of European thinking, particularly in Eastern countries, while the Communists should have realized what kind of danger lurked behind their oppressive regime, and tried to alleviate the bitter hate in their people lest the Communists themselves fall victims to extremists of a different hue, albeit no less vicious.

The Hungarian revolutionaries were not nationalists of the type so familiar in the history of Europe, when throughout the ages nationalism simply meant the enslavement of nationalities by one nation. They were trying to evolve something of which apparently both the East and the West strongly disapproved. The West offered the revolutionaries a handful of discredited émigrés, and the East more of the same thing which the Hungarians had had for eight weary years.

Certainly there was no name for Imre Nagy's program. It was simply intended to give the Hungarians a chance to evolve toward a free, democratic political structure—something they had never had before. There was no question of reestablishing Hungarian freedom; for the Hungarians, except for brief revolutionary periods, never had known freedom, either under Horthy or under the monarchy before him, and least of all under the Communists.

The Hungarian freedom fighter vainly looked toward the West or the East for moral support—which was the only kind that would have helped after the revolution reached its climax. Instead of helping to consolidate the gains, voices coming from the West incessantly pushed the Hungarians toward extremes, although this was neither the wish of the Western people nor of their responsible governments. But the Soviets and their Hungarian stooges accepted what appeared to be Western intervention on behalf of the Fascists at its face value. The bell tolled in Hungary for both the East and the West, and both became blind and deaf while Hungarians went down in defeat.

12

The Final Stages

On my return from Vienna on Tuesday morning, October 30th, the government was announcing thoroughgoing reforms and the Communist party had voted its own dissolution. A new party was to carry on the communist ideology, but intense negotiations were under way to create a government of national coalition. A few days later a new cabinet was announced by Imre Nagy which contained three Communists, three Small Holders' party leaders, three Social Democrats, and three members of the Peasant party (which was renamed Petofi party), with Pal Maleter, the minister of defense, representing, by that time, a group of Christian parties.

Among the concessions and reforms were: Withdrawal of Soviet forces from Budapest and the opening of negotiations for their complete withdrawal from Hungary; agreement with Moscow on the renegotiation of Soviet-Hungarian commercial treaties, including the Uranium Concessions; establishment of a free press which immediately gave birth to six new daily newspapers and several in process of organization; the establishment of political freedom which resulted in the formation of a number of parties which I shall describe later; complete amnesty for all who fought against the Soviet or the AVH and the dissolution of the AVH itself; AVH personnel were asked to appear before the examiners of the state attorney's office to establish their former roles as members of a proscribed organization or accept a free passage to the Soviet Union; all workers were to be paid full wages for time lost during the revolution; Cardinal Mindszenty's trial was annulled by ministerial decree; important economic concessions were made to the peasants, who were given permission to withdraw their land from cooperatives if they so desired; and political power was temporarily transferred to National Councils and Workers' Councils until the new elections, which were to be held in January, 1957, could produce a national constitutional assembly.

These were some of the major achievements of the revolution when it entered its fourth phase.

For emphasis let me repeat that this fourth phase, after the revolutionary students and workers had retired victoriously from combat, was the one in which all AVH killing, hooliganism, lawlessness, and plundering took place. This was the phase when heavily armed "heroes" appeared to gun down unarmed people and when swaggering hoodlums were organized in mysterious formations.

This was also the time when the West could have helped most by hailing the miracle that had been wrought by a handful of people, by rushing in with good will and offers of help, by recognizing with praise Soviet withdrawal and inviting Russia to join in an international effort to bind the wounds, and, above all, by silencing the discordant, goading, hateful voices of émigré radios. If the West was at any time serious about having a democratic Hungary, and was concerned with the welfare of a sorely tried people, this was the time to show it by decisive moves.

Instead, what happened was this. The revolutionary government of Hungary was snowed under by hostile propaganda from the outside, by deliberately fomented disorders at home, and by the malfunctioning of its own Defense Ministry. Even so, with the odds so heavily against it, the government could have survived and could have brought the saboteurs under control had it not been for the fact that Soviet troops in great numbers began to stream into Hungary during the night of October 31st, and thereby forced Imre Nagy's hand. I have been told that the Soviet troops originally were brought in to protect the orderly withdrawal of the remnants of the Soviet forces in Hungary. How true this was I do not know, although, considering the inordinate pride of the Red Army and some of the humiliating experiences of the Russians at the hands of the Hungarians, that may have been their first consideration.

I learned something about the entrance of hooligans into the picture from a railroad inspector whom I picked up at the border on my return from Vienna. He told me that several truckloads of relief goods had disappeared between the border and Budapest. He also gave me a good description of what had been going on during the day and a half that I had been away.

Just as soon as the consolidation of the revolution began, a number of so-called Christian parties, some without membership, appeared to claim the spoils. The Hungarian Christian party, Christian Youth Association, Christian Democratic People's party, Christian Youth Society, and the Christian Democratic party were among the conspicuous ones. There were other political movements: something called National Association of Partyless People, Metropolitan National Committee and, last but not least, the Fraternal Association of Hungarian Political Prisoners, a large number of whose members were former Nazi-Nyilas war criminals.

Among the newly published newspapers was one called *Magyar Honved* (Hungarian Guardian), which said on its masthead that it was the organ of the Hungarian Guardians and the newly formed National Guard. This was Pal Maleter's newspaper. After I read the issues from October 30th to November 3rd, its role became clear: to cut through official formations and create a new armed force largely made up of roving bands.

One by one, all revolutionary leaders took to the microphone to urge their followers to end the strike which had begun on the second day of the revolt and help restore order in the city. Workers, intellectuals, and students held meetings, formed councils, and proclaimed the end of the struggle. Even as intransigent, anti-Nagy a revolutionary figure as Jozsef Dudas issued a call ending with, "Now we say it: Cease fire! Don't shoot! Now morality, justice will protect you and also our brotherhood, and, yes, I write it: God."

Preparations were made to resume work in all plants on Monday, November 5th. The government, as well as all exposed and visible mass organizations, was trying to stop the spreading lawlessness—that is, all except the Defense Ministry under Pal Maleter. There is no profit in speculating on Maleter's unwillingness or inability to dispatch armed forces to trouble spots; the fact was that all the sporadic outbursts fomented by nondescript armed bands could easily have been dealt with. Moreover, there were not many. I have read the statistics of the Kadar regime regarding "White" atrocities with care. Reckoning liberally, there were no more than seventy AVH fatalities at the hands of the lawless mobs. I saw a dozen corpses of AVH personnel during that fourth phase of the revolution.

Suddenly there was an announcement that all Christian parties were to act as one under the general command of the "Christian Front." My next statement will have to be taken on faith: I learned from a person who was part of the movement that Pal Maleter was being groomed as a dictator of Hungary with the backing of the Christian Front. Since some people who were involved in this plan are still alive, I can not go beyond this statement, but long before I was certain that something was up I had sensed the trend and discussed it with Minister of State Geza Losonczi in the presence of Tamas Aczel, the novelist. Losonczi seemed taken aback when I asked him to explain Maleter's role. He wanted to know my reason for asking, and I explained briefly that I had investigated Maleter, since he appeared in a dubious light, and had found that he was first a Horthy officer, later a Soviet volunteer who became a trusted Soviet officer, and that now I had seen him commanding a group of his former colleagues from the Horthy army with a phenomenal rise in power. Colonel, brigadier, lieutenant-general, undersecretary of defense, secretary of defense, commander of all armed forces—all in one week's time. Moreover, I pointed out that though the roving bands had some kind of new identification cards making them members of Maleter's organization, these were the bands which prevented the restoration of order in the city.

"It seems to me," I said, "that Maleter could stop the atrocities if he wanted to by issuing an order to his own men, unless he prefers to let them go on and use the disorders as a reason for grabbing all power himself."

Losonczi seemed aghast, and later I found Imre Nagy equally bewildered. But by then it was too late, anyway.

This conversation with Losonczi took place early in the morning on Thursday, November 1st. Aczel and I went to see him because I wanted a clarification of ideological trends, for by then it appeared to me that Hungary was definitely out of the satellite group. What would replace Hungary's ties to Russia? Titoism, Gomulkaism, some kind of Western orientation, or what? We found Losonczi in deep gloom. He said he did not want to talk about anything except what had happened the night before. Soviet armored columns were pouring into Hungary through Zahony, and what was the Hungarian government to do?

Since this conversation and my subsequent discussion with Nagy became known to the Kadar regime and became part of the protest Kadar sent to America about "an American journalist's intervention in Hungarian affairs," and "performing a courier service for Cardinal Mindszenty," I can only guess that Losonczi or Nagy repeated what I had said at the cabinet meeting that noon and that later a distorted version of it reached the new Hungarian Communist regime.

Briefly, we discussed the problem of immediately proclaiming Hungary's neutrality and its desire to leave the Warsaw Pact. I understood from Losonczi that although Nagy and his associates were willing, the method of doing it and the possible consequences of such steps were sources of great anxiety.

My analysis of the situation was this: A Hungarian neutrality declaration might not stop the Soviets from crushing the revolution. But if that was to be the case, the government had nothing to lose because it would be crushed anyway; on the other hand, it would clearly mark the Soviet move as an aggression. If the Soviets wanted to risk that, then their determination to return was stronger than any other consideration, and there was nothing to be done about it. However, there was still a chance that the Soviets would not risk such a palpably aggressive move if they realized that world-wide condemnation would follow. To nail this down, Imre Nagy should address a personal plea to the heads of the Big Four asking them to realize and accept Hungary's new position.

Losonczi made notes of this conversation. The idea of an appeal to the heads of states was particularly attractive to him and to the cabinet. I may have overstated my case, because I never had a moment's doubt that America, France, and Britain would react immediately and accept the Hungarian declaration; and the Soviet Union might reluctantly follow if the pressure of the West were sufficiently strong. In this I was greatly mistaken. The West did not react to the declaration until after it was too late, and its last-minute effort only aggravated Imre Nagy's position. Perhaps it cost him his life.

Later, around noon, I met Seymour Freidin of the *New York Post*, and gave him an outline of the situation since I was not in Hungary for the purpose of getting spot news. I met him again at five in the afternoon, and he told me that there had been a news conference earlier in the afternoon and that Nagy had issued the appeal, proclaiming Hungary's neutrality.

At any rate, from that moment on, only a concentrated effort from the West, as well as from the Hungarians, to restore order could have saved the revolution. The West failed; the radios from Germany and elsewhere prodded and goaded the Hungarians to refuse to work or to accept the government's orders until certain demands, which were manifestly impossible to fulfill, were accepted. Among them the most prominent was one which every responsible person ought to have known was not possible to achieve: the immediate, unilateral tearing up of the Warsaw Pact accompanied by the immediate withdrawal of Soviet forces. Politically, logistically, and legally it was not possible to meet this demand, and Western propagandists knew it well. Among the roving bands, this demand was embroidered with the afterthought that the Red Army must march out with white flags flying or else it would be attacked. Cardinal Mindszenty was to be named premier, and wholesale martial law should dispose of every Communist Jew in Hungary.

While none of the Western governments spoke up at this

critical moment, the Hungarians, listening to Western radios, accepted the extremists' words as the official Western attitude. No one in the West seemed to have a good word for the Hungarian Revolution until after it was crushed. The few liberal voices were drowned out by the shrill propaganda which floated over Hungary in those days.

Hungarian hatred for the Soviets needed no prodding from the West; it was virulent and abiding. No one in Hungary had a good word for the Russian type of colonialism which was in effect before the revolution. Even the handful of pro-Soviet high Communists was silent or spoke in approval of Imre Nagy's effort to establish Hungarian independence, among them the present first secretary Janos Kadar and the current prime minister, Ferencz Munnich.

From what I had been able to learn, I believed that the Soviet Union was willing to make drastic changes in its ties with Hungary, and Moscow officially announced that negotiations were to begin immediately.

What, then, went wrong? Certainly the Russians did not risk a major political defeat for a handful of lynched AVH men. There were signs of an incipient White terror, and undoubtedly it would have increased, but not beyond the point which the Hungarian government could control once Maleter was removed from the helm of the armed forces.

The most plausible explanation I could find was that the Red Army decided to stop the Hungarian Revolution, and the political leadership of the Soviet Union fell in line.

The Red Army is an immensely proud organization, and fanatically devoted to what Red Army men call the honor of their armed services. Militarists of all countries have special pride in their service tradition and virtues, but perhaps the Red Army is quicker to take offense than most on these scores. And serious offenses had been committed against the Red Army, after the revolution came to a victorious climax, by superpatriotic heroes who strutted around at will. The desecration of the Red Army cemeteries of those who had fallen in World War II was one major offense to the Red Army. The stoning of and spitting upon of their wives and children during their embarkation on a Danubian steamer to take them out of Hungary was another. The destruction of memorials erected to commemorate the heroic exploits of the Red Army against Hitler's hordes was still another. Added to these, the not unnatural resentment of the Red Army for their misunderstood role in the Thursday massacre was, I believed, enough to awaken their wrath. For that matter, American troops could not have been insulted in that manner without arousing their resentment, even though the political background of the insults was understandable.

That something of this sort did happen and that the Red Army made the decision was clear from the conditions which were handed to Maleter on November 3rd during the Soviet-Hungarian negotiations for Soviet withdrawal. The three points were: the withdrawing Soviet Army should be given military honors; Red Army memorials should be restored; and the Hungarian government should guarantee that Soviet Army cemeteries on Hungarian soil remain sacred forever.

Perhaps the real answer to the question of why the Russians returned to Budapest to crush the revolution will never be known; nor is it quite as clear as some may think that Janos Kadar volunteered for the role he subsequently played or even agreed to it. As I shall try to show, Kadar for some time believed that he could carry out Nagy's program with some modifications in regard to Soviet-Hungarian military ties. The decision was made in Moscow, and if the Hungarians played a role at all it was very likely a minor one.

I spent the days between my return to Vienna and November 4th, when the Russians suddenly infested the city, in attending meetings of various political groups and generally keeping in touch with developments at the Parliament House, where the government was in continuous session.

Accompanied by a band of enthusiastic AVH hunters, I visited the Rakosi villa and explored the luxuriously equipped tunnel beneath it. The cellars of the AVH headquarters produced some grisly stories connected with a sinister-looking machine which was installed in the cellar to pulverize discarded documents and papers. According to an old woman whom we met there, prisoners were chained behind the machine where they choked to death by inhaling the paper dust which the machine produced. At the villa of Count Istvan Tisza, the prime minister of Hungary at the outbreak of the

First World War, we found radio-jamming equipment, also in a tunnel. I watched excavators at Republic Square in front of the Party Building, where the massacre of some AVH men occurred, searching for a tunnel which, according to engineers and builders, extended under the park and where, according to the people assembled there, some AVH prisoners were still alive and waiting to be liberated.

Thus the rise of a superpatriotic temper fomented from abroad and at home did not escape attention. My own judgment of the situation was expressed by Bela Kovacs during our last meeting after the return of the Russians. Kovacs said that there had been a possibility that a White terror might have gained the upper hand in Hungary, but only for a short time. His reasoning was that there was no chance of reconstituting large landed estates, or returning the mines, factories, and installations to private ownership; the economic power behind a Fascist regime would be missing. I thought Kovacs was right, although by then it was clear to me that some kind of dictatorship of the Right had been in the making, with Maleter at the helm. But I also believed that a Hungarian Fascist regime would not have been tolerated by the West and would not have been helped economically by the democracies. I had in mind the end of Mannerheim's Fascism in Finland after the First World War which had to give way to a democratic regime because none of the Western powers, prominently America, would extend much-needed credit to Mannerheim's Finland. Something of that sort would have happened, I believe, if the Hungarians had established a terror regime.

On Friday, November 2nd, the day following my talk with Losonczi and Nagy, Kadar and Munnich disappeared. I heard about it late at night, and was told that the best guess was that the two had gone to Szolnok, where Soviet military headquarters was established. Rumors of an impending Soviet move were spreading all over the city, and the American Legation sent off a convoy of legation dependents to Vienna.

For some reason which in retrospect I cannot explain, I did not believe that the Soviets would return and crush the revolution. However grievous they may have considered the loss of Hungary, I could not imagine that they would commit such stupidity after their experiences with their earlier effort to stop the Hungarian Revolution. Despite mounting signs, I still could not bring myself to believe that such a raw rape of a nation was in the making. Even if I were willing to disregard every consideration but the great damage to the Soviet Union which such a move would bring, it seemed to me that they would be coolheaded enough to balance the gains against the losses and make the best of the situation. There was a chance until the very last that Soviet-Hungarian relations would remain friendly even after Nagy's denunciation of the Warsaw Pact—if tempers were held in check.

I was awakened by heavy cannonading at dawn, Sunday, November 4th, and stared at the ring of fire surrounding the city with an amazed disbelief that hundreds of thousands of others shared. Angry flashes of yellow and red flames encircled Budapest. The fifth phase of the Hungarian Revolution was beginning.

The city was quickly occupied, and thousands of tanks, armored cars, and troop transports raced to their predetermined posts. By 9:00 A.M. a heavy steel vise held every section of the city, and it seemed that the occupation was so complete that all resistance would be futile from a military standpoint. But the Hungarians were not military experts. They were an outraged people possessed by an anger beyond reason and logic. They were quiet now; their hate was so deep in them that they became curt and solemn. There were no speeches or rallies—everyone was his own commander and his own armed force. If a few met together they joined. But, alone or in groups, all those who had weapons were out hunting Russians.

Soon after the cannonading announced the return of Soviet troops, Imre Nagy recorded a call to arms and ordered the Hungarian Army to resist. The radio, until silenced, poured out poignant calls for help to save the revolution. Writers, intellectuals, students, workers, and all those who had started the rebellion sprang into action to save it. Of course, the revolution was beyond saving; the problem which confronted the Hungarians now was: how to kill more Russians. In reality very few with whom I maintained contact during subsequent days cared anything about political, social, or economic programs for the future. All they were interested in was

164

how to get hold of more guns, how to fight more effectively without the slightest hope of achieving anything.

This was the period when Westerners were bitterly berated for not sending arms and troops. The argument of whether to send arms to Hungary flared up during those days and has been debated ever since. The whole question was argued on the wrong premise: the West could not have sent arms even if the West had wanted to, because of Austrian neutrality. The Soviet Union would have been entitled to reoccupy Austria the moment her territory or air space was used for military action hostile to the Soviet Union. Neither air-drop nor overland delivery of arms was possible under the circumstances, and Soviet forces were concentrated in western Hungary for just such an eventuality.

During the subsequent days the Soviet Army nearly reduced Budapest to its 1945 state, when 70 per cent of the houses in the city were destroyed or damaged during the battle between the German-Hungarian forces and the Red Army. Now the house-for-a-bullet policy was adopted, which meant that if a sniper bullet was fired from any building the whole building was razed. Soviet tanks roared up and down the avenues, boulevards, streets, and squares blowing gaping holes in buildings and making them uninhabitable. It was a grim policy which in one week's time turned the city into a shambles. The battle, or whatever it may be called technically, lasted for five days, and for several days thereafter isolated pockets of resistance continued, withering away slowly and finally dying out altogether.

The week following the Russians' return had been a busy one for me. On the morning of November 4th, all American newsmen moved to the legation, where we were given a large room on the main floor in which to make ourselves at home. And that was what we did. The room was for about thirty of us—our study, bedroom, and office, with a few blankets spread around to make life easier. Miraculously, the telephone system of Budapest worked throughout the siege, and we were able to make contacts.

With the permission of the legation officials, I called the Soviet Embassy to protest in the name of the American press corps our enforced idleness and to demand safe conduct out of Budapest. My first contact was Press Attaché Fishoff of the Soviet Embassy, a courteous and unfailingly punctual man who did his best for us. Through Fishoff, I got myself involved with a number of Russian civilian and army officers and received one night an offer of a special Soviet tank convoy through the center of the city.

On the second day of the siege, Mr. Andropov, the Soviet ambassador, assured me that there was no reason why we should not leave Budapest, and said that he would telephone immediately to the commandant of the city, General K. Grebennyik, and arrange the matter. I drove to the Soviet military command and met Colonel Kuznyinyov, the chief of staff. From that day until November 10th, when I finally left Budapest, I was in daily contact with the Russians. From the first I adopted the attrition method of dealing with them. I reasoned that if I wore them down, kept after them, and followed their instructions, sooner or later they would run out of excuses and alibis, and would either let us go or assume responsibility for keeping us there.

This led to a great many amusing incidents, and one that was not humorous. One day the commandant blandly assured me that the Soviet forces holding the Margaret Bridge had orders to let me through. I drove to the bridge and was immediately surrounded by Mongol soldiers brandishing Tommy guns. I drove back to the commandant. "Sorry, sir," I said, "you were mistaken." The commandant grabbed the phone, and after some embarrassed discussion with someone at the bridge he said that he was sorry but there was some mistake. "Would you like to give me a piece of paper with an order to let our convoy through so that there should be no mistakes?" I asked. Well, he thought that might be possible, and after much hemming and hawing he unearthed a tank corps major to write out the pass. The major and I had had several earlier talks, and either he knew that I was to be given a runaround or he really did not know what to do. He required two full hours to write five lines on a sheet of paper. In the meantime, the hour of curfew had passed, and outside everything was ominously dark. The major reread his masterpiece several times until at last he was satisfied that it said, "This convoy of International Newspapermen shall be permitted to pass through Budapest." Then he thought of a problem: He had no jurisdiction outside Budapest, and what would happen to us once we left the city? I assured him that we would take care of ourselves. This gave him another hour of deep worry. Finally, he roused himself and began to look for the seal.

There was no seal. He sent two orderlies for it. It could not be found. Then someone thought that the seal was somewhere else. There on the desk was the coveted paper, but it was useless without the seal of the command. By this time it was three hours beyond the curfew, which in those days read: "Everything moving between 6:00 P.M. and 6:00 A.M. shall be fired upon without challenge."

The major was desolate. There was nothing for me to do, he said, but come back in the morning. By then the commandant and Colonel Kuznyinyov had left, and I could not appeal to them.

A discussion began as to how I was to drive back to the legation. The major assured me that there was nothing to worry about. On cue, all hell broke loose outside the building. Machine guns began to chatter, intermingled with the booming of tank cannons. The major and I looked at each other, grinning.

After a while the firing stopped, and the major said that he would provide two tanks to escort my car, one ahead and one behind me. This, I told him, would be an engraved invitation for the rebels to spray my car, regardless of the Stars and Stripes I had on my radio antenna, which could not have been seen in the dark in any event. There was nothing to do but risk it.

Not unlike the Ford worker who was said to have been trained to employ all his limbs, and more, simultaneously, I drove through the city at the rate of five miles an hour. My right hand was on the steering wheel, while my left held a flashlight outside the window playing on the flag; my right foot was on the gas and my left kept the blinker going without interruption. I kept to the middle of the road everywhere and selected the widest avenues. All the roads were heavily blanketed with broken window glass crossed by sharp cables. On both sides of the streets fires were burning where Russian soldiers were warming themselves. In some places, where once a café or a large store had stood, camp fires were burning inside the buildings. To make sure that my flag was recognized I had fastened a wire on its loose end to spread it out fully.

It must have been an astonishing sight for the Russians to see a car creeping along with the American flag lit up in the beam of my flashlight. At any rate, it worked. Only once did I hear shots, just as I crossed Octogone Square, but I did not stop to find out who was shooting at whom. The marine on duty at the legation gate was a surprised young man when I dashed in and gave him a big hug.

Needless to say, the Soviet command had another story for me the following day. "You see," the colonel said, "we have no right to give you a pass; the Hungarians must give you one. We are here merely at their request as an auxiliary police force. The Hungarians rule the country."

I solemnly took his word and drove to the Hungarian Foreign Office, knowing full well what the answer would be. Several hours later I returned to report to the colonel that there was no Hungarian government anywhere around, that the Foreign Office was closed, and that the offices of the cabinet at the Parliament were deserted. This gave the colonel another chance to invent a story. He chose a bad one. "You should see," he said with a smile, "the Soviet ambassador." I told him that the ambassador had sent me to General Grebennyik in the first place, and would he like to check by calling him?

This went on for five days. Finally I persuaded a Hungarian official to issue for us passes in Hungarian and Russian which I could take to the Soviet command for their approval.

This again led to a revealing encounter. The Foreign Office, which finally opened for limited business on the fifth day, assigned to me a young attaché named Metzner, who was to accompany me to the Soviet Command with the passes. There no one wanted to speak to him. I kept urging him: "But they told me that the Hungarian government exercises authority over the country and that you are representing an authority which they acknowledge to have power over them."

Metzner looked at me as though I were crazy, and said, "Are you joking?"

But there we were. We had Hungarian passes, and all they had to do was to put their seal on them. Again they invented all kinds of stories, but for two days I kept after them. They said that the Hungarian pass was enough. So I drove to a check point and was sent back. "No," I reported, "it isn't enough."

At that point I sneaked out of Budapest, and the rest of the press corps did have their passes validated on the following day by the

Russians. My pass was without the Soviet seal when I left Budapest.

During the many hours I spent with Soviet Army men, we discussed their role in Hungary. I asked a colonel in command of the armored cars: Why the senseless destruction of the city? Why the cruel and often seemingly sadistic behavior of the troops? I recounted to him how on that very morning I stood in line just before the curfew was lifted with several hundred people waiting outside a bakery. Six tanks raced through the streets shooting with their machine guns just above our heads while screaming and cursing Hungarians threw themselves on the ground. Was all this necessary?

The colonel agreed that what was happening in Budapest was unusual. "But you must understand our side," he said, and continued: "We were ordered to restore peace here and disarm the troublemakers, who are, after all, only prolonging their agony. I and my men did not come here to die as heroes. We don't want people to shoot at us, but they do shoot. In an ordinary war I know who is the enemy. I recognize his uniform, and I know how he would behave under given conditions. But there are no rules here. Everyone is an enemy. I have no way of knowing who would or would not throw a grenade at my men, so we spray the roads ahead of us to scare people off the streets and keep their windows closed.

"As for the order to destroy any building where a sniper may be hiding," he explained, "that became a necessity too. We used to send patrols up in buildings from which snipers fired at us. But, more often than not, the patrols were thrown through the windows from the upper floors. So we don't send them in any more. We make sure that the building comes down with the sniper."

The colonel readily admitted that the Soviet command had to replace its regular garrison in Hungary because of severe breaches of discipline. What he meant was that some Russian soldiers had changed into civilian clothes and joined Hungarian revolutionary bands.

The major, who had begun to accept me as a permanent fixture, told me the dates of their departure for Hungary. He and his tank group had crossed into Hungary from Romania on the 21st of October, with orders to dawdle along the road to Budapest until further orders were given to enter the city. This led us to the speculation that perhaps the whole revolution—that is, the shooting part of it—was deliberately provoked by Erno Gero to wipe out discontented elements. The major, who was obviously familiar with the inner working of the Soviet system, thought this was possible, althought he believed that the Red Army had been against entering the Hungarian fray from the beginning, and that only after the grievous insults which the Hungarians had heaped upon them was there any enthusiasm shown in Red Army circles for the task of subduing the rebels.

Apparently, from what I was able to learn, the Soviet militarists made the same mistake militarists the world over are apt to make: compute the logistics of a siege but neglect to calculate the x factor, the reaction of the human beings they have set out to conquer. Budapest was so thoroughly occupied that it seemed impossible to make a move without running into heavy Soviet fire; nevertheless, the Hungarians somehow managed to destroy during the first few days of the second Russian intervention 120 combat vehicles, including seventy tanks.

An incident which had its beginning at dawn on November 4th illustrates the quality and determination of the rebels. The Ferihegy airport was guarded by a regiment of Hungarian artillerymen, when Soviet troops suddenly swooped down and disarmed it. After the artillerymen surrendered their arms, they were turned loose. Without prearranged plan, they all went up to the Castle Hill where they obtained new weapons and entrenched themselves. Four days later, Cardinal Mindszenty and I were watching Soviet artillery pounding Castle Hill, where the artillerymen were still fighting. The cardinal's residence was near a spot from which black smoke curled. A dearly-beloved old couple, friends of mine, were hiding in a cellar of a building which, we guessed, was also close to the fire. I told the cardinal about their kindness, undaunted courage throughout the years of adversity, and their unfailing faith in a better future. Mindszenty prayed for them at the window and blessed my old friends whom he had never seen, even though I told him they were Protestants.

My dealing with Cardinal Mindszenty was another subject of protest by the Hungarian government to the American government, and I have seen a number of references in the world press and in

Hungarian publications to myself and to the cardinal. The truth was that I tried to help the cardinal, who was a free man as far as I knew. He was not a part of the "counterrevolution," which the present regime in Hungary claims to have destroyed; he had no political ambitions; he did not want to lead a crusade; and at the time the Russians returned he was exerting himself to calm the Hungarians, and asking them for a quick restoration of order. I was not unmindful that Cardinal Mindszenty's name had been used by elements with which the cardinal had no connection and that there was a movement afoot to install him as regent of Hungary, but the cardinal did not know about these things. I know that Mindszenty was seriously trying to find a way to evolve a peaceful, democratic Hungary, though I also knew that he had rather reactionary political ideas which he accepted as a matter of expediency from people who possibly were not as politically naïve as Cardinal Mindszenty certainly was. Furthermore, I was aware that Pal Maleter was represented, for the cardinal's benefit, in glowing colors.

I have spent long hours discussing social and political problems with the cardinal. And having heard him with great sincerity expounding on the future of Hungary, I left him in Budapest with a genuine regret that so many of us, including myself, had misunderstood him so long. The man is a Catholic prince, a Hungarian patriot, and a great humanitarian who had been politically sinned against far more than he sinned himself. The Hungarian peasant in him is astonishingly gullible, unwilling to ascribe unworthy motives to men who carry historic names. But beyond all this, he was trying his ineffective best to pour oil on troubled Hungarian waters; had he been politically counseled, I believe he would have taken the lead to stop any use of his name by groups of Fascist orientation.

I had not seen Mindszenty since 1946, although I had had many near misses during his years in prison. The Hungarian government, beginning with 1954, alternately agreed and then reneged on a promise to permit me to interview the cardinal in prison. I had had correspondence with and made personal pleas to the Hungarian government dozens of times, and in 1955 actually came so near to being permitted to see him that I had made an arrangement with NANA to prepare a special release on the interview. When he was brought to Budapest, on October 31st, I did not go to see him because I received a message from him saying that in a few days, when things would be calmer, he would have more time for me.

We met again during the early-morning hours on Sunday, November 4th. He arrived at the Parliament Building, which by then was surrounded by Soviet troops, in response to an urgent call from Imre Nagy. Whether the prime minister did send for him or he was called into a trap I was not able to learn, and the cardinal himself did not know.

During the days of Hungary's desperate resistance against Soviet troops, the cardinal and I met almost daily. The story he wanted to tell the world does not belong here because one day he may be able to tell it himself. I read his memoirs for two reasons: one, because he wanted me to read them in case he should never be able to tell his story, and, second, because he asked me to help market them. As Mindszenty explained, most of the Catholic schools were burned or plundered; the students needed textbooks and the teachers needed food. He did not want to use relief funds for starting up schools, and needed money from elsewhere to do it. "That is the only reason I am willing to bare myself," he said.

His secretary was Monsignor Dr. Egon Turchanyi, who was dragged out of my car by AVH men while we were on our way to the border on November 10th, and who is now serving a life sentence in a Hungarian prison. Arrested at the same time, I was turned over to the Soviet NKVD, but next day, by a margin of a few minutes, I managed to cross the Austrian border.

If the Kadar regime had not been so grimly devoted to the profitless pursuance of non-existent Western conspirators, Monsignor Dr. Turchanyi might have had a chance. For our trip was innocent enough. Before I agreed to take Dr. Turchanyi with me, I consulted the Hungarian Foreign Office and told them that the Austrian Caritas, a Catholic welfare organization devoted to collecting relief supplies (mostly expensive medicines) for the Hungarians, had asked that a responsible Catholic official take charge of the next shipment of antitetanus serum at the border because several earlier shipments had been stolen. Monsignor Dr. Turchanyi, a white-haired, elderly man, was selected to go because, as the cardinal ruefully said, "Not having anything to do these days, I can get along without a secretary."

I had agreed to take him, provided I was shown the documents relating to the trip. Dr. Turchanyi showed me his orders from two leading hospitals in Budapest and the note from Caritas. It so happened that my efforts to arrange safe conduct for the press corps came to a head at that time, and the Hungarian Foreign Office agreed to accept a list from me. I included Monsignor Dr. Albert Egon Turchanyi on that list. More than that, whenever I discussed the list with officials I called their attention to him to make sure that they understood that I was not trying to slip something over on them. On the 10th of November, when I became fed up with Soviet tactics and wanted to get out at all costs, I told Monsignor Turchanyi that I was leaving, though without a valid permit, and that I had a rendezvous with John MacCormac and Seymour Freidin on the square facing the American Legation.

Monsignor Turchanyi insisted that he wanted to accompany me. I pointed out that we would be taking great risks and that, being an American, I had a better chance of escaping than he, a Hungarian. I tried to picture the eventualities, but he appeared to think that I was worried about myself being caught with him. I assured him that if he wanted to come I would take him, and he silenced me with, "If you are afraid to take me I will stay, but if you let me take a chance with you, I'll go."

We waited in vain for MacCormac and Freidin. I wanted to reach the border before dark, so we drove off shortly after 2:00 P.M.

We successfully negotiated a number of Soviet and Hungarian check points with my unstamped pass. Then, where the main road to Vienna forks into the road leading to Tatabanya, it happened.

If I were a novelist trying to dramatize two coarse, grim, brutal-faced AVH men I could not do justice to the two who stopped my car. At earlier check points I had asked Monsignor Turchanyi not to talk or ask any questions. He was inclined to engage everyone in a conversation, somewhat incautiously, regarding the Hungarian tragedy.

Because the men were in civilian clothes, I asked them whom they were representing: the government, the rebels, or the Soviet authorities. One of them replied, "We are Hungarians." This sounded nationalistic enough to Monsignor Turchanyi, and he exclaimed, relieved, "Thanks to the God of the Hungarians!" The AVH men ripped open the car doors and dragged Monsignor Turchanyi out. I protested, and told them that I was taking him to the border to receive much-needed serum and that hundreds of people were in danger of dying in Budapest from lack of necessary medicines. Just as Monsignor Turchanyi hit the pavement, he was seized by a heart attack. The two AVH men lifted him up by his shoulders and legs and threw him on a truck parked across the road. Then one of them got into my car and delivered me to a Soviet major a few hundred yards up the road.

The Soviet encampment consisted of a number of tanks, anti-aircraft units, and troops. The major was in command, and he had me surrounded by Mongolian soldiers. I was ordered to open all my luggage, and the car was nearly ripped apart. I don't know what they were searching for, but since nothing was taken from me except my passport and identification papers I guessed that they were after weapons. It was bitterly cold, and after sunset I had to start the engine to keep the heater going. They held me there four hours. Then a bit of luck came my way. The AVH men stopped two more foreign cars, and later three additional cars were intercepted. As long as I was alone, things did not look so well, especially if the AVH had discovered who Monsignor Turchanyi really was, for his papers merely read, "Dr. Albert Egon Turchanyi." Now, with other newspapermen around me, I felt safer. It was pitch dark by the time a convoy was organized. With a tank preceding and another following us, we were escorted to the barracks at Tatabanya, headquarters of the district NKVD. The others were told that after identification they would be released, but nothing was said to me. Just as soon as we were herded into a large room I saw two prominent newspapermen, the correspondent of the Italian communist newspaper *L'Unita* and the secretary general of the Italian Socialist party, Matteo Matteotti, correspondent for a number of Italian magazines. In a loud voice I addressed Matteotti: "My dear colleague, I am being held here and my papers have been taken away from me. Would you be good enough to file for me at Radio

Austria?" and handed over a number of stories, including my interview with Cardinal Mindszenty.

The NKVD colonel who heard and saw was upset. He realized immediately that I was building a back fire under him by asking Matteotti to give the alarm in Vienna. He quickly went through the examination of the others but did not speak to me. Addressing Matteotti the colonel said: "Hungarian roads are still not safe after dark and you may run into an ambush of gangsters. I would like you all to accept my hospitality for dinner and an overnight stay. Of course, you would be free to leave as early as you like in the morning."

Matteotti and the others who knew of my detention were not fooled. They knew that the colonel wanted time with me and wanted to consult higher Soviet authorities. I gathered during the night that he did actually talk several times to Ambassador Andropov, the Soviet commander in Budapest, and his own superiors in Moscow. When the others left for dinner my examination began. From the first question it was clear that the colonel knew who my companion was. I wanted to keep the story simple; he wanted it complicated. "When he came to your car, from which side of the street did he come? What was the first thing he said?" and on and on, hundreds of insignificant questions. I knew the trick but was powerless to do anything about it. He wanted to collect so many conflicting details that it would be clear that our story was an invented one. "How many times did you see him before you left?" "What was said at each time?" The colonel even wanted to know whether Monsignor Turchanyi was shaven each time I saw him and what he was wearing. There too I was in trouble. Because Turchanyi did not have any clothes but his clerical garb, on the road I had taken off my sweater and my overcoat and he had put them on. He was twice my size, but that did not matter, since most Hungarians were wearing castoffs. I had no way of knowing what Turchanyi was answering to all these questions—if he were able to answer them—and I had a feeling that we would be held on some kind of conspiracy charge. The only hope was that somehow he would manage to avoid answering questions. If his heart attack was a serious one, he might not be in condition to talk.

Around two in the morning I heard screams of pain from the cellar of the building in which I was held. Whether it was Monsignor Turchanyi I did not know, and still do not. I was numb with cold. I had nothing on but a shirt, a pair of trousers, and a jacket, and the night was one of the coldest I had ever experienced. The colonel went to his quarters around three, and I was led to an empty room, which I guessed was part of the dispensary. A Soviet guard was stationed at my door. Sleep was out of the question. Alternately stamping my feet on the floor to keep my blood circulating and trying to curl into a tight knot to keep my limbs warm, I awaited the dawn.

It must have been before six when I heard doors opening in the corridor and the voices of the other newsmen who had spent the night there. A lieutenant came to collect us, returning passports and travel passes to all of them. But he gave me only my passport. Matteotti quickly told me that meant the colonel wanted to send me on without a pass so that other Soviet guards would arrest me along the way. He drove a Fiat, and I had a powerful Sunbeam Talbot. I could make 160 to 200 kilometers an hour but he could not. So we quickly agreed that I would keep behind him and he would get the most out of his car. Then, just as we drove off, I had another lucky break. There were two English students with us who had been trapped in Budapest, and when I had made up the list for the safe-conduct passes I included them. I asked them whether they still had their passes. They did. So I got them into my car and took from one of them his pass. Then I stepped on the gas.

We sailed through several Soviet check points while I waved my borrowed pass at them. The boys in the car remained silent. At Gyor we were flagged by a civilian who told me that several American and English correspondents were interned at the hotel and that the Soviet commandant would not let anyone through. He brought a message from the newsmen for me to go and see them. I told the man that I could not stop but that I would wait if he would run to them and get me their names. A few agonizing minutes later he came back with two handwritten appeals, one addressed to the American Embassy in Vienna and the other to the British ambassador. I delivered them by phone an hour later.

I grabbed the papers and drove on. I felt that if the colonel had expected me to be arrested away from the prying eyes of other newsmen, I must be out of Hungary within minutes.

The automobile performed magnificently. I crossed the two hundred kilometers of Hungary in an hour and a half, and this included several rolling stops to wave my pass at Soviet sentries. The technique was not to stop but to take it for granted that a mere whiff of the paper should be enough and to indicate with a lordly manner that anything else would be considered insolence.

It worked for me, but not for the unlucky Hungarian border guard. I cleared through in seconds because I saw a Soviet jeep driving fast toward us along the long, gently curving road between Hegyeshalom and the border. Just as I drove off into Austria the jeep arrived and several Soviet soldiers under the command of a lieutenant went to the guardhouse to check the book in which automobile license numbers are registered. Half an hour later, in Austria, I learned that the border guard had been arrested for letting me through.

The reason I tell the story of Monsignor Turchanyi in such detail is that the aftermath of our trip brought grievous harm to him, and my story may, even at this late date, induce the Hungarian government to reconsider his sentence. A few days later in Vienna I met Freidin and MacCormac, who knew that I had left Budapest with Turchanyi and that I had arrived in Austria without him. They wanted to know what had happened.

I described our unlucky trip, and the three of us agreed not to send the story to our papers because it might expose Monsignor Turchanyi, if he were still alive—I did not know the outcome of his heart attack—to Hungarian wrath. A few days later, early one morning in New York, I was listening to a newscaster reading a story datelined Budapest, telling of the arrest of Monsignor Egon Turchanyi, secretary to Cardinal Mindszenty, in the company of an American newspaperman and saying that Turchanyi was trying to escape while carrying important messages to Cardinal Spellman of New York and others. I called the U.P., whose story it was, and they read me the text of the entire release. It could not have been worse. The same irresponsible agency reporter who sent out the story of the fake American hand grenades had sent this one too.

And, except for the fact that Turchanyi had been arrested, the rest was sheer embroidery. Now the Hungarian prosecutors could point to an American report to prove that the unlucky Turchanyi was a secret messenger, a conspirator, and heaven knows what else. The truth, despite the news report, was that Turchanyi did not carry any kind of message for anyone. I did. Before I left Budapest, Cardinal Mindszenty handed four documents to me and asked me to read them. One was a message to President Dwight D. Eisenhower in Washington; one was for Archbishop König in Vienna, asking him to put his apostolic seal on the documents inasmuch as Cardinal Mindszenty's own seal was out of reach; another was addressed to Father Jozsef Vecsey, asking him not to undertake anything concerning Cardinal Mindszenty's memoirs or anything else without first consulting with Monsignor Turchanyi; and the fourth was a power of attorney for Monsignor Albert Egon Turchanyi empowering him to act in all matters for the cardinal. This last document was to be left with Archbishop König, who was asked to keep in touch with Turchanyi by phone or by mail. There was no written message for Cardinal Spellman, but I had an oral one for him, which, owing to circumstances, I could not deliver. He was in Korea at the time of my arrival in New York.

Cardinal Mindszenty wanted me to read these documents to assure me that they did not contain anything compromising. He also asked me to undertake negotiations concerning his memoirs, get in touch with Turchanyi in Budapest or anywhere else he might be, or, if I were unable to do that, to use my best judgment, provided I would honor his previously made promise to an American newsman that all syndicates and news organizations who might be interested in the manuscript would be given a chance to bid.

During the time I was held on the highway I destroyed these documents, except the one addressed to President Eisenhower. My reason was that if the papers were found on me, Turchanyi would be exposed immediately as Cardinal Mindszenty's secretary, even though he had a legitimate reason for going to the border. It may be argued that surely Monsignor Turchanyi would have escaped across the border if he had a chance. I had no opinion on this, because I was sure that he wanted to get the antitetanus serum to Budapest and if he had any thoughts about escaping he kept them to himself. But I was also sure that if he had entertained such thoughts he would have tried to escape only after he had returned to Budapest with the medicines. I do know that both the cardinal and his secretary spoke eagerly about visiting His Holiness the Pope, but my impression was that they intended to go to Rome as representatives from Hungary rather than as refugees.

I offered to return to Hungary to testify on behalf of Turchanyi if he were to be put on trial, but Foreign Minister Imre Horvath, who was in New York at that time, declined my offer.

This, in brief, was the story which was embroidered by the Hungarians until it became a sinister Western conspiracy involving furtive agents, a Machiavellian journalist-diplomat (that was supposed to be me), the Vatican, Wall Street warmongers and their agent, Cardinal Spellman. Poor Monsignor Turchanyi, who had pieced together a living during the years of Communism in Hungary by writing fairy tales for children and making toys for them, with all his talents for fairy tales could not have invented a more ironic one. His only concern was to get some sorely needed serum to the desperately ill, but he received a life sentence as recompense. The AVH and the NKVD were out gunning for scapegoats to justify what they were doing to Hungary, and the three of us—Cardinal Mindszenty, Turchanyi, and myself—were too good a chance for them to miss.

Until our departure from Budapest, Hungarian police power was restricted to a few uniformed city policemen whose main concern was to keep out of the way of Soviet patrols. Fear gripped the people, although arrests, except of those with firearms, were few. The crusade for revenge had not yet begun, partly because it was unsafe for the AVH to circulate among the people and partly because Kadar during the first days of his rule believed that he could win over the revolutionaries. He envisaged a coalition government to include Imre Nagy and some of his associates, among them Bela Kovacs, leader of the Small Holders; withal, however, a basically Communist-dominated cabinet. To Kadar it was clear that the Rakosi-Stalin type of Communism had to go; and whether he believed himself capable of evolving a new one or was ordered to do so by the Red Army, he ended by surpassing Rakosi and instituting a terror of which Stalin in his heyday would have been proud.

In the interest of historic justice, it must also be pointed out that Kadar was forced to retreat from this program step by step because of the people's fanatical hatred for all those who had anything to do with the return of the Soviet Army. They would not stand still long enough for Kadar to talk to them, let alone to win their confidence. The Soviet Union could have sent two chickens for every Hungarian pot—as they nearly did—and it would not have been enough to make a small dent in the accumulated hatred of the people toward the Soviets. The inhabitants of Budapest had never been so well fed as during the first weeks and months of Kadar's regime. From all Communist countries food poured in, and the Soviet Union sent large-scale help in materials and tools to repair the damages caused by their tanks; still the Hungarians would not accept Janos Kadar. First reluctantly, and then with increased vindictiveness, Kadar began to press the strikers and the still-intact Workers' Councils.

Perhaps Kadar became personally resentful of the people's doubts of his integrity and honesty. He made speeches, gave promises in line with the original revolutionary demands, all to no result. Kadar obviously did not understand the true state of the Hungarian mind; he was trying to deal with problems which no longer existed. True, a scant few days earlier those problems were important, but Kadar did not realize that history had outstripped the calendar by a ratio of a thousand to one.

The first leaflet issued by the Kadar regime is before me as I write. It is itself a historic relic, a memento of a long-gone era which existed only briefly, to be buried by a cataclysmic earthquake. It reads in part: "Young Workers! Students! Universities! WHAT DO YOU WANT? The return of the White Terror of 1919? The downfall of the workers' rule? The restoration of capitalists and landlords in power? No! YOU DO NOT WANT THIS! For an independent, free Hungary, for the prevention of the return of the Gero-Rakosi clique, for a democratic evolution, for the discontinuance of the old erroneous political economy, for the freedom of the people, for its welfare—you rose in battle. WE, TOO, WANT THESE! That is why now you must stand by the revolutionary worker-peasant government, the government of Janos Kadar!"

The Soviet authorities, too, tried to join the Hungarian Revolution, only to be met with derision and disgust. The first leaflet issued by the Soviet command was full of praise for Hungarian effort to do away with the old misrule and establish an honest, just, and prosperous state. It said that the Soviet Army was there merely to help them to gain these ends. It promised cooperation and large-scale help, liberally spiced with protestations of love for the Hungarian people. The second one was more to the point. It asked Hungarian cooperation against White terrorists, bandits, Western agents, and the like. It reminded me of the young freedom fighter who, thirsty and exhausted, appeared at a rear door of a restaurant where I happened to be, asking for a drink. Because the water was turned off, the manager gave him a glass of raspberry soda. The young man offered to pay, but the manager refused it, whereupon the youngster, shouldering his rifle, placed the money on the table and said: "This came from a worker of Csepel, the kind of capitalistic bandit the radio is talking about."

The third proclamation, issued by General Grebennyik, minced no words. "I order . . . I command . . . I direct you . . . stern retaliation and martial law. . . ." It finally penetrated the Soviet mind that the Hungarians did not want them at any price, and from that day to this, naked terror rules Hungary.

If the Soviets did not realize that they were dealing with a world which they did not understand, neither did the West. We were still doing business on the old stand: The only good Communist was a dead Communist, and once a Communist always a Communist, and a Communist was something lower than the lowest devil in the Bible. Men and women who led the revolution, and later the resistance against the Soviets and Kadar, were all Communists; therefore we either had to promote them to the rank of "patriotic nationalists," a name the émigrés called themselves, or demote them to some kind of fakers who had fooled the Communist hierarchy successfully and so, hurrah for them! The American hallmark for a reformed Communist was the Chambers-Bentley-Crouch type of penitence. Any other kind of non-Communist Communist was incomprehensible, hence unacceptable.

But the incontrovertible fact was that not a single non-Communist participated in the organization and leadership of the revolution, and only a few non-Communists were prominent in the resistance which met Kadar and his Soviet mentors. Not crypto-Communists or fakers, but honest-to-goodness Communists who joined the party not for advancement and luxury, as so many did, but because they were sincere idealists and because they sought a just and humane world. The opportunists stayed away, awaiting the outcome of the struggle; the betrayed and outraged young men and women whose ideals the Communist hierarchy tried to destroy were those who moved from meeting halls to the streets and finally into hastily thrown-up barricades.

Surely they were Communists who went through it, and came out immune as a child after a bout with the measles. But they were not penitent; they did not think of themselves as sinners; and they were horrified at the idea the Americans had of them. To them, freedom meant to be free to become Communists or leave Communism behind, as their consciences dictated, and they contrasted bitterly the readiness with which ex-Nazis and ex-Fascists were embraced by the West with the treatment they themselves received from Western sources. "What do you want us to do," asked a bitter young woman, "appear before your un-American activities Committee and bare ourselves to be acceptable?"

America's problem in dealing with Hungarian events went deeper than that; the foundation of America's foreign and domestic policies received a jolt in Hungary. To admit that Communists could conceivably be fine human beings and that the intellectual leadership of the Communists, as distinguished from the bureaucratic leadership of the Communists, was made up of people devoted to ideals of freedom and humanism, even as we are, was to admit that American domestic encroachments on social, political, and economic freedoms in the name of anti-Communism, and the Western crusade for freedom against Communist enslavement in the world, rested on contrived moral grounds. We had to keep our devils black and our saints white at all costs, or President Eisenhower's fine words and Ambassador Lodge's gallant speeches would lose their impact. To say that a brutal, dictatorial oligarchy was holding in its relentless grip fine upstanding Communists whom we would like to help to regain their freedom would merely compound the existing moral and political confusion.

America wanted no Djilases and Aczels, whose spiritual qualities first led them toward Communism and later led them away from it, but Chamberses and Crouches, pillars of the American thesis of low-down bomb-throwing conspiracies, whose facile imaginations could fulfill nearly any kind of demand made on them.

But Djilas and Aczel are real, and there are many thousands of them involved in the struggle to break the inhuman chains with which theologians of Soviet Communism and its Apostolate are trying to hold in bondage man's innate decency and humaneness, while Chambers and Crouch are but infections on the Communist as well as on the democratic body. To understand this and say it nowadays amounts to heresy, yet there is no effective way for the West to deal with the Communist problem except through understanding it. During its short history Soviet Communism has shown that it cannot exist among free men and that the prerequisite to its existence is spiritual, political, and economic slavery; nevertheless, a large majority of its intellectual elite is still engaged in trying to wrest the promises of Communism from those at its helm whose only interest is to exploit it. The kind of struggle which exists in the Christian West resembles that of the Communist East in that on both sides there are thousands who are willing to do battle for their faith until, as in Hungary, faith itself betrayed them. There it became clear to them that not only the men who led them were bad, but also that the elaborate theology with which the leaders tried to justify themselves and inspire their followers was false. Even so, finding their leaders cruel tyrants and their theology wanting did not alter the impulse which led them to Communism. On the contrary, their desire for a free, decent, and just society became sharper and more insistent.

That Communism brought about a great moral revulsion in Hungary and will bring about similar upheavals in other Communist countries is understandable, and, in my view, inevitable. The failure of the West throughout the revolution and during its aftermath, however, was not easy to understand and certainly was not inevitable. Was it symbolic that the envoy of neutral Austria was the only foreign representative in Budapest who responded to the demands of the revolution with humanity and gallantry? Dr.

Walther Peinsipp, the Austrian ambassador, was the Western hero during the revolution and the dark days of its suppression. He rode from hospitals to battle stations distributing food and medicine, was accessible at all times to Hungarians and to his own people who turned to him for help and advice. He defied Soviet restrictions on crossing forbidden areas on his missions, and kept his embassy open for refugees, while in other Western embassies and legations confusion and uncertainty reigned behind tightly locked doors.

The American Legation seemed to have exhausted itself by extending hospitality to Cardinal Mindszenty, and soon became frightened by its own generosity and tried to keep the cardinal under wraps. That was the extent of our tangible help to the Hungarians during the revolution and its aftermath. In view of our long-standing leadership of the free world and our strong advocacy of the rollback of the Soviets, added to our often declared intention to help people who wanted to free themselves, we presented an embarrassingly sorry sight to the Hungarians. Many of us cringed inwardly when Hungarians surrounded us eagerly, asking what we were doing to help them. Early one morning, after the reentry of the Russians, Seymour Freidin and I went around a market place to talk to people. We progressed slowly thoughout the empty streets, because Freidin had a sore foot and I was scouting ahead, taking placards off the walls for my collection. We got to a nearly bare, enclosed market where a number of Hungarians, some of whom spoke English, happily surrounded us. They were all glad to see us and asked questions eagerly. Freidin tried his best to explain our position but failed, for it sounded hollow even to him. He hobbled away, and we walked silently for several blocks toward the legation. Freidin is a great hulking man next to whom I look like a pygmy. After a while I stole a glance at his face and saw that he had tears in his eyes.

I have written and said many harsh words about our role in the Hungarian struggle, and some things I have written have been resented by the legation staff in Budapest. If I have singled out particular persons, I have meant only to illustrate the policy to which we were wedded, and not to castigate them personally. They and their wonderful wives who fed us, as well as we, their guests, were living together at the legation under great emotional stress.

With a calmer and longer view I can now see that they were overly secretive and uncertain because they were operating in an atmosphere which left little room for any one of them to use his own judgment and to respond to his own humane instincts. I am sorry if I have offended any of them.

13

Aftermath—The Failures of the West

When I arrived in Vienna on November 11th, the Hungarian struggle was over. But for many months thereafter the Hungarians at home and we in the West wrestled with the aftermath of the revolution.

First it seemed important for me to learn as much as I could of Western reaction to Hungarian events and then visit other Communist countries to evaluate the impact of the disintegration of Communism in Hungary. The first feverish forty-eight hours after my arrival in Vienna will always remain with me as the craziest I have ever lived through. First to arrive were the military intelligence people from the American and British embassies in response to the messages I relayed from the interned journalists at Gyor. In quick succession came Radio Free Europe representatives to renew the feud we had started two weeks earlier during my quick dash to Vienna; press associations; friends of friends; relatives of people I had never heard of; important and unimportant phone calls, while editors from America were asking how long I intended to sleep and how soon I could get to work. After my arrival it was five hours before I could bathe and shave, and not until days later was I able to take time out to buy an overcoat to replace the one I had left with Monsignor Turchanyi.

Refugees coming from Hungary soon became a problem of international proportions. Here was an issue that dramatically called the world's attention to Hungary's plight, although only a very small proportion of the refugees represented the revolutionaries and not more than 10 per cent were representative of Hungary as a nation. The rest were opportunists who came out to seek their fortunes elsewhere, posing as freedom fighters. Ambitious scientists, workers, and peasants made up half of this group, and the other half consisted of juvenile delinquents, hoodlums, escaped convicts, prostitutes and ne'er-do-wells. A knowledgeable Hungarian journalist, who also escaped, told me that within one week he met in the hotels and cafés of Vienna all the prostitutes the AVH used in Budapest to spy on foreigners.

Here was another dilemma for the West. To explain that a large proportion of the heroic freedom fighters who made such good copy in the world press were scum, and to refuse them, would have created an impossible situation. There was nothing for the West to do but to accept them and cover up the ugly picture visible below the surface.

The real harm of the refugees was in their attempt to palm themselves off with fantastic yarns which distorted events in Hungary and made all the harder the task of evaluating them. There is a good deal of acting ability in the Hungarian make-up, and this led inexperienced Western investigators into difficult situations. The Hungarian refugees were not slow in exploiting the halo around their heads. The extraordinary thing was that the leftover refugees in Vienna, after the West absorbed nearly four-fifths of the two hundred thousand, had more genuine freedom fighters among them than there were among those who were accepted for immigration during the first months of the exodus.

Another aspect of the refugee problem was the large number of abandoned children in Hungary. Thousands of mothers and fathers swapped mates and walked out on their children to begin a new life in the West. Soon "bird dogs" of white slavers appeared in Vienna and, with the help of Hungarian pimps, began to recruit single girls. By the time I got around to investigating the situation in March, 1957, a Viennese police inspector estimated that over five thousand Hungarian girls had been shipped out to become voluntary or involuntary prostitutes in houses from Dakar to Tokyo.

With every passing day the moral issues that earlier had shone crystal clear became confused in Vienna. While European countries went about the refugee problems with traditional simplicity and humanity, American countries north and south (with the notable and praiseworthy exception of Canada) lost themselves in endless complications, maneuvering, and political byplay. Naturally, everyone looked expectantly toward Washington. Weeks passed, and it appeared that the United States wanted no part of leadership. Not until Vice President Nixon's well-photographed visit to Austrian refugee camps was any serious effort made to have America take part in the rescue. Subtly but effectively a change came over Vienna during the weeks of American hesitation, which became overt and pronounced when it became known that the United States proportionally would take a much smaller part in the work than any of the European countries. The record, as it stood in the spring of 1957, when large-scale relocation of refugees came to a halt, showed that Great Britain had accepted proportionally five times more refugees than the United States, France fifteen times more, Switzerland eighteen times, Germany ten times, Sweden, Norway, and Denmark eight to ten times more, Yugoslavia five times more, and Austria thirty-five times more than the United States.

There were curious sidelights to this situation. Most of those accepted by America were in the first October-November groups who fled from the revolution rather than from its suppression. While most of the countries, notably France, Britain, and Switzerland, simply accepted trainloads of them, they received proportionally a much higher caliber of refugees than did the United States, despite careful screening.

Three incidents involving American handling of refugees, among the many I investigated, show the ludicrousness of our approach.

Three sisters arrived in Vienna late in December. The eldest was a leader of the university group she belonged to, and counted as one of the inner core. Her younger sister, also a university student, performed courier service throughout the revolution; and the youngest was a high-school girl without much of a revolutionary background. The girls had always been close and devoted to each other. Registering for America involved a church affiliation or a pretended one. The three had had no religious education; their parents were freethinkers, and the girls were advised to "accept" a religious affiliation for the purpose of registering for American acceptance. (None of the other countries required religious affiliation in their refugee work.)

American officials claimed that the youngest needed parental consent and that they could not issue a visa until they could find the legal guardian appointed after the death of the girls' parents or until the girls applied to an Austrian court for appointment of a new guardian. (The Austrian courts declared themselves powerless in the matter.)

The girls would not be separated. I came upon the case in a Catholic hospital where the youngest was taken after the police rescued her from a gang of Hungarian "heroes" who hired out as bird dogs for white slavers. She was bleeding severely, and the doctors feared a hemorrhage. After two days of devoted nursing by the mother superior herself, the girl was saved.

The police supplied the rest of the story. The three girls had been ravished and the two older ones had disappeared—the police guessed into the net of the flourishing girl traders who came to Vienna to fill orders from houses for desirable Hungarian girls. The youngest was bleeding too badly and had been abandoned in a park when the police found her.

Another case involved a professor of engineering and his family. An American scientific body assigned to evaluate refugee scientists gave the professor the highest rating. In addition, the Freemasons interceded on his behalf because in Hungary he kept alive the proscribed organization by conducting meetings and helping fellow Masons. He was suspected in Hungary as a determined anti-Communist, and it would have been impossible for him to survive the harsh regime of the Hungarian Stalinists were it not for his wife.

His wife was a member of the Communist party. Her first husband having been executed by the Nazi-Nyilas government, she was informed after the liberation that she and the son born of her first marriage were assured of a state pension sufficient to provide for the son's education if she joined the party. When she met and married her present husband in 1948, her membership in the party was a convenient cover for his anti-Communist activities. I had known the couple and their three sturdy sons before the revolution.

In Vienna the professor received his American visa, and as he was leaving the office he tured to the consul and said: "I do not wish to sail under false colors, and certainly I do not wish to be sent back, so I tell you now that my wife was a member of the Communist party."

The official, as well as the professor's sponsors, assured him that that would not matter but that the case must be reinvestigated. Weeks passed, and no word from the American Consulate came to them. The Freemasons of Vienna and Switzerland offered to guarantee the man and his family. Nevertheless, his visa was withdrawn.

Curious as to the reason, I talked to the man who handled the case at the American Consulate. He insisted that no Communist could be permitted to enter the United States and that he was there "to protect our country from such enemies." I pointed out that she was not a Communist, whereupon I was told: "She could have left the party any time she wanted, but she did not."

The professor today is one of the most valuable members of the University of Vienna, and, if the official is to be believed, America is safe from contamination.

The third typical case was that of an army captain, his wife and their two intelligent, well-mannered children. The captain was a professional soldier, and when the Reds took the helm of Hungary in 1948 and the first series of purges was staged a number of his commanding officers were executed. He himself was cashiered. I first met the man walking behind the coffin of his rehabilitated superior officer, who was ceremoniously reburied in 1956.

In Vienna the captain went to the American Embassy where he was told that he had to register through a religious organization. The captain also had a former colleague, now a well-to-do Wisconsin manufacturer, as a sponsor. Everything went swimmingly until someone discovered that he was anti-West. This came about in the following manner:

Many refugee camps in and around Vienna were a mere half-notch above pigsties. The captain and his family were quartered at the Rothschild Spital, an abandoned structure formerly used by the Nazis as a torture camp for Jews and other unreliable persons. The place was filthy and, like many of the hastily opened refugee camps, was never intended to be used for human habitation. Moreover, refugees assigned to the camps were indiscriminately thrown together in halls and hallways, and the mixing of the sexes inevitably led to nightly bed hopping by many of the boys and girls who lived practically on top of each other. The commandant of the Rothschild Spital was a Swiss Red Cross official, a warmhearted, always helpful, intelligent man who had selected the captain as his aide.

The condition of the camps, the haphazard way their inmates were fed, and the obvious graft which went into the distribution of relief supplies moved the commandant to protest in various quarters. The Austrian authorities, who did their level best during those impossible weeks, were powerless to do more. Little Austria was not prepared for the sudden influx of over two hundred thousand guests; even if the guests had had money the situation would not have been much better, because there simply was not enough of anything needed to sustain so many people. Even so, the delay of promised financial help from Western countries handicapped the Austrian government in its superhuman effort to alleviate conditions.

Soon the Swiss commandant and his aide, the captain, became known as martinets and busybodies who interfered with the nightly orgies at the camp and became nuisances to the authorities by their endless protests. The Swiss commandant was sent home at the end of his temporary assignment, and the captain became the victim of indiscriminate stoolies. One of the more questionable practices of the American authorities was their employment of Hungarian stoolies, mostly unreliable and immoral practitioners of the art of denunciation. Both the Reds and the Americans imported their "security" measures to Austria to deal with the refugees. The Hungarian kaders, trash cans of unverified and often malicious gossip, were filled with reports from Red stoolies, and similar American files were collected by American authorities through glib-talking, oily "freedom fighters." Both the American- and Red-employed collectors cared nothing about human values, but were after political data at five dollars a day, gleaned through listening to conversations at camps and cafés.

The captain, who often cracked down on strutting "heroes" and chiseling panhandlers, fell victim to the system. After eight years of active opposition to the Reds in Hungary and eight years of miserable hiding in damp cellars and mansard cubicles to escape the wrath of the AVH, he was pronounced unreliable by the American security system.

One of the captain's exploits drew me into a scandal which the Austrians extinguished with great tact and persistence. A General Kovacs of the Dominican Republic showed up in Vienna and sent word to the camps that he was interested in agricultural workers and single females for emigration to the republic. He promised a family-size farm to the peasants and "brilliant opportunities" for the females. The list of volunteers grew. General Kovacs interrogated most of the volunteers in person, and it developed that he wanted illiterate workers and unattached personable young females, preferably without family or kin. Those in charge of the camps who knew something about Trujillo's Dominica became uneasy. They remonstrated with the Austrian Refugee Committee and asked them to interest themselves in the matter. The Austrians rightly pointed out that they had no authority over the refugees, since the committee was an advisory group; as for the government, it could not question the special envoy of a country which enjoyed friendly relations with Austria. What all the official statements amounted to was that the refugees were a people without a country, on their own, and that no authority existed to deal with their problems.

My captain challenged General Kovacs' statement that he was a former colonel of the Hungarian Hussars, an especially proud outfit of the old monarchy, and demanded that the general account for the Jewish refugees Trujillo accepted after the war. Kovacs brusquely rejected the captain's challenge and complained to the authorities. At this point the captain got in touch with me and told me about his misgivings and Kovacs' elusive promises and unsubstantiated statements.

I tried to interest several Austrian members of the committee, and one of them, a well known Viennese publisher, promised to expose the matter if the general appeared to be successful in his quest. In the meantime the captain and several other outraged refugees sent notices to all refugee camps to warn them against General Kovacs, and for a while it looked as if the scandal might break out in print. However, Kovacs suddenly left Vienna with nearly four hundred refugees, half of them meeting specifications: attractive, unattached females between the ages of eighteen and thirty.

One type of case where the Austrian authorities felt compelled to intervene was that of the repeated outbreaks of anti-Semitic violence, mostly in American transient camps. The Salzburg camp, which was used for refugees who were in possession of American visas and who were awaiting transportation, was repeatedly occupied by Austrian gendarmes at the request of American camp officials. That the anti-Semitic outbreaks occurred in American establishments was understandable on two scores. One was the fact that no Hungarian Leftist of any hue, whether he was part of the uprising or not, found favor with American authorities except those Stalinists who fled from the revolution with forged papers. The other was the atmosphere which Americans created about the Hungarian Revolution, labeling it a revolt of the Rightists.

Of course, American officials in Vienna trying to deal with the aftermath of the Hungarian Revolution were just as much the prisoners of the Washington security craze as were the State Department employees who all over the world isolated themselves from contemporary realities for fear of being contaminated. General Joe Swing, the Commissioner of Immigration, came personally to Vienna to be helpful. No greater contradiction could have been imagined than Joseph M. Swing, a typical high-minded, warmhearted American enmeshed in a maze of fears and suspicions. He believed, as did his subordinates, that reformed and rebelling Communists were a greater danger to the United States than the many delinquent pseudo heroes who managed to get their approval. As it subsequently developed, except for political reasons, none of the immoral, predatory people who arrived as refugees in the United States and ran afoul of American laws and mores were deportable.

There was one American activity during those days in Vienna which caused a great deal of comment and perhaps helped a good many young men and women. Partly as a denominational competition and partly to counter the widespread sexual excesses in camps, certain American religious denominations offered one thousand Austrian shillings ($40) to couples who wished to marry. Thousands did, some more than once; but undoubtedly many who took advantage of the offers found stability in marriage and a new start in life in a new home.

A memorable discussion I had with a group of refugees in Vienna revolved around the difference between the behavior of Austria and Switzerland, two really neutral nations, toward the refugees, in trying to be helpful, and that of the other Western countries affected by the cold war. The Swiss and the Austrians performed magnificently in a quiet, businesslike manner without pages of questionnaires or hired stoolies. The Austrians, particularly, were aware of the quality and composition of great masses of people streaming across the frontiers, but it did not seem to daunt them; human beings without food and shelter were the problem, and they applied themselves to it to the limit of their capacity.

The Swiss surprised me, since I knew how cramped their living space was and how carefully they had to dole out their facilities to the never-ending streams of refugees who for centuries had sought refuge in the protected peace of Switzerland. This time, however, the Swiss had no consideration except that of rescuing as many as they could transport across the border.

A Hungarian novelist said, "The thing that bothered us during the past weeks in Budapest, and now that we live among you, is this. We know that America and the West have been the beacons of our civilizations and that all we want and all we hope for is to be like you. But why, with all you know and with your great traditions, do you permit pygmies to distort your ideals and dictate such clumsy and harmful behavior? After all, we are merely trying to get where you are; therefore you have much more to lose than we from this unbelievable deterioration of values."

The novelist referred to the behavior of Western agencies trying to exploit the Hungarian Revolution. Long after that discussion, going over my notes, I found myself trying to gloss over that and many similar discussions. But there was no escaping them and the lesson they brought home.

Those who did play a significant part in the revolution were Communists and therefore unacceptable to America. The elite of the revolutionaries, largely because of American restrictions, went to London and Paris, and many of them remained in Vienna. Among them were a number of scientists, writers, professional people, and army officers. In one sense, all the refugees were legitimate: They were fed up with life in Hungary. However, the large majority of those who felt responsible for the revolution remained in Hungary to be able to defend and justify their actions, regardless of personal consequences. Time only will show whether Paloczi Horvath, Ignotus, Aczel, and others like them were right to escape, for they belonged to the intellectual elite of Hungary, and by associating themselves with the West they lost much of their former high standing in Hungary. The view of the West from Communist countries has undergone a great revision as a result of the Hungarian Revolution, for many of those Communists who looked toward the West and hoped for leadership were sorely disappointed. The disappointment did not arise from the inability of the West to help the Hungarians with arms, but from lack of comprehension of their problem, and the political and moral bankruptcy of Western anti-Communism. The seething and fermenting anti-Communist Communists realized during the weeks and months following the Hungarian Revolution that henceforth they must find their own way, and that instead of joining the main stream of Western political and social thinking they must create a pattern of their own. This pattern, as it evolved during my conversations with people in Yugoslavia, Czechoslovakia, and Poland, will very likely be the one that will operate within the Communist framework. Instead of revolution, the fight will be for reformism; instead of accepting Western ideas and Western leadership, the Communist dissidents will turn toward party leaders sympathetic to liberal Communist ideas. Thus the split between the East and the West deepened considerably as a result of Hungary. Before the revolution a large majority of the dissidents believed a good deal of the Western protestation of moral excellence, even though the subsidized émigrés manning Western propaganda outlets acted as brakes on their enthusiasm for the West. The discontented elements of Communism now realize, however, that the West is not interested in moral and humanistic issues, but only in tactical maneuvers in that suicidal race best known as the cold war.

Perhaps, on balance, the West lost more in Hungary and during the aftermath of the revolution than the Russians: Soviet practice, ideology, and leadership were already discredited at the outbreak of the revolution; but the West, despite reservations some of the revolutionary leaders had toward it, still was untested. The Russians merely added roughly 10 billion forints ($850 million at the official exchange) worth of material damage to Hungary: 2,217 totally destroyed apartment houses and multiple dwelling places, 21,000 severely damaged buildings, 3,000 destroyed shops and stores together with their machinery and inventory. As for casualties, a reliable figure has never been compiled, but my own guess is that the Hungarians had 3,000 dead and more than 10,000 wounded, largely as the result of indiscriminate shooting, while the Russian casualties were no more than a thousand dead and wounded.

I do not know how to relate material damage to moral values, but houses can be repaired and casualties converted to become national assets of tremendous moral significance on which generations thrive. Thus, a realistic estimate would show that the Soviets and their satellite henchmen sank lower than they were before the outbreak of the Hungarian Revolution in the eyes of their own people as well as in the estimation of neutral nations. Even though this is true, what really happened was that the captive people stiffened their backs, and now it will take longer and greater exertion for Soviet leaders to win them to their ways. But as long as the satellites remain captive audiences for Soviet propaganda, and if a more humane approach is employed in wooing them, it is possible for Soviet Communists to achieve a measure of success.

On the other hand, years of Western effort to win satellite peoples with promises of support toward a freer and more humane life went down in defeat solely because of the inability or un-willingness of the West to live up to its promises in a crisis. Thus, while the Soviets experienced a setback, the West lost nearly all of its standing and now must begin all over again. Better under-standing of the problems and a new approach to them are called for because the Hungarian Revolution underlined the bankruptcy of the cold war both as a tactical and as a moral weapon. If the Hungarian Revolution was an eloquent and irrefutable proof of the inhumanity of the Soviet brand of cold war technique, it also presented a humiliatingly shoddy and futile image of the Western version.

It would have been far better if the Western propaganda radios had been manned by the moral and intellectual leaders of the West during the Hungarian affair than by the experts of Radio Free Europe, Voice of America, NTS, and others. Instead of advanced Western ideas which would have left a deep imprint on Hungarians as well as on Communists of other nations, the West beamed trick political speeches toward them which were quickly discovered to be spurious. This in itself was a major contribution toward the suppression of the Hungarian revolt. The suppression of a revolution fought for human values and political decency would have been far harder for the Soviets than the one which Western propaganda covered with increasingly intransigent nationalistic overtones. An inspiring revolution was fought and won on moral grounds, and to overturn it the Soviets would have been hard put to find an acceptable excuse to place before world opinion. The West and people intoxicated by Western words urging heroism and gallantry—when gallantry should have expressed itself in magnanimity toward the erstwhile foe, and heroism in patience and restraint—were to a very large degree responsible for the destruction of the Hungarian revolt. The height of political amorality was reached when the world press reported, and it was duly transmitted to Hungary, that Republican "truth squads" in America, electioneering for Eisenhower, asserted that Eisenhower's policies were responsible for the Hungarian Revolution. What was the West trying to prove: that the Hungarian intellectuals and students were engaged in carrying out Eisenhower's policies? If that was the idea it succeeded, for it was readily accepted by the Soviets and used as an excuse to crush the revolution and to hang some of the finest people Hungary ever produced. Even though they may one day be rehabilitated and ceremoniously reburied, it is doubtful that the West will have anything to do with it.

Nearly a year before the Hungarian Revolution I suggested to my editor that we run a series of articles on Western anti-Communist propaganda institutions such as Radio Free Europe and the Voice of America. I had accumulated a good deal of material which indicated that, unknown to the American people, our propaganda was misleading and harmful. Pressure of other events, however, prevented the project from being carried out, but the notes were with me in Hungary when the revolution broke.

Earlier in this book I tried to indicate the tremendous damage caused by RFE and others in falsely accusing Imre Nagy of having brought in the Russians to suppress the revolt. During my quick dash to Vienna on Sunday, October 28th, two men from RFE, both named Koch, came to my hotel to discuss the revolution, inasmuch as I was the first newsman out of Hungary who had been there from the beginning of the outbreak. Although snowed under with work, I gave them as much of my time as they wanted, and explained what was going on in Budapest and the baleful effect RFE's broadcasts were having on events. Both were enthusiastic, and they repeated over and over again, "This is what we want; this ought to help us!" Before they left to consult with Munich, they got my promise to tape-record what I had said for the benefit of the RFE staff. Needless to say, what I said to them was not what they wanted to hear, and at the time of my return to Budapest I found a note, signed "Koch and Koch," saying, "Sorry, Munich already has your stuff. . . ."

Two of my reports from Hungary, "Budapest: Interview in a Basement Hideaway" and "How We Failed in Hungary," both published in *The Reporter* magazine, especially aroused RFE. In the first article, I quoted Bela Kovacs as follows:

. . . "True, there was a small fringe of extremists in the streets and there was also evidence of a movement which seemed to have ties with the exiled Nazis and Nyilas of former days. But at no time was their strength such as to cause concern. No one in Hungary cares for those who fled to the West after their own corrupt terror regime was finished—and then got their financing from the West. Had there been an attempt to put them in power, all Hungary would have risen instantly."

I told Kovacs that this analysis agreed with my own observation during the first phase of the revolution. For the first time during the night Kovacs smiled. He told me:

"I wish you could convince the West and make them keep the re-actionaries out of our hair. Many of the exiles the Americans are backing are men who are marked because of their war crimes. Some of the voices that come to us over Radio Free Europe in particular are not welcome here. I understand the Americans' eagerness to fight Communism, but this is not the way to do it. As long as the West continues to maintain ties with Hungarian feudalists and fascists, we are handicapped in our effort to seek ties with you. Tell your people to help us by selling democracy to the Hungarians, rather than White reaction."

My story about RFE was even more restrained. In the meantime I had met several RFE executives and had seen a great number of documents relating to their activities, and I realized that these people were unaware of the true significance of their activities and their consequences. In part I said:

In Vienna and later in New York I met several executives of R.F.E. and Crusade for Freedom, the parent of R.F.E., all of whom were trying to prove that what I had heard was not so, that other West German stations, notably NTS, had been used by former Hungarian Nazi-fascists to confuse the Hungarians.

They claimed that R.F.E. was always helpful to the Hungarians and their brave attempt to free themselves from Soviet domination. But nothing they have said to date could change the notes I made while listening to R.F.E. in Budapest. These notes are confirmed by a set of instructions sent by its New York office to Munich and a set of "task reports" returned by Munich, most of them proving the very thing that we who had been there had been saying all along: that Radio Free Europe and to some extent the Voice of America greatly embarrassed the Nagy revolutionary government with their broadcasts by insisting on goals which by no stretch of the imagination that government could ever have reached.

R.F.E., in a letter to me enclosing the instruction sheets, said that it was merely relaying demands of "Hungarian freedom fighters." Who those fighters were we have no way of knowing. I have a great pile of news-papers, throwaways, and placards from Budapest issued by the revolution-ary groups, begging the handful of extremists to stop all fighting, return to work, and give the Nagy government a chance to consolidate the gains of the victorious revolution. Meanwhile R.F.E. kept on broadcasting in-creasingly extreme and impossible demands from what it called "revolu-tionary groups."

199

Of course, it is quite possible that R.F.E. itself was misled by confusing voices reaching it from Hungary. Elementary precaution should have been taken, however, to establish the exact source of the transmitters that R.F.E. was quoting in its broadcasts.

However, the major fault of R.F.E. was much more in the tone and emphasis of its broadcasts than in the words it used. When it rebroadcast excerpts from Ambassador Lodge's speech before the United Nations, it stressed over and again Lodge's sentence: "We shall not fail them"— meaning the Hungarian revolutionaries. The emphasis of R.F.E. was always on "American willingness, readiness, and eagerness to help" captive people to free themselves.

R.F.E. claims that it never promised help to the Hungarian rebels, which is true. Explicitly, no one said that military help would be forthcoming. But promises of all-out help were implicit in the broadcasts, and if the Hungarians understood that to mean military aid, the fault lies in the ambiguity of the broadcasts. Actually, military help was not wanted by the most responsible Hungarians, who did not wish to make a second Korea out of their country.

R.F.E.'s behavior was particularly unfortunate in the fateful days from October 30 to November 4—the days that had seen the re-establishment of political parties, complete official exoneration of Mindszenty, Soviet withdrawal from Budapest, the announcement of a general election in January—in short the days when the revolutionary government swiftly went about establishing democratic processes in Hungary. The broadcasts heard in Hungary from R.F.E. were demanding that Nagy honor all its promises immediately, including the one he made about Russian withdrawal from Hungary. Nagy could only promise to negotiate for withdrawal, and the Russians agreed. But no one in his right mind expected that the Hungarian government could unilaterally nullify a treaty with the Soviets.

John MacCormac, in the November 25 issue of the *New York Times*, said that R.F.E. and the Voice were "merely mouthpieces" of American foreign policy, which in the last analysis was at the root of the whole trouble.

I agree with this view and have something else to add. The American personnel of R.F.E., so far as I have been able to judge them from brief meetings and discussions, are sincerely dedicated men, who under no condition would knowingly mislead or misinform people fighting for their freedom. But the American personnel of R.F.E. were just as unprepared as the State Department and the Legation in Budapest. These men could not help depending on Hungarian advisers, and among the advisers only those could be hired who, according to the prevailing security regulations, could be considered "safe."

The R.F.E., like the Department of State and other public and private organizations dealing with Hungarian affairs throughout the years, has been so occupied with the question of security that it has to consider as safe only those who proved 100 per cent anti-Communist with no dissenting opinion even murmured. Any newspaperman who has worked in Europe can testify to the fact that during the postwar years the tendency has been to look with jaundiced eye on European liberals, progressives, and socialists—all considered, if not Communists, at least near-Communists. It so happens that former war criminals, escaped Nazis, double and triple agents, and dubious characters of all sorts have been counted as allies in our crusade against Communism.

Following the publication of the Kovacs interview, an exchange of correspondence ensued in the pages of *The Reporter* regarding R.F.E.'s role:

R.F.E. AND HUNGARY

To the Editor: We find it impossible to believe that Bela Kovacs had Radio Free Europe in mind when he spoke of "reactionaries," "feudalists," "fascists," and "men who are marked because of their war crimes" in the passage quoted by Leslie B. Bain in "Budapest: Interview in a Basement Hideaway" (*The Reporter*, December 13).

The writers, editors, and broadcasters with R.F.E.'s Voice of Free Hungary include no one in any of such categories, nor has R.F.E. ever broadcast to Hungary programs that by any stretch of imagination could be classified as "White reaction," whatever the precise meaning may be.

A large number of R.F.E.'s Hungarian personnel were members of Bela Kovac's own Independent Small Holders Party, and many of them were close personal friends as well as political colleagues and admirers of this fine and decent Hungarian leader.

In the circumstances it is impossible to verify Mr. Bain's quotes, but we would like to ask him this question: Who are some of these undesirable Hungarians employed by R.F.E.? Did he ask Mr. Kovacs to identify them?

The fact is that the individual political beliefs of members of R.F.E.'s Hungarian staff range from conservative to liberal. Neither the extreme Right nor the extreme Left of the political spectrum is represented. Furthermore, R.F.E. broadcasts do not advocate the cause of particular individuals or parties in or out of Hungary. We support simply the right of the Hungarian people to select, through free elections, their own form of government.

It may be relevant to note that for six years the U.S.S.R., in concert with its worldwide Soviet bloc, has hurled at R.F.E. the charges of "fascist," "reactionary," "war criminals," "feudalists," etc., in an endeavor to put R.F.E. out of business.

> W. J. Convery Egan
> Director
> Radio Free Europe

Mr. Bain replies:

I have read Mr. Egan's letter with interest and I am sorry for not being able to give him a detailed answer. Neither Kovacs nor other Hungarian revolutionary figures spoke of Radio Free Europe in terms of personalities. I am sure Kovacs knows nothing of the organization and its personnel. The views expressed to me by Hungarians were based on Radio Free Europe's performance before, during, and after the revolution.

Specifically, R.F.E.'s efforts to undermine the standing of Nagy's government, question its honesty, and influence the population to make impossible demands on it were considered nefarious by the revolutionary leaders.

I am surprised that Mr. Egan finds it necessary to defend Radio Free Europe with Soviet hostility to it. The relevancy of Soviet charges against R.F.E. may be apparent to Mr. Egan but escapes me when juxtaposed with Kovac's remarks.

Again in the March 15, 1957, issue of *Look* I wrote:

It also developed that, instead of strengthening Nagy and helping him negotiate some settlement with the Russians, we worked to undermine his prestige. U.S. financed radio transmitters in Munich broadcast attacks by Hungarian émigrés—many of whom, in the opinion of the freedom fighters, were discredited Fascists and war criminals. . . .

Even more disheartening to an American was the bitterness of Hungarians who had been led to believe that we would help them in their struggle for freedom. Words of encouragement and talk of liberation from across the Atlantic had raised their hopes. When the tanks of returning Russian forces first rumbled into Budapest, American newspapermen were surrounded by crowds asking when help would arrive. I remember a man grabbing me by the arm. "Is it possible," he cried, "that you are abandoning us now?"

As it can be seen from these extensive quotations, my approach to the problem of the Western role in the affairs of Eastern Europe was to consider its usefulness and helpfulness to the people entrapped in the Communist quagmire. It may be argued that this was the wrong approach, that the first consideration of any policy must be its usefulness to the current foreign policy of the United States. This was the Dulles doctrine. In the long view, the argument was valid, for obviously a free Eastern Europe would greatly strengthen America's hand vis-à-vis the Soviet Union. However, the trouble with the Dulles doctrine was that it accomplished the reverse; it alienated rather than attracted; instead of helping people to free themselves it tightened the Soviet hold on the Eastern Europeans and, perhaps, on the Asian people. Apart from the quality of the personnel employed by American propaganda agencies, the fact was that the operation of these agencies was based on the Dulles doctrine.

It would be easy to quote extensively from American newspaper editorials and reports of observations by outstanding American writers and newspapermen to prove that the RFE was an important factor in the debacle in Hungary; instead I shall call upon RFE itself to make the point.

I had been given carefully chosen excerpts from RFE's directives in New York and Munich, as well as a number of press releases issued by RFE. Strangely enough, they bear out every contention I had made concerning RFE's activities during the Hungarian Revolution.

To start with, in a press release dated November 16, 1957, former Ambassador Joseph C. Grew, chairman of the Board of Directors of Free Europe Committee, Inc., which operates (that's what the release said, "which operates") Radio Free Europe, said that RFE had been falsely accused of inciting the rebellion in Hungary. Then Mr. Grew quoted part of a directive issued in 1951 to the émigrés employed by RFE in Munich: "Speakers are warned not to yield to a natural impulse to bring hope to their compatriots by promising armed intervention by the West. . . ." Thus, already in 1951 RFE was aware of the fact that it did employ people whose natural impulse was to build false hope in their compatriots. Why was it necessary to employ people who had to be restrained *not* to mislead and misinform their own people and drive them into dangerous adventures? The directive went on to say: "To raise the hopes of our audiences in this fashion would be to do them a cruel disservice; it would also constitute radical misrepresentation of the present policies of the Western powers." This directive was issued in 1951, but after 1952 the restriction did not apply because Eisenhower declared that United States policy was to roll back Soviet power from eastern Europe, and every child knew that the only way a reluctant "rollee" can be made to roll back was to apply force. Consequently, the RFE dutifully (not to say with dramatic emphasis) repeated the Eisenhower doctrine as a direct incitement. In one week's time I heard in Hungary more about American determination to help, by all available means, freedom-seeking people than during the previous four years of the Eisenhower administration.

On page 9 of the RFE's report on its role in Hungary I found: ". . . it urged them to unify, to concentrate their efforts on their most urgent goals rather than dissipating them on political maneuvers (get the Russian troops out first, assess the conduct of individual government personalities later). . . ." This I found in the section called highlights of RFE's treatment of the Hungarian revolt. In another section RFE quotes this paragraph from Radio Moscow: "With a view of insuring the mutual security of the Socialist countries, the Soviet government is ready to examine with other Socialist countries which are participants in the Warsaw Treaty, the question of the Soviet troops stationed on the territory of the above-mentioned countries." The two quotes show that the RFE issued a directive to its employees to egg the Hungarians on to demand first the removal of Soviet troops, while at the same time it knew that this was impossible, without the renegotiation of the Warsaw Treaty which the Soviets—at least so it was said—were willing to do.

The report on page 16, recounting events on October 24th, and the Guidance for that day, reads: ". . . we immediately counteracted natural impulses of our writers to go all out in condemning Nagy." Again we come to those peculiar writers who did not care about examining the chronology of events, as I have shown earlier, but who had trouble with their natural impulses to go on to condemn Nagy. The business of condemning Nagy was the business of the Hungarians; strangely enough, the RFE people, and later the Soviets, had the same kind of impulse toward Nagy, with the result that he was hanged on Russian orders. On the same page the RFE report says: "one of RFE's first problems was caused by Imre Nagy's early identification with the policy of using Soviet troops to maintain order." Who identified Nagy with that policy? Certainly no one in Hungary, until the RFE began to identify him with bringing in Soviet troops. The Guidance I referred to above continues to say: "That Nagy called upon foreign troops to restore 'order' is a fact he will have to live down." It was not a fact; it never arose, and the inventors of the canard would not permit Nagy to live it down because it seemed to permit them to loosen their natural impulse.

The next day's Guidance, that of October 25th, was more explicit, and included not only Nagy but all the Communists who led the revolt against Soviet colonialism: "To repeat: The guilt for the shedding of Hungarian blood lies with the Kremlin and with the Hungarian and other satellite leaders who helped to strengthen and perpetuate the Soviet Empire." Every Communist I met in meeting halls or on the barricades at one time or another did strengthen the Soviet Empire at least by helping it to defeat the Nazis and the Fascists. Again in the Guidance for October 29th, when the Soviets already had agreed to withdraw from Budapest, the center of the revolt: "It is recommended that cross-reports give widest publicity to the minimum demands of the Hungarian patriots, with which the RFE wholly identifies itself. (1) Immediate and total withdrawal of all Soviet troops from Hungarian soil. . . ."

The people of natural political impulses in Munich did not need these directives; they joyfully kept on broadcasting impossible demands by "Hungarian patriots," while in Budapest every patriot, Communist or non-Communist, begged for a cease-fire and the restoration of order.

Who were those patriotic groups? From October 29th, when the revolution itself reached its successful climax, and wide political, social, and economic concessions were announced, including a general election in January, the RFE increasingly fell back on those mysterious groups. I met a few of them myself.

One day RFE rebroadcast reports, inflammatory demands, and descriptions of battles from a "Radio Rakoczy," ostensibly originating from Budapest. The lady who monitored radio broadcasts for me and I were sitting listening to these broadcasts, gazing out the window on deserted streets and a large square, the very location at the very time RFE was "rebroadcasting" a great battle in that location. The broadcast ended with a cry for help and the pledge, "We are ready to fight unto death."

I was visiting Gyor where a 40-watt ultra-short-wave station was used by a group of people calling themselves the "Revolutionary Council," elected by a town meeting. Another group appeared at the transmitter, also calling themselves "Revolutionary Council," and demanding to be heard. Part of the ensuing fist fight went out on the air. Subsequently, one of these groups was elevated by RFE to the chair of "true Hungarian patriots," while the other, the elected council, was called "Red-dominated."

In this, too, RFE's own release gives us a revealing insight of the busy men of Munich. The directive of November 4th said, "Have for present discontinued commentaries, in favor of news, messages from freedom radios, etc. . . ." By then the commentaries became international scandal, and the RFE found an easy way to circumvent its own responsibility. The formula was simple; it consisted of relaying messages regardless of their sources. Part II Section 5, lists eight relayed messages as typical. Four of the eight messages were said to have been received from "unknown radio." One was identified as having been received on the wave length of Dunapentele, one from a rebel radio in Vac, and the rest from what was called Radio Csokonai. When I called RFE's attention to this and pointed out that any provacateur outfit could and undoubtedly had used RFE facilities by simply putting on the air harmful calls and depending on RFE to give them wide circulation, I was told that slip-ups occurred but that these were confused times.

Several months later I visited RFE's headquarters in Munich where I had a brief interview with the director of the organization, William Griffith, a political officer of the State Department, in charge of Radio Free Europe. The man knew so much and was so sure that what he knew was worth knowing that it was useless to talk to him. Whether we discussed Poland, Romania, or Hungary, Griffith knew the answers positively and the policy to be followed regarding these countries unerringly. After all, he represented the State Department.

Several others at RFE headquarters in quiet conversations admitted that they were not at all sure but that they were powerless because the State Department determined the policies of Radio Free Europe. We all laughed about the best *known* secret in East and West: namely, that RFE was supposedly a voluntarily supported organization maintained from donations by the American people. The real secret which amused us all was that it was a secret only to the American people that only a small part of RFE's budget came from the annual solicitation of the Crusade for Freedom; the large part of its operation was paid for by the State Department, and of course all of its operation was controlled by Mr. Dulles.

The maintenance of this fiction about RFE was the basic reason for its malfunction; under the circumstances it could not become what it should have been, a free forum for the people of Europe. It was neither fish nor fowl, neither an official organ of the United States nor representative of European thought.

The most important reason, however, for the confusion which prevailed at RFE was the lack of understanding and sympathy for the problems of the satellite people. The Warsaw newspaper *Sztandar Mlodych,* in an editorial rebuke to RFE for presuming to tell the Polish people how to vote, said, "It is not you who will be given ballots but we, and it is we, not you, who will have a better or worse life in this unlucky Polish land." If the RFE had been interested in helping satellite nations to break their chains, then they should have printed on every Directive and Guidance, in capital letters and italics, "*ONLY COMMUNISTS CAN DEFEAT THE COMMUNIST OLIGARCHY AND FREE THE PEOPLES OF EASTERN EUROPE.*" This is true, even though to explain the paradox would take two essays, one on semantics and one on the prevailing political confusion. Had this been understood, there would have been no point to the bitter remark made by a Hungarian refugee in Vienna: "It would be sheer ingratitude on the part of the Soviets not to decorate the directors of Radio Free Europe with the Order of Lenin."

It is manifestly impossible to reproduce in this book more than a few waves of the vast backwash churning in the wake of the Hungarian Revolution inside and outside that unhappy land. My judgment may have been faulty in selecting events, incidents, personalities, and statements with which to reproduce so important an upheaval with a few strokes. However, a total view can be obtained only by a minute examination or by the selection of revealing high lights without partisan considerations. Yet, to be unpartisan these days is to live in a vacuum, an impossible and certainly undesirable state. Therefore I have tried to express my partisanship by selecting material which would show the disaster ahead for both the West and the East if the present precipitous trends are further maintained.

No matter how I try to view the Hungarian Revolution then and now, the conclusion becomes inescapable that by the intervention of the principal protagonists of the cold war, the Hungarian Revolution and its aftermath, as well as the efforts to extinguish it, went far beyond necessity: the dynamics of events, that incalculable x factor of the alchemy of history, overtook both—the revolution for liberty and justice threatened to become, at least for a short time, a passionate anarchy; the counterrevolution, first intended merely as a break, became a vicious, revengeful tyranny. And that intervention also managed to grind reason, logic, justice, and self-interest into dust which is destined to sting the eyes of mankind for a long time to come.

PART THREE

Repercussions

14

Hungary and Her Sister Satellites— Interaction

For many months after the Hungarian debacle, top Yugoslav Communists were still debating and second guessing the role of the principals of the revolution. Newspapermen, writers, and state officials to a man had pet theories and quick remedies. The trend, however, was unmistakable: the Yugoslav Communists believed that events in the Soviet Union were forcing Khrushchev back toward Stalinism and that the Yugoslavs had better watch their step. Many Yugoslavs felt as though a dear cousin had done something disgraceful; they were sorry for Khrushchev, whose ascendancy to power and exposure of Stalin had been hailed as a new approach to socialism.

The dilemma had a special Yugoslav flavor. Top Communists

knew all along that the Yugoslav people had to be controlled tightly to make them hew to the Communist line; at the same time they also had to be anti-Stalinists, which meant antiterror, anticoercion, antistate. As one of the editors of *Borba* said: "We would like to achieve socialism without pressure but we know that it cannot be done. Thus the Soviet Union forces us to retreat to some extent from socialism because we cannot afford to be identified with Stalinism even in its mildest form." The Yugoslavs were beginning to be afraid of what would happen if they were forced to face Kadar's choice: widespread relaxation of the relentless pressure on the people—or Stalinism.

Except for the sizable Hungarian minority and the Yugoslav elite, the rest of the country reacted to events in Budapest as though they had occurred on the moon. Tito's zigzag policy toward Imre Nagy and his cautious endorsement of Janos Kadar convinced the Yugoslavs that what happened in Hungary was a minor falling out between Communist factions. The retrial of Milovan Djilas, on the other hand, was a major sensation. None of his heresies was published in Yugoslavia, only the fact that he was sentenced to seven years in prison for debasing the Yugoslav state. Djilas, despite the official attitude toward him, remained a beloved figure among the Communist elite and among the people of Yugoslavia. His exploits during the war were legendary, and his compassion for the underdog and his willingness to fight oppression under any label endeared him to the traditionally oppressed people of Yugoslavia. With Tito alive, the affair of Djilas could not cause a major upheaval. But after the Hungarian Revolution the lines in Yugoslavia did become more visible: on the one hand were the orthodox bureaucratic Communist functionaries whose loyalty to the handful on top was and will remain unquestioned, while on the other were intellectuals and the younger elements among whom the validity of the whole Communist theory was receiving a searching analysis along the lines of Djilas' criticism.

Apart from the manifest clumsiness of the Communist economic plan, the Yugoslavs were beginning to show recognizable signs of political uncertainty and unease. Not only were those restive who wished a stronger orientation toward Western liberalism, but also the pro-Soviet forces who worried lest Yugoslavia crawl too far away from the Soviet Union and in a major crisis be driven out of the socialist orbit altogether. I found the lines sharper in Yugoslavia after the Hungarian Revolution than they were before. That revolution may not have been as strong a catalyst in Yugoslavia as in Poland; nevertheless, even the short time I spent in Belgrade, Zagreb, and other cities showed a marked change in the tempo of events.

Yugoslavia, after all, had been independent among Communist states since 1948; therefore the Hungarian Revolution, which was essentially an attempt to establish independent Hungarian national policies, was not so deeply felt in Yugoslavia as in Poland. Poland was, is, and will remain anti-Soviet and antitotalitarian in her attitude toward Communism. If these terms are severally contradictory, so they are, but the Poles believed they could work a miracle and reconcile them, if permitted to evolve their own brand of Communism.

I wish that I could write freely of the wonderful people I met in Poland without endangering their lives. Going over my notes, I came across names which brought back warm memories and nights of long and largely indiscreet discussions. Often we met for tea, stayed for dinner, and reluctantly parted at dawn. Things have changed in Poland since those days, and now I face the choice of either writing about those people or merely reporting what they said without mentioning anything about them that could lead to their being identified. True, things are not yet back where they were in pre-Gomulka days in Poland. But time is running out on them; and, who knows? what I write here may one day be read in court by a "People's Prosecutor." However, I emphatically do not wish to imply that I was given governmental secrets or that our talks were treasonous.

Poland's revolutionary bid to free herself began on October 19, 1956, four days before the Hungarian rebellion erupted. Next day, on October 20th, Wladyslaw Gomulka made his historic speech before the Central Committee of the Communist party (United Polish Workers' Party) which took the wind out of revolutionary sails. Speeches by politicians rarely make good reading, especially by Communists, who manage to contrive the dullest of texts for all of their utterances. This Gomulka address before the Eighth

213

Plenary Session of the Central Committee, however, merits a second look if for no other reason than that of comparing it with what was said in Hungary just about that time and what happened as its consequence.

Gomulka, fresh out of jail, minced no words. He began to point out the lies and statistical juggling of the Communist economic reports. He showed that instead of advancing, as reported, the coal industry had retrogressed; the automobile industry was turning out economically insupportable, obsolete models at high cost; machines and equipment bought with the lifeblood of the Polish workers were rusting and rotting away without even a hope of ever being useful to Poland; all this, said Gomulka, had to be paid for by the Polish workers; and the Communist party leadership was responsible for such bad management. He continued with agriculture, showing that the only efficient farms were those which were privately owned; but he said that those were taxed out of production by political hatchet men who poured billions into inefficient cooperatives and state-owned farms. Exposing the big lie regarding Poznan, he said: "The causes of the Poznan tragedy and of the profound dissatisfaction of the entire working class are to be found in ourselves, in the leadership of the Party, the government. . . . There is no escaping from truth. If you try to hide it, it comes to the fore in the threatening shape of a ghost which haunts, terrifies, rebels and raves."

Gomulka went further than any Communist leader during those hectic days in laying down the basis for Communist rule: "Governing the country requires that the working class and working masses should place their trust in the representatives, in those who are at the helm of state power. This is the moral basis for exercising power in the name of the working masses. This trust can be continuously renewed only on condition that obligations toward those granting it are fulfilled. The loss of trust granted by the working class means the loss of the moral basis for power."

Then Gomulka castigated the idea that only the Communist way was the true way to socialism and that doctrinaire principles were necessarily superior to the thinking and feeling of the people. He condemned all the Communist practices of the past and urged the committee, which was listening to him in abashed silence, to

214

get on with the job of making Polish socialism humanistic and acceptable to the masses.

This was what the Poles wanted to hear. When Gomulka, toward the end of his address, raised the question of equality with the Soviet Union and insisted that each must respect the other's independence, he won the revolution singlehandedly. He, at long last, had said "Nyet" to the Russians.

By the time I got to Poland in April, 1957, the honeymoon between Gomulka and the Polish people was in its last phase. Gomulka, however sincere he may have been, could not begin to fulfill his promise, and his true role became apparent. He was both the last hope of the Stalinists who faced a bloody revolution and the white knight of the anti-Stalinists who were looking for a leader. But by trying to appease everyone he succeeded in satisfying no one.

When a friend of Gomulka's reported to him that "all Gomulka-ites in Poland seem to be optimists except Gomulka himself," he agreed ruefully. Gomulka had to retreat slowly from his October 20th speech under the relentless pressure of Polish realities. He stubbornly believed in trying to compromise the irreconcilable, and maintained against overwhelming odds that such a course offered Poland's best hope. The trouble with the Gomulka hope was that nearly all ingredients of the synthesis he hoped to develop were unreal.

A close friend and collaborator of Gomulka's said: "What the chief does not seem to realize is that, at the moment, both the East and the West are interested in maintaining the status quo for Poland. Washington and Moscow are sending us driblets of relief to make us stay put, but that merely postpones the evil hour."

"Why do you believe that Washington and Moscow want to keep the Poles in their present state?" I asked.

"The answer is Germany," my informant said, and continued: "We are constantly on the verge of a revolution which the major powers fear might touch off a world war. If we rise and try to steer away from the Eastern bloc, the Soviets would intervene if for no better reason than that we are their lifeline to East Germany. In that case, the Polish Army would fight fanatically against the Soviet Army, and before our revolution would be many hours old, East Germany would also rise. In that event, there would be no way of preventing West Germans from pouring across the border to help their East German brothers. That would come close to an East-West war situation, and both sides are frightened at the prospect."

In that case, I wanted to know, what of Poland? "If she must stay still what can you do to relieve the misery of your people?" He told me to go to see Oscar Lange, the economist, former professor at the University of Chicago, who was a member of the State Council and Gomulka's first economic advisor.

Calling on Mr. Lange, I took along data I had collected on the many idle plants on my way to Warsaw. In the areas around Katowice, Ostrow, Poznan, Lodz, and Warsaw I had seen large industrial installations in which no wheels turned, although workers came to the plants but got no pay for their trouble.

Lange did not try to evade the problem which arose from the crazy planning of the previous regime. He freely admitted that Poland built factories and large plants dependent entirely upon imported raw and processed materials. He mentioned cotton looms, electronics plants, and a number of medium and heavy industries which were idle owing to lack of foreign exchange with which to buy the needed materials. As to why these plants were built, Lange explained that at the time they were planned the cold war was in its inception and no one believed that it would materially influence the development of Poland's economy.

"Even so, why was it necessary to build plants entirely dependent on foreign raw materials instead of developing Poland's own resources?" I asked.

Lange said that many mistakes had been made, and mentioned the great number of machines which were ordered but which could never be used. He came as close to agreeing with me that all Communist planners were touched by a frenzy or megalomania as a high Communist functionary could without committing treason. "Yes, yes," he said, "we all make mistakes." I told him about my experiences with Hungarian, Romanian, Yugoslav, and Czechoslovak planners, and asked him whether he thought that those planners could have held such important jobs in Western countries. He said that what happened was not so much the planners' fault as that the political direction of the Communist countries was infected by Stalin's Caesaromania.

216

Item by item, we went over Poland's economic difficulties: exaggerated industrialization without ready sources of raw materials or markets; top-heavy bureaucracy; the maintenance of a large military establishment, estimated at 350,000 men of whom about a third had mechanized equipment; the support of armament industries, including not only small and medium arms but heavy equipment such as tanks and jet planes; the cost of maintaining the Catholic clergy and churches; and the political necessity of freeing the peasants from compulsory deliveries. The last item was at that time the most urgent. Poland's agriculture was in such bad shape that once the peasants were freed they would naturally hoard their produce to extract higher prices. Poland needed grain immediately to stabilize spiraling food prices.

The deeper Professor Lange got into the economic problems the clearer it became that Poland was in far worse state than was Hungary before and after the revolution. With all her difficulties, Hungary could feed herself, and were it not for the wasteful bureaucracy and unfavorable Soviet-Hungarian trade, she could even enjoy a fair prosperity. On the other hand Poland's food production was not enough for the country's needs, and her industries were unproductive and uneconomical. Coal, as Professor Lange pointed out, was Poland's only marketable export. "Coal, our mainstay, is also our biggest headache," he said. "We either need to produce more coal for export or electrify our railroads to have more left for export. But we cannot do either one without capital investments. The machinery of our colliers is obsolete, and we need to modernize it to produce more coal. As for the electrification of our railroads, that, too, would call for an enormous amount of capital investment."

Discussing the worth of such investment, it appeared that Poland's coal industry could become a prosperous business; but, as Lange pointed out, investment loans from the Soviet Union or from America would have major political consequences. The Soviet Union was willing to help at the price of re-Stalinization and the integration of Polish economy with that of Russia. The price America was asking would amount to the abandonment of the Warsaw Pact, a requirement to which no Pole, Communist or non-Communist, would agree unless the Oder-Neisse border was guaranteed by all the major powers.

I had earlier had the impression that fear of German resurgence kept Poland in the Eastern bloc, and I found confirmation of this during my talks with Catholic officials. This partly explained Gomulka's huge majority at the polls; he meant every word of his fateful utterance on the eve of the election: "If you cross off the candidates of the United Workers' Party from the list, you will cross off Poland from the map of Europe." What he meant, and what every Pole understood, was that the Soviet Union was Poland's only protection against the visibly rising German power.

Another Polish economist with whom I argued the point that war between Poland and Germany was unthinkable said, "Granted that the military fear is unreal, but the great power that Germany wields through American support is enough to smother us all and make us vassals of Germany. As long as America supports a dominant Germany there can be no break in the Eastern bloc."

Aid presently received by Poland from Washington and Moscow was enough to drag her bankrupt economy along but left nothing for solution of her long-range problems. The dilemma of Poland was described to me by a Communist editor in these words: "The reintroduction of Stalinism in Poland, even though tied to economic help, would be a signal for most of the Communists themselves to revolt. The abandonment of the Warsaw Pact, without Western guarantees, would also lead to the overthrow of Gomulka and the likely return of a strongly pro-Soviet regime. Thus the problem is: Who can help us without engendering a revolution?"

This was the fatal choice which Gomulka was trying to avoid through his endless compromises. One need not be an economist to see the utter misery of the Poles: there were signs of it everywhere. It seemed that every economic remedy applied by Gomulka somehow backfired: wage increases began an inflationary spiral which was, for a while, nearly impossible to hold; the amount of foreign aid merely gave the black marketeers a boost; reorganization of agriculture nearly wrecked the country because the peasants withheld their produce from the markets; relieving the misery of idle workers by regularly paying wages to them reduced the value of the zloty nearly three-fourths. One of the major difficulties in regard to American aid was the repayment of loans. Poland could not produce in quantity anything of value for the West, and the products of her consumer-goods industry were of such low quality—especially cotton goods—that only Asian countries could be counted as customers. Thus, American loans had to be arranged through a third country: America loaned to Poland; Poland repaid the loan with goods for France; France sold the goods in Asia and paid America with her own products.

I found corruption in Poland more widespread than in any other Communist country, and it was not only accepted but defended by officials. A high police official with whom I talked about it said, "How can I expect my men to be honest when their monthly pay covers their minimum needs for at most ten days?" Even higher officials in the 2,000 to 4,000 zloty class were often willing to accept bribes. In stores, factories, and other state enterprises stealing was endemic. Unless it had become too obvious, it was generally accepted as an unavoidable evil. A new twist in black marketeering was prevalent in Poland during my stay. Licensed private entrepreneurs bought up every desirable item in state stores the day they were put on sale; later, when the item became scarce, they sold it to the public at 200 to 400 per cent profit. State-produced shoes, for instance, could rarely be bought in a state store. No sooner was a shipment received than private store owners bought up the stock. A newspaperman and I went all over Warsaw one day to buy a light bulb because we heard that a shipment was sent in from the factory. After an all-day search we bought a 200-watt bulb; the smaller ones disappeared inside the first hour. A major sanitation crisis hit Warsaw when black marketeers cornered all supplies of toilet tissue and plumbing broke down all over the city. From all I hear, the black market is even worse today.

There were two major forces at work in Poland whose influence no one was able to measure with any degree of accuracy for me: the Church and the Army.

Stefan Cardinal Wyszynski, in sharp contrast to his nervous and high-strung staff, was a soft-spoken, calm man to whom the years had been kind. He had the diplomat's knack for saying meaningful things innocuously. Only a careful analysis of his words showed what he really wanted to convey in the smooth generalities he spoke. Cardinal Wyszynski and his two trusted aides, Bishops Bavanek and Choromanski, made up the high command of the Polish Catholic hierarchy. I heard Wyszynski widely praised for his stand during the elections, which according to many observers saved Poland from a civil war. Wyszynski and Gomulka had one thing in common: they were both patriotic Poles first and leaders of their followers second. Wyszynski believed that the only road to freedom was a tortuous one and that only great caution could prevent a fall into an abyss. He made a deal with Gomulka whereby the Church would send its followers to the polls in exchange for an assurance that the Church would have more freedom. Five days before the election Cardinal Wyszynski kept his word: the Church urged the faithful to do their duty by the state.

The Polish Catholic Church, except for Cardinal Wyzynski himself, resembled the Hungarian in many ways. The lower and upper clergy were increasing their political activities, thereby giving powerful support to the Stalinists, who, in satellite countries, often tried to justify their terror regime by pointing to the allegedly conspiratorial activities of the Catholic clergy. The most innocent Church-led activity became a sinister plot in the eyes of the orthodox Communists. Yet both in Poland and in Hungary a large part of the people, even Communists, owed some kind of allegiance to the Church, and without a modus vivendi between Church and state a peaceful social pattern was unthinkable. Wyszynski said that this compromise with reality as it existed in Poland did not mean that he was unaware of the basic incompatibilities that separated Catholicism from Communism but that he believed that continued coexistence was possible.

Actually, I found that the immediate future of Poland rested on those two hard-pressed leaders Wladyslaw Gomulka and Stefan Cardinal Wyszynski. Both were at the mercy of inexorable forces around them, and so were those who looked to them for leadership. The Communists were pressing Gomulka to be less tolerant about the activities of the Church and to cut its large state subsidies. Wyszynski fought daily battles with his more fanatical subordinates and followers to maintain the precarious status quo. In candid discussions both realized that the present state of affairs was untenable but that it had to be maintained.

The position of the Church had been strengthened lately by an unexpected development in the Polish Army. The army has undergone considerable changes since October, 1956, under the Command of General Marian Spychalski. Following the replacement of Russian officers with Polish professional soldiers, the army became strongly nationalistic—too strongly, according to some Communists. Nationalism in Poland has always had a deeply religious quality; thus, whether Spychalski planned it or not, the army began to drift toward the Church, and religious influence in the army became considerable. General Spychalski himself, a former architectural engineer and partisan officer during the war, who was jailed for five years by the Stalinists, is nationalist in feeling but Communist in profession. Spychalski knows that in the event of Soviet intervention, such as occurred in Hungary, his army would fight with fanatical determination against the Russians. In such a war the army's morale would be heightened by religious influences, and since such a war was a real possibility he was not doing anything to counter this clearly visible tendency in the army.

With Gomulka's prestige and influence lessening, he also faced Kadar's fatal choice. Despite his capacity to stand up under unbearable pressure, his personal popularity was losing ground because he was unable to fulfill the high hopes of October, 1956. The poverty-stricken peasants and workers wanted a larger piece of bread, the restless intellectuals a larger measure of freedom, and the rebellious youth a hope and faith in which they could believe. All have been disappointed to varying extents.

Disillusionment with Gomulka would have set in more rapidly were it not for his personal qualities. He is modest, hard-working, devoted, and loyal. Although Gomulka is markedly anti-intellectual and distrusts the intellectual elite, a very large part of his supporters belong to that classification. To the masses he is the man who *also* suffered from the Communists and who, above all, said the long-yearned-for "Nyet" to the Russians. In reality, however, Gomulka never said No to Khrushchev and Bulganin; he merely pointed out the necessity for compromising with the mounting unrest to save Communist rule in Poland.

Officially, the Polish United Workers' party exercised governmental authority by default. It would be truer to say that governmental authority in Poland was exercised by Gomulka, who through his personal prestige in the country still managed, but with increased difficulty, to cover up the fact that the party in power was hopelessly split, had no authority or mass support, and was but a shadow which would have disappeared, as in Hungary, were it not for the circumstance that there was nothing to take its place. The party was split four ways: the Natolin group (named after a summer place of the Russian Embassy where Polish Communists used to meet), which was openly Stalinist; the neo-Stalinists, who wanted to improve the methods of Stalinism while retaining the essentially monolithic power of the orthodox Communists; the Gomulkaites, who hoped to continue the tightrope waltz begun in October, 1956, and the fourth group, those who were trying to enlarge the Gomulka doctrine and extend freedom to an ever-greater degree.

The Natolins and the neo-Stalinists controlled the party organization; they were natural allies, and enjoyed the confidence of the Russians, who used them to relay Soviet disapproval of certain party functionaries and members of the government.

The Gomulkaites had no clear program beyond wishing to avoid trouble and somehow consolidate the fermenting forces in Poland to make orderly economic growth possible. Faced with nearly impossible odds, the Gomulkaites echo Gomulka: "We can't give more than we have but what we have belongs to the people." It was a good slogan and would have been effective if "what we have" were not so alarmingly small and were not getting smaller every day.

Although not adequately represented in high party circles, the fourth group was the strongest throughout the country. These people would still like to follow Gomulka, but they want him to go faster and further. Slowly the realization grew among them that Gomulka would not lead but that he would, if forced to, become a reluctant follower. Hence they were hammering away at him at every available opportunity.

What I really looked for in Poland was some kind of reliable guide by which to measure the influence Hungarian events had on the Poles. The ferment which existed in all Communist countries was highest in Hungary and Poland, and it seemed to me that the fate of one would profoundly affect the other. Stopping in several places in Czechoslovakia on my way to Poland, I was able to recognize the tightening of the Communist grip on that country, particularly in the care with which Czechs avoided discussing Hungarian events. Many of them realized that their role in suppressing the revolution was a shameful one, and they were not anxious to explain it. The Czechs, somewhat like the Prussians, have always responded to regimentation more readily than other European people, and their thinking followed the official party line. My brief tour of Czechoslovakia was twice interrupted by my arrest for inadvertently driving through forbidden areas. In both instances they let me go after a few hours, since the roads were not marked with warning signs and I had no way of knowing when I had strayed from the main road. During one of the interrogations, an army captain engaged me in a conversation about Hungary. He, like the group of county officials I had had lunch with that day, wholly accepted the view that Western—to him it meant American and German—agents fomented the revolt and that it was aimed at the restoration of Nazi rule in Central Europe. He was willing to bet with me that the Germans would be Nazis again within ten years. "Since there is very little likelihood that either of us will be in a position ten years from now to collect from the other, we had better not bet," I said.

But if the Czechs were reluctant to discuss Hungary, the Poles were overly eager. Nearly all the meetings I had with Poles somehow turned into debates about Hungary. I had even prepared an opening gambit, an article by Tibor Dery which was written on the 30th of October and which appeared on the streets in the November 2nd issue of *The Literary Journal*. I was with Dery when he wrote it, and I knew of the anguish with which he watched the rapidly deteriorating events. And since he was in many ways the spirit of the revolution, I had used his article in Yugoslavia, Czechoslovakia, and Poland to start the conversation on Hungary, and to watch the reaction his words evoked. This was the article:

My Friends:
It was a hard decision for me to speak out; when the first rifle bullet was heard my blood drained from my head: for this, you too are responsible. You made speeches, you called for revolt; how are you going to account for the dead? On the streets the number of unburied increased:

go out and stop the hands of the murderers! I could not accept the simple fact that there can be no revolution without bloodshed. With the sound of every rifle fire I felt as though I pulled the trigger. I believe in human conscience and I place myself in the dock as a defendant.

My friends, I accept the responsibility. It makes me happy and proud that my colleagues and I were the first to hear and first to write the voice of the nation. In the annals of Hungarian history this was the greatest and the first successful revolution on the record. Not single persons, not political groups, not particular beliefs or opinions fomented it and carried it through but the will of the people. With horror I awaken to the realization of what we but vaguely felt, suspected, of which we spoke with half-words which now shakes us to our very marrows: how merciless the deathly pressure must have been upon our people to bring forth such universal and complete response to face tanks with bare hands! They said this was a revolution of the juveniles! From this day the word "juvenile" shall be sacred to me! Throughout the years I watched in despair the Hungarian youth, silent, in coma. On the 23rd of October it stood up and restored the honor of the nation. With respect and awe, I bow to them. As I had wished, asked, and hoped: our nation now has the Youth of '56 to match that of '48.

First of all I wish to speak to them, for the fate of the revolution is in their hands. I am old, past sixty-two, and I have participated in two lost revolutions. In '45 I believed that the workers, peasants and the rest of us who were always outsiders had found a home within the nation. But during the past ten years, step by step, they managed to steal the ground beneath our feet. We believed that we would be permitted to build socialism; instead we were locked in a prison whose walls were built of lies and blood. I feel also responsible for having opened my eyes so late. And when they finally opened I could not increase either my silence or my voice that all could understand me. But we have one excuse, we Hungarian writers; even though late, still earlier than anyone else, we took up the struggle against tyranny.

My friends, if my words merit your credit, listen now to me: Safeguard our revolution! Until now it had such a nobility which only justice and humanity could lend to a cause. Let us concentrate on one thing: this is not the hour of revenge but of justice. The guilty shall be judged by the courts. But do not torture those who erred; we must not forget that hundreds of thousands have erred because they were led into their errors.

The revolution is victorious, but it could collapse if we do not give it time to gather its strength. It could also be embezzled by those whose interest it is to steal it. Let us hold together: we have one life and one country. If my words merit your credit: let us hold now together and let us not fight each other! Let us trust in the decency and power of the people. Stop the flow of blood! Respect the dead!

Tibor Dery

Dery, who by then was in prison, could not have spoken to a more understanding and affectionate audience than the Poles in Warsaw. Even those who had disagreed with the Hungarians had nothing but praise for their gallantry and sincerity. The Poles understood the Hungarians, for there was much in common in their attitude and approach to social, moral, and political problems. Positive in their love and hate, intolerant of faint hearts, emotional and tense, apt to be carried away by intoxicating words, the Poles relived with me the heady days of October, 1956, in Budapest, and several times we found ourselves toward dawn, with excellent Polish vodka making the rounds, holding the wake of Hungary.

Once, when the discussion got very confusing, I said to a writer: "You remarked that the reason Polish writers would not feel as Dery did was that the fatal words which aroused the Hungarians were originally spoken by Gomulka. But since that time you have been constantly hammering away at Gomulka for not living up to his promises. Moreover, censorship, however devious, has been reinstated, and the outspoken *Pro Postu*, a magazine of the students and intellectuals, suppressed. Now, if this retrogression continues, and you feel compelled to do as Dery did, would you, in the light of what happened in Hungary, go as far?"

First there was an attempt to show that Gomulka would never be a Gero or a Kadar, but after some analysis of the Polish situation it was admitted that stronger measures would be justified under what he might consider provocation.

"It is true," he continued, "that Hungary sobered us considerably. But the events in Hungary also had another effect on us—there is a considerable feeling among the younger element to seek revenge on the Russians for what they have done to the Hungarians. None of us, for instance, believe that the Hungarian comrades would have permitted the return of fascism in Hungary, no matter what the Russians and Kadar are saying. In fact if we take on face value all the Russians have said on this subject, still there is not an iota of

225

proof that Hungarian socialists behaved otherwise than as socialists during the revolution. We are not so naïve as not to see that predatory people tried to take over as they would here too; but essentially we are against predators from the Left as well as from the Right, and we, as we believe the Hungarians, would fight against them.

"As for what we would do if the situation should further deteriorate—and I don't see how it can—the answer is that we, the Communists of Poland, would rise against it. Non-Communists would undoubtedly help us, but it was Gomulka himself who said that we Poles of various political beliefs ought to work together. In speaking of the Catholics I would differentiate between the higher and the lower clergy. The majority of the lower clergy, as well as the Catholic mass organizations, would fight with us and after victory would stay with us. Now, some of the bishops are reactionaries and so is the Vatican, but we are not afraid of them!"

"Assuming that the status quo could be maintained, is it acceptable?" I asked.

Another writer, a woman of great attainments, replied: "No, it is not; nor is it possible to maintain the status quo, because life itself never stands still. We are moving constantly, and those who would not are being dragged along. Now, the question is, Which way are we going? I believe the wrong way."

A member of the Council of State who joined us said: "If both America and the Soviet Union would realize what is at stake here they might change their attitudes. If not, Poland will go through a terrible ordeal. But in the end we will have a free socialist country."

Quoting a close associate of Cardinal Wyszynski, I said, "My understanding of the attitude of the Church is that unless it gets a greater and freer role in molding the lives of the intensely Catholic Poles the country may face a civil war." Almost everyone denied this. What they said was that a revolution of Catholics versus the State could never get off the ground without the workers and peasants, who, while Catholics, are also anti-clerical.

"You speak of the status quo not being tenable and you say that things are moving," I said. "Nevertheless, your economy is still overburdened with parasites and drones. Can something be done about them to bring production costs down to a more acceptable level? After all, the ratio of producers to nonproducers in your economy is still two to one. Here is an example: I talked to a brigade foreman in Katowice who told me that he had to get permission from three different offices to move a pile of refuse from one corner of the factory yard to another."

An economist said: "The question is not an economic one. We do know how to correct the situation and did know all along. The question is political, and it is: What are we going to do with the superfluous personnel? We have to pay them no matter what they do, and there are not enough jobs at the moment. We will have jobs for everyone once our factories and plants operate in response to the market instead of in response to some crazy political scheme. But right now we would gladly swap three of our 'great socialist achievement' type of factories for one which could actually use available labor and indigenous raw materials."

"Soviet economists say that you can't live by yourselves and that you would be far more prosperous if you would coordinate your economy with that of the Soviet Union," I said.

This was the time when the nationalist Pole in them somehow broke through every Communist present. They would not hear, consider, or discuss any idea, plan, or scheme that would lessen Polish independence. What seemed hard to reconcile was Communist internationalism—in which all professed to believe—and the intransigent nationalism they displayed. I had the distinct impression that ideologically these people had reached a point where all was confusion. I remembered the night in Hungary when I watched the revolutionary Communists sit around trying to evolve a national program in a session which ended with nearly all the cherished Communist dogmas being pitched through the window into the blazing streets. The Poles, too, knew what they wanted, and were perhaps willing to fight for it—but what they wanted belied their words. I said as much to them and a Communist functionary present pointed out that "That is precisely the trouble. That is why we are all unreliable. We know what we want to tear down but we are not clear about what we want to build."

The politically-minded youth of Poland were astonishingly like the Hungarians. Their newspaper, *Sztandar Mlodych*, got some unexpected replies from its readers during a survey conducted to probe the minds of the youth. Two thirds of the answers were emphatically pessimistic about Polish politics and a similar percentage answered the question, "What is your aim in life?" with a blunt "To live like human beings."

Another memorable twilight-to-dawn session with constantly changing participants revolved around the cul-de-sac in which the Poles found themselves as a result of the Hungarian Revolution and its aftermath. The Poles said that since the Hungarian Revolution Radio Free Europe had taken a more realistic view of their problems and was less intolerant than it used to be. Several who knew the people at RFE's Polish desk in Munich claimed that a liaison had been established with Munich and that the Polish desk was more inclined to take advice from Warsaw about economic and political matters than heretofore.

"Just as the toleration of freedom here at home may be temporary, Munich, too, may be free only as long as the U.S.S.R. and America find it expedient to leave us alone," was the opening statement made by a newspaperwoman.

"Today we may talk freely, but for the same words tomorrow we may be sent to Siberia. Today the West may be helpful and sympathetic—tomorrow we may again be dirty bomb-throwing, conniving Communist conspirators. We are leaves blown hither and thither by any casual wind from Moscow or Washington. A plague on both their houses." The speaker was a magazine writer, just back from Paris.

The ensuing discussion brought forth the ambivalence of the Poles toward the West. Spiritually and culturally the Poles always wanted to be a part of the West; Paris was their Mecca, the fountainhead of their nourishment. But Paris was in eclipse and Washington ruled the West, a capital which had nothing for the Poles but rock-and-roll, push-button refrigerators, H-bombs, and moneybags. The law in America said that Poles could not be admitted even as visitors because they were tainted; they were lepers, untouchables. This was the program Washington was trying to foist on Paris and London, and the Poles were outraged.

"It would not be so bad if you would offer something with which to replace our ideals, but you give us nothing but pious words, admonishments, and threats. You seem to think it is our fault that we can't produce as well as you do, that we are industrially backward, scientifically clumsy, and that we can't devote our time to building better and newer refrigerators. If we told you that we were trying to get into the twentieth century, you would tell us that we should emulate you and be more efficient in commerce and industry. As if prosperous commerce and industry were something we could will!" said one writer.

The discussion became pointedly sharp on America and the West. It was embarrassing as well as unjust. "Why are you so critical of us instead of the Soviet Union whence all your troubles seem to stem?" I asked. An elderly man who spoke little during the night and who later turned out to be one of the most prominent professors of history answered: "We have all the right to be more critical of you. We are a part of the West, your beliefs are our beliefs—we have contributed to the treasures of the West as much as any comparable people. We have the right to ask you not to let us down. We never expected anything from the Russians, because we look upon them as barbarians who occupied our land. But when we speak of the West we are speaking of our brothers and sisters. From Christians we expect Christian behavior. When you fail us, when you betray us, you are betraying yourselves. We expected you Americans to live up to your faith, but you are playing shoddy politics with us. The civilization which rests on the beliefs of Franklin, Washington, Jefferson, Lincoln, and other illustrious founders of your Republic is morally bound, and when you transgress you break faith with the essential morality of mankind."

There it was. In the eyes of the Poles we were guiltier than the Russians because the Russians made no bones about what they wanted and how they intended to get it, but we of the West had no right to play fast and loose with them.

All seemed to be experts on Eisenhower and Dulles. They could quote both of them extensively and accurately. They were greatly irked by what they regarded as contradictions between what American leaders have said in regard to freeing the enslaved world and what they have done. One laughed at my objection and my reference to Soviet contradictions, and said, "They have special Marxian dispensation to say one thing and do another, but you are stuck with Christian and human morality—you claim to be guardians of Western heritage."

A strange note reoccurred during these conversations. The Poles were inclined to identify themselves with neutralist countries such as India, Indonesia and, to some extent, Yugoslavia, rather than with the Eastern or the Western blocs. They felt more at home discussing Nehru than Khrushchev or Eisenhower. They acknowledged that Polish thinking and hopes were centered upon a vaguely defined third force, some emerging new humanistic approach to life which they believed was developing in Asia. We spent a good deal of time on this subject; and it appeared to me that partly because they felt betrayed both by the Soviets and by America, the Poles were groping toward ways to escape from their geographic and political prison.

During most of the talk about neutralism and the third force, a Communist party functionary kept frowning and making derisive grimaces. Finally she could contain herself no longer, and said: "Comrades, we are all professional revolutionaries. We are willing to fight and die for a cause, but we are not willing to live and work for it. You talk about the coming revolution, mooning over ways to fight across Europe and Asia to join up with India; you are full of plans, talk, high resolves, and dramatic speeches while there are thousands of tasks right here at home which we could undertake if we would be willing to stop talking and get down to work." She was laughingly ruled out of order because she was quoting herself from a speech she delivered that morning at an activist meeting. But there was something in what she said. These lively, charming, intelligent Communists of Poland were given to strong words and overidealism but had little appreciation of reality. Perhaps I was unfair to them, for I have not seen them on the barracades like their Hungarian colleagues, exchanging words for bullets. And when I hazarded a cautious comparison I was told that they were realists. "The trouble with the Hungarians was that they believed in the West, and instead of getting moral support they got condolences and crocodile tears. We know we must rely on ourselves alone. Perhaps because of that, our means and methods seem incomprehensible to you. But we shall get there."

It would have been grossly impolite to inquire just where the "there" was, but even though I was convinced that they could not have put it in words they did have an idea of where it was. This was Hungary after all, but without the tanks and guns: searching, seething intellects carelessly cutting across ideologies in a determined effort to get "somewhere."

In Poland the past did not seem to impede the present as much as it did in Hungary. Political exiles, past leaders and ideologies, feudalism, clericalism, fascism, and the whole paraphernalia of the past appeared to be dead to Communists and non-Communists alike. Mindful of the marginal groups in Hungary which tried to take over the revolution, I paid special attention in Poland to people and movements which were oriented toward the past. Except for some of the higher clergy and old discarded officeholders of bygone regimes, I found very little to indicate that there was any rightist movement in Poland. I found plausible explanation in the Nazi devastation of Poland. The Germans did not destroy physical Poland alone, but managed to wipe out the past too. Polish history seemed to begin with the Nazi attack in 1939; everything that happened before that was remote and unreal. But I did find a good deal of anti-Semitism; strangely enough, it was most virulent among the pro-Soviet Communists. Jews were leaving Poland in droves, and those still there were making frantic efforts to get passports and visas. One of my anti-Communist Communist friends explained the phenomenon. "After the Poznan riots," he said, "Bulganin and Zhukov came to Warsaw to discuss the problem. They readily admitted that the riots were the result of bad economic conditions and police terror. But who caused these things? The Jew Hilary Minc who was the chief economic planner and the Jew Jakub Berman who was the chief of the political police! Let them be tried in open court, and the people will quiet down. The majority of the party turned the suggestion down. But the Natolin group began a systematic campaign to shift all responsibility for the prevailing misery on the Jews."

Just before my arrival, the Soviet cultural attaché, Masljenikov, in a talk to Polish newspapermen, said that the Polish press was in the hands of "terrible Jewish traitors," and when one of his hearers asked him what was the difference between what he said and what Hitler had said, Masljenikov pointed out that Hitler was an anti-Semite, while "we are merely regulating the roles of minorities." The upshot of the incident was that the Polish Federation of

231

Newspapermen asked the Soviet ambassador for the recall of the cultural attaché.

That pro-Soviet groups were not loath to resort to anti-Semitism in Poland was in interesting contrast with Imre Nagy's behavior in Hungary. Both Poland and Hungary have been traditionally anti-Semitic. When, during the revolution in Budapest, signs of anti-Semitism appeared, Nagy and his associates took great care to weed out the Jews from the government and from the high command of the party in order to lessen the effectiveness of the anti-Semitic agitation. This is not to say that Gomulka was encouraging anti-Semitism in Poland, but it did appear that the government was not interested in meeting it.

What was the Polish government interested in? It is doubtful that in all history Poland ever had a government more secretive than Gomulka's. It was not hard to meet them and engage them in conversation, but it was nearly impossible to have an interview with any of them on record. Gomulka himself was readily accessible and so were others of his government, but apart from Poland's economic problems no one was willing to say anything for publication. Some said that there was nothing to say because the government did not know from day to day what it was going to do, while others believed that Gomulka was so afraid to rock the boat that he ordered everyone to stand still and be silent.

One could talk to every antigovernment person and group quite freely but not with supporters of the government. When I asked about this curious situation, I was told that even the normal propaganda agencies of the government were not functioning properly and that no one cared. Facts and figures were available, but they were just as misleading and meaningless as the ones Gomulka complained about to the Eighth Plenum of the Central Committee on October 20, 1956. In absence of reliable statistics, one had to go about measuring Poland in terms of everyday life of her citizens. But that was misleading too, for if one had to base his opinions on what the Poles in all walks of life were saying, one would have to come to the conclusion that revolution was just around the corner. And that would not have been true. A Polish revolution was in the making, and conceivably may erupt someday, but if it comes it will be an all-encompassing national movement which would challenge the Soviet Union either to exterminate all Poles or get out of Poland. The restricted quality of the Hungarian Revolution did not escape the Poles, and the indifference of the Hungarian peasants was recognized as a major factor which enabled the Soviets to crush the revolution with less risk than if the whole country had risen simultaneously. The Polish revolution, if it comes, will not be fought to break with Moscow and join Washington, but to break with both.

Since the notes for this book have been gathered, the inexorable dynamism of life in the Eastern countries has compelled the people and their governments to continue their chosen paths. I had hoped that in time more could be written about them and with greater freedom. Today it is clear that for the time being no peaceful evolution is possible for the satellite nations, and perhaps not for the Soviet people.

To those dead pioneers and to those in prison who, in this immoral century, first demonstrated the moral excellence of man by refusing to yield to bribes or terror, this and future generations owe a great deal. They have made it possible for men to believe in themselves and to renew their faith in the decency, humanity, and spiritual greatness of their kind.